BEHIND THE THRONE

Behind the Throne

Servants of Power to Imperial Presidents, 1898-1968

Edited by

THOMAS J. McCORMICK

and

WALTER LaFEBER

The University of Wisconsin Press

The University of Wisconsin Press
114 North Murray Street
Madison, Wisconsin 53715

3 Henrietta Street
London WC2E 8LU, England

"Brooks Adams and American Expansion," by William A. Williams, first
appeared in *The New England Quarterly* 25, no. 2 (June 1952): 217–232.

Library of Congress Cataloging-in-Publication Data
Behind the throne: servants of power to imperial presidents,
  1898–1968 / edited by Thomas J. McCormick and Walter LaFeber.
    286 p.   cm.
    Includes bibliographical references (p.) and index.
    ISBN 0-299-13740-6
    1. United States—Foreign relations—20th century. 2. United States—
    Territorial expansion. 3. Presidents—United States—Staff—
  History—20th century. 4. United States—Officials and employees—
  Biography. I. McCormick. Thomas J. II. LaFeber, Walter.
  E744.B436   1993
  327.73—dc20   93-18754

For Fred Harvey Harrington,
in whose honor these essays
have been contributed

Contents

Contributors

WAYNE S. COLE is Professor Emeritus of History at the University of Maryland–College Park. His most recent books include *Roosevelt and the Isolationists, 1932–1945* (1983), and *Norway and the United States, 1905–1955: Two Democracies in Peace and War* (1989).

LLOYD C. GARDNER is Charles and Mary Beard Professor of History at Rutgers University, where he has taught since 1963. He has been a Guggenheim Fellow, and Fulbright Professor in England and Finland. His most recent publications are: *Approaching Vietnam: From World War II through Dienbienphu* (1988), and *Spheres of Influence: The Great Powers Partition Europe from Munich to Yalta* (1993).

DAVID HEALY is Professor Emeritus of History at the University of Wisconsin–Milwaukee. He is the author of, most recently, *Drive to Hegemony: the United States in the Caribbean, 1898–1917*, the University of Wisconsin Press, 1988.

WALTER LAFEBER is Noll Professor of History at Cornell University. His publications include *America, Russia and the Cold War, 1945–1992* (1992), *The American Age, 1750 to the Present* (1989, 1993), and *The American Search for Opportunity, 1865–1913* (1993).

THOMAS J. McCORMICK is Professor of History at the University of Wisconsin–Madison. His most recent book is *America's Half-Century: United States Foreign Policy in the Cold War* (1989).

CARL PARRINI is Professor of History at Northern Illinois University. His publications include "Theories of Imperialism," in *Redefining the Past: Essays in Diplomatic History in Honor of William Appleman Williams*, Lloyd C. Gardner, ed. (1986), and, with Martin J. Sklar, "New Thinking about the Market, 1896–1904: Some American Economists on Investment and the Theory of Surplus Capital," in *Journal of Economic History* (September 1983). He is currently at work on a book, *The United States in China, 1896–1911*.

ROBERT FREEMAN SMITH is Distinguished University Professor of History at the University of Toledo. He is the author of *The United States and the Latin American Sphere of Influence: The Era of Good Neighbors, Cold Warriors, and Hair Shirts* (1983), "Latin America, the United States, and the European Powers," in *Cambridge History of Latin America: 1870–1930*, Vol. IV, Leslie Bethel, ed. (1986), and "La deuda externa de Mexico, 1920–1943," in *Pasada y Presente de la Deuda Externa de Mexico*, Fernando Rosenzweig, ed. (1988).

WILLIAM APPLEMAN WILLIAMS was Professor Emeritus of History at Oregon State University, a former Professor of History at the University of Wisconsin–Madison, President of the Organization of American Historians (1981), and author of such influential books as *The Tragedy of American Diplomacy* (1959), and *The Contours of American History* (1961). Professor Williams died in 1990.

Introduction

THOMAS J. McCORMICK

This book explores the ideas and actions of nine archetypal servants of power who advised American presidents and influenced their foreign policy choices between 1898 and 1968. The time frame spans the period between America's emergence as a world power during the Spanish-American War and the beginning of America's decline as global hegemon with the slow, tragic denouement of the Vietnam War.

This period also encompasses two parallel developments. First, the growth of the so-called Imperial Presidency witnessed the increasing concentration of foreign policy decisions in the executive branch at the expense of the Congress and the public. Second, the evolution of that strong, global-minded presidency fostered the need for a new breed of presidential advisers whose first loyalties were to the chief executive, not to the traditional bureaucracy in the State Department or to congressional bodies like the Senate Foreign Relations Committee. As "action intellectuals," their primary responsibility was to employ their considerable intellects to provide those imperial executives with the global, big picture; to ascertain the state of the world and to project a vision of how it might be altered and what America's role in that alteration process might be. Some bore the additional responsibility of selling decisions to the private sector, to the legislative branch, and to the public.

In the seven decades of America's "rise to globalism," such responsibilities had not yet been fully bureaucratized and institutionalized. That tendency would emerge with the evolution of the National Security Council and especially the office of National Security Adviser in the 1950s and 1960s. Before the 1970s, however, presidential advising on foreign policy was informal and ad hoc. Many of those "servants of power" operated without portfolio or held positions of authority that far exceeded their nominal bureaucratic office. Most had direct and often routine access to the president. Most famous and most studied among those presidential advisers were Colonel Edward House, confidant to Woodrow Wilson, and Harry Hopkins, who enjoyed a similar relationship with Franklin Roosevelt.

The essays in this volume focus on nine such servants of power. Less well known than House or Hopkins, their ideas and actions, nonetheless, played a vital role in shaping and often implementing modern American foreign policy. The essays generally seek to reconstruct the *Weltanschauungs* of these key actors and to analyze the relationship between their ideas and their actions. In some instances, the difficulty of being an action intellectual constitutes an important subtheme. Is it possible to serve power and still remain true to oneself as a creative, original thinker?

These precursors of today's "national security managers" followed no single bureaucratic track in reaching their positions of influence. Brooks Adams was America's preeminent turn-of-the-century intellectual. Brother of Henry Adams and descendant of two presidents, Adams was intellectual mentor to the movers and shakers of the William McKinley and Theodore Roosevelt administrations (including Roosevelt himself). Moreover, his legendary articles and books, like *The Law of Civilization and Decay* and *America's Economic Supremacy,* had wide impact on American expansionist thought. Charles Conant, the leading economic theoretician of his day, was another adviser to those same Republican presidents—especially in the structuring of America's economic relationship with Third World countries in Asia and Latin America. An early action intellectual, he played a hands-on role in implementing that relationship in the Philippines and China. Admiral William Caperton was a career naval officer and a disciple of Alfred Thayer Mahan, whose views influenced American policy in the Caribbean and Latin America as a whole. As a quasi-colonial bureaucrat in the 1910s, he presided over American military government in Haiti and the Dominican Republic, and he engineered a "demonstration election" in Nicaragua. Thomas Lamont was the quintessential Dollar Diplomat. In charge of J. P. Morgan's overseas investment activities, Lamont acted as minister without portfolio for both the American government and his banking partners in Mexico, Cuba, Japan, China, Manchuria, and elsewhere. A sophisticated intellectual, Lamont had direct access to and considerable influence on every American president in the 1920s and 1930s.

Adolf Berle was author of *The Modern Corporation and Private Property* (one of the most influential books of this century) and a member of Franklin Roosevelt's original brain trust. Later, as assistant secretary of state, he played a major role in planning America's economic and security policies for the post-World War II world, preparing the way for the World Bank, the International Monetary Fund, and the International Civil Aviation Organization. Senator Arthur Vandenberg, isolationist turned internationalist, used his position as ranking Republican on the Senate Foreign Relations Committee to promote bipartisanship and congressional acceptance of presidential prerogatives in foreign relations. His special relationship to President Harry Truman gave him significant influence in the formation of the United Nations and the Organization of American States as well as later cold war strategies in the Truman Doctrine, the Marshall Plan, and NATO. Thomas Mann, career diplomat, played a key role as undersecretary of state for Latin American affairs in both the Kennedy and Johnson administrations. An early skeptic of the Alliance for Progress, he still played a key role in its conceptualization and implementation. Later, he led the retrenchment that manifested itself especially in America's intervention in the Dominican Republic in 1965. McGeorge Bundy, former Harvard dean and protégé of Henry Stimson, epitomized the action intellectuals—the "best and the brightest"—that became synonymous with the Kennedy-Johnson experiments in global social engineering, climaxing in Bundy's key role in escalating the Vietnam War. Bundy, whose relationship to Kennedy approximated that between Hopkins and Roosevelt, was a transition figure between the ad hoc, informal advisers who characterized America's rise to globalism and the more bureaucratized, institutionalized national security managers who characterized its zenith and decline. Like Berle, who left government to chair the Twentieth Century Fund, Bundy moved on to chair the Ford Foundation.

The authors of these eight essays have based their work on extensive research in archival and manuscript materials. Their interpretations are fresh, and they often introduce subjects whose significance has not been previously appreciated. The essays themselves are original and heretofore unpublished. The one exception is the opening essay by William Appleman Williams, which is reprinted here with the kind permission of the *New England Quarterly*. Williams died before completion of his essay for this volume, but it seemed important that his work be represented. Like the other authors, Williams was one of Fred Harvey Harrington's doctoral students at the University of Wisconsin–Madison. As Walter LaFeber's essay of appreciation will suggest, all the authors owe much to Harrington's training and influence—the rigorous use of primary materials, the skeptical turn of mind, the willingness to entertain unconventional hypotheses, and the fascination with power and its behind-the-scenes practitioners. Given Harrington's tolerance of all points of view, provided they are systematically grounded in historical evidence, it is fitting that these essays reflect the diversity and the consensus that are both part of the Wisconsin School of Diplomatic History.

BEHIND THE THRONE

Fred Harvey Harrington,
Teacher and Friend
An Appreciation

WALTER LaFEBER

As a scholar, teacher, chair of one of the nation's largest and most influential departments of history, President of the University of Wisconsin system, and a leader of the Ford Foundation's programs in South Asia, Fred Harvey Harrington has been a dominant voice in American higher education over the past half-century. As the University of Wisconsin's president in the 1960s, he was, indeed, often *the* dominant voice in the national university community. With the voice has come an arresting presence: a commanding 6'4" frame, rapid speech, pointed words, and an energy-charged style even after heart bypass surgery at age seventy-five. Harrington's graduate students, most of whom he trained at Madison between 1946 and 1960, quickly learned to appreciate both the academic (and administrative) talent and the presence. They also soon appreciated his willingness to break intellectual molds, to think the unconventional, to question the accepted, and, perhaps above all, to deal with the roots, transformations, and effects of power in an American society that, as Harrington reached full speed in his career, had become the most powerful in history. Because of his influence, many of those students have devoted their own careers to charting the historic course of U.S. dominance.

Harrington, given his own ambitions, matured intellectually at the perfect time—that is, in the 1940s as the United States assumed superpower status; as American universities (especially such state-related schools as the University of Wisconsin) struck off on new national

3

Fred Harvey Harrington

and international missions; and as burgeoning graduate programs fueled by the GI bill and newly created fellowships required the gifts that Harrington exhibited as a teacher. His timing was also right when his publications and graduate seminars began to reshape the writing of American diplomatic history. Developed in the 1930s, especially through the multiarchival researches of Samuel Flagg Bemis of Yale and the highly popular textbook of Thomas A. Bailey of Stanford, the field of United States diplomatic history had become important and appealing to students. It had also become nationalistic. Focused mainly on political rather than intellectual, economic, or cultural influences, it was part of a growing consensus school in the writing of American History that deadened the discipline during the early cold war years by narrowing debate.

As historian John Higham observed, a veritable "cult" dominated the historical profession, a cult that genuflected before consensus history and damned the Progressive history of the century's first forty-five years. This Progressivism had stressed the importance of economics, class divisions, racial animosity, and the need to question all power in American life. After World War II, however, historians joined other scholars and journalistic pundits, and they in turn followed national officials, as all rushed off to find the vital center of American society so they could, like so many publicists on the head of a pin, cluster to fight the cold war. As one discouraged Progressive historian lamented, "Our university scholars are but made of flesh." If even Supreme Court Justices' opinions supposedly "follow the election returns," Matthew Josephson continued, "should historians lag far behind in judging the shift of political power to conservative hands?"[1]

THE BACKGROUND

"The only major diplomatic historian" who taught from a progressive perspective, in Peter Novick's words,[2] Harrington used the 1950s not to praise a temporary (as it proved) consensus, but to prepare students for a quite different, post-1960 era by coming to terms with the American past. That also required coming to terms with the Bemis-Bailey legacies.

Bemis demonstrated the importance of using multiarchival research to lay bare international relationships, and he presented, especially in his work on John Quincy Adams, the elite policymaker's view of those relationships. Bailey turned Bemis inside out. Spending remarkably little time in foreign archives, Bailey forced us to look more closely at the internal causes of American foreign policy. His major contribution was to make readers aware of the attentive public's role in policymaking, especially as that opinion was manifested in Congress, newspapers, and periodicals. Bailey and his time, in this regard, were perfectly matched. The internal mainsprings of U.S. foreign policy became more important precisely during Bailey's heyday of the 1940s and 1950s when the American superpower forced other nations largely to react to its initiatives. When problems arose with Bailey's approach (as Bernard Cohen and others have noted), they related to his reluctance to ask which groups more precisely shaped public opinion, and—most crucial—whether and how that opinion influenced those who wielded ultimate political power in American society.[3]

Fred Harrington made serious observers aware of the need to ask these last questions. By approaching them from a different direction, he carried Bailey's concerns to another level. Harrington forced his students to read the rather exotic literature (at least exotic for most diplomatic historians) that discussed how ethnic and interest groups perceived and influenced foreign policy. In a paper presented at the 1984 American Historical Association's annual meeting, Professor Lloyd Gardner related his shock when, in his first traumatic meeting with Harrington to discuss the initial chapter of Gardner's Master's thesis, Harrington abruptly asked: "Where's the economics?"[4]

Because Harrington forced his students to investigate the nature, hierarchy, and influence of ethnic and interest groups and how their ideologies shaped diplomatic history, he made an important impact on the profession. Such a view of his importance goes far beyond the too-simple notion that his significance was acting as the father to a supposed "Wisconsin School of Diplomatic History." True, a group of young scholars who studied at Wisconsin under Harrington and later under William Appleman Williams in the 1950s and 1960s agreed on certain essentials that were then nearly heresies in the field. But many who were supposedly members of that "School," although proud that they would be singled out as heretics in a profession that always seems in need of a few more, have since believed that the term was too narrow in several respects. Important scholars who were never inside the state of Wisconsin were making many of the same arguments.[5] Harrington's influence, moreover, went beyond any supposed school. Out of his seminars came Wayne Cole as well as William Appleman Williams, Thomas McCormick as well as David Healy, Vivian Munson as well as Walter Heacock, Barbara Welter as well as Charles Vevier, Carl Parrini as well as Robert Freeman

Smith, Lloyd Gardner as well as John Burke (a foreign service officer who during the 1980s headed the much criticized Classification-Declassification Division at the Department of State that was responsible for declassifying State Department documents). Personally, Harrington had early condemned monocausal history. As he phrased it in a review of Frank Tannenbaum's *The American Tradition in Foreign Policy* in 1955, the author's emphasis on moralistic-legalistic motives in explaining U.S. policy had some virtues. But, Harrington emphasized, "This is single-factor interpretation carried to an extreme. . . . This is unfortunate; for human beings and nations are complex. In striving toward understanding, we must ever beware of oversimplification."[6] In Harrington's intellectual house there were, therefore, many rooms—although, as will be noted shortly, most of the furniture was modern Progressive.

THE PREPARATION

This architect of much of the post-1960 writing in American diplomatic history had been born in Watertown, New York on June 24, 1912. Harrington traveled 150 miles south to attend Cornell University. He went to Ithaca with the intention of becoming a Foreign Service officer, but a distinguished historian, Arthur Whitaker, convinced him that he should become a scholar of American diplomacy. Harrington has testified that during those undergraduate days he learned how to write (and, apparently, how to teach writing) from Carl Becker, but it also seems that somewhere Harrington heard Becker define—or witnessed Becker exemplify—a professor's purpose as Becker saw it: "to think otherwise."

After graduating with honors from Cornell, he accepted the Frederic Courtland Penfield Fellowship from New York University and obtained a Masters (1934) and Ph. D. (1937) while working under Henry Steele Commager. In 1937 he became an Instructor of History at the University of Wisconsin and was promoted to Assistant Professor in the 1939–1940 academic year. Then, however, the University of Arkansas' young President, J. William Fulbright, asked Professor William Hesseltine, of the Wisconsin history faculty, for suggestions about candidates who could chair the Arkansas History and Political Science Department. Hesseltine nominated both his prize student, T. Harry Williams, and Harrington. Hesseltine was hoping that Harrington would receive an offer and use it to raise his salary at Madison, and that Williams would go to Fayetteville. Fulbright's offer, however, proved so attractive, and the possibilities of rapid promo-

tion in Wisconsin's department (that contained mostly senior professors) so slim, that Harrington went to Arkansas—and then saw to it
that Williams was placed at Louisiana State University, where over
the next generation he became one of the most distinguished historians of southern politics and the Civil War.

For Harrington and his family, the Arkansas years "were special for
us: we enjoyed campus social life there more than anywhere else,"
and "in the four years there," he recalled in 1990, "I launched a state
historical society and an historical quarterly, both of which still exist."
In 1944, Paul Knaplund, the renowned historian of the British Empire
and, in Harrington's words, "the main force" in the Wisconsin History Department, brought the Arkansas professor back to Madison—
"the only case in the Wisconsin Department's history in which a faculty member was invited back after defecting," as Harrington
recalled.

THE WRITINGS

Harrington quickly became a popular and highly influential teacher
at both the undergraduate and graduate levels. Indeed, he later
claimed that his influence had been little felt beyond the work of his
students. "I never became a major figure in U.S. diplomatic [studies]
myself," Harrington wrote in a personal letter. That statement, however, requires considerable qualification. His earliest essays, published in the 1930s when he was a very young scholar, opened the
1898–1900 anti-imperialist movement to its first serious scrutiny,
peeled back the rhetoric of the late 1890s to reveal the various factions that were trying to capture the movement, became a starting
point for the analyses of other scholars during the Vietnam War
years, and remain major mileposts in the field. Jerald Combs's sweeping survey of *American Diplomatic History* since 1750 correctly notes
that Harrington's work "revived the reputation of the anti-imperialist
movement."[7]

A decade later the first of Harrington's three major books appeared.
These volumes revealed the characteristics that marked his teaching
as well as his writing: the use of persons, previously considered to be
of second-rank in historical importance, to open fresh insights into
an era (not to mention the revival of some of the most fascinating
characters in American History); a revisionist view that stripped away
the easy assumptions, indeed the illusions, that had marked earlier
writing on the era and/or subject; a sensitivity to economics that had
been lacking in the scholarship of American diplomatic history; and a
writing style that was direct and sharp.

The first book, *God, Mammon, and the Japanese: Dr. Horace Allen and Korean-American Relations, 1884–1905* (University of Wisconsin Press, 1944, 1961), probably contributed more than any other volume to initiating the study of the U.S.-Korean relationship. Harrington told the fascinating story of how the religious missionary and the robber baron combined in the single person of Horace Allen to open Korean resources to U.S. interests and ultimately (in a most instructive irony), to the Japanese Empire. Tyler Dennett, no amateur in the field, began his review of the book in the *American Historical Review* by noting "its lurid though correct title," and concluded that the volume not only was an "important chapter" in the long history of Western powers in Asia, but "for those who would understand the Korean problem," it is "an indispensable book."[8] After Harrington finished this work on the seminal years of 1890 to 1905, it was difficult to conclude that Americans had stumbled into Asian commitments as mere mouthpieces for the more worldly British, or that Americans were only "sentimental imperialists" in Asia. Harrington had not only installed Korean relations as a part of American diplomatic history, he had installed as well the role of economics in that relationship with Asia. It would, however, take the field nearly twenty years to catch up with his latter insight.

Four years later he used another figure, previously considered secondary, to throw a brighter light on an era that the profession thought it knew well. *Fighting Politician: Major General N. P. Banks* (University of Pennsylvania Press, 1984) colorfully analyzed the life and times of the man who outranked Ulysses S. Grant for three-quarters of the Civil War, was a ten-term congressman from Massachusetts, and served as the state's governor. It was Banks's leadership of the House Foreign Affairs Committee, however, that proved especially important, for, with a driving political ambition, he had switched from the moderate Republicans to the Radicals and became a rabid manifest-destiny expansionist in the late 1860s. The period marked the last gasp of the nation's landed expansionism (with the purchase of Alaska), and the transition to the overseas commercial expansion that shaped the next century of American foreign policy. Banks personally emerged from the account as indecisive. He held titles that were considerably higher than his capacities and was unable to get his military or political timing right—in all, always "late to battle," in Harrington's words. As Paul Buck of Harvard wrote in his review in the *American Historical Review*," . . . [O]ut of such material as he, a good deal of the history of the Civil War generation was made, and it must be understood if the period is to have a complete meaning." Buck gave the work a rave review: it "is almost clinical in its precise analysis. . . . This is a work which the professional scholar can depend upon with the confidence that all the available evidence has been used effectively."[9]

Harrington explored the years (and the territory) linking Banks and Allen in *Hanging Judge* (Paxton Press, 1951), the story of Judge Isaac C. Parker who dispatched seventy-nine men to the gallows and would have sent twice as many except that after 1889 the Supreme Court ruled that thirty-six of the forty-six condemned had not received fair trials from Judge Parker's ham-fisted justice. Reviewers focused on Harrington's depiction of an American West that was not only wild, but at wild variance with the West portrayed by Harrington's famous predecessor at Madison, Frederick Jackson Turner. In this "graphic portrayal" of the Fort Smith-Indiana Territory frontier, Carl Coke Rister wrote in the *American Historical Review*, "Harrington gives us a brutally frank, but needfully realistic narrative." Quite "unlike fiction writers and cinema producers, he presents outlaws . . . as 'the refuse of humanity' . . . and not as unfortunate Robin Hoods. For example, Belle Starr [who had just been the title figure in a romantic and fawning Hollywood movie] 'had no conscience . . . no beauty, but was a crude and ugly nymphomaniac,'" to use Harrington's description. "This book is in a pioneer field and is a unique contribution to western history," Rister concluded. "The author has pointed the way for the doing of other needful studies." A young professor at the University of Mississippi, James Silver, concurred in admiring Harrington's portrayal of Belle Starr (once convicted for stealing a horse from a crippled boy), Starr's daughter (another person given a romantic turn in a Hollywood film but also nothing more than a common prostitute), and the distinctly unTurnerian West. "But it is doubtful," Silver lamented, "if all this will have much effect on the Saturday afternoon menu at the local picture house."[10]

Harrington was also challenging the conventional wisdom in outspoken, often stunning, book reviews. One of his most striking attacks was a 1944 *Mississippi Valley Historical Review* critique of Pitirim Sorokin's widely read, and highly fashionable, *Russia and the United States*. First came Harrington's sensitivity to sources. "Professor Sorokin's book," he wrote, "shows the author's sincerity and . . . also his self-confidence: thirty-four of the forty-three footnote references are to Sorokin's own works." Then came a remarkable paragraph:

Citing lack of fundamental conflicts, Sorokin claims that Russia has been historically our greatest friend and that Americans and Russians are "sociocul-turally" in tune. . . . Stalin's country should be our chief partner [Sorokin argues] in the fight for a better world. . . . This reads smoothly; by calling indifference friendship, by stressing similarities and explaining away contrasts, one can make any two peoples seem alike. But that is word magic. Besides, co-operation could be promoted better by discussing than by dismissing Russian-American conflicts, as in Asia. Trade, which Sorokin neglects, will affect the diplomatic future more than similarities in family patterns, which are discussed at length.[11]

In this passage, Harrington revealed his ability to use history to judge critically the easy generalities of the day, his concern that economic conflict not be obscured by "word magic," and, more implicitly, a sensitivity to power that, when placed in this arena of U.S.–USSR relations, sets off alarm bells. (It also seems that at this time he was considerably more suspicious of the Soviets than were others, including Samuel Flagg Bemis.)

THE SEMINAR

The qualities that marked his writing turned his teaching into, literally, a seminal experience. When someone with his sharp views and breadth of knowledge, his physical presence and intensity, strode up and down restlessly before undergraduate classes, rapidly laying out the evolution of American global power and doing so without any notes before 450 students at one time, his impact could be considerable. Wayne Cole recalled that "the most valuable part of my graduate training" was assisting Harrington in a two-semester undergraduate course. Cole already had been a U.S. Army Air Force flight instructor and a high-school social studies teacher, "but I learned all over again under Harrington's guidance and example." Others, who never assisted but only watched, had the same reaction. Thomas A. Bailey's popular lectures at Stanford were beautifully crafted, timed to the second, sprinkled with humor, and delivered with skill, industry, and much practice. Harrington's lectures were intense, sprawling, and cut through with a humor that was more piercing, thrusting, overwhelming. If Bailey's performance resembled that of an interesting, entertaining Elizabethan playwright, Harrington's was that of a slashing and deadly serious Sir Francis Drake.

Harrington's graduate seminar was similarly notable for its everpresent assumption that it was concerned not only with mastering books, but understanding—and reshaping—the ideas that divided and drove societies. At the same time, however, the seminar was also notable for both the diversity of its students and its duration. As Harrington noted later in a personal letter, "I handled doctoral students in diplomatic [studies] less than a dozen years, perhaps a third as long as Bailey and Bemis." That in such brief time he was able to turn out a number of published scholars occurred in part because of the Wisconsin History Department itself. Graduate work at Madison was a collective effort. Working with Harrington also meant possibly working with Merle Curti, Howard K. Beale, William Hesseltine, Paul Knaplund, Philip Curtin, or Merrill Jensen, among others. The American scholars within the department were especially linked by ideological attachments to Progressive history, notably the history written by Turner, Vernon Parrington, and, especially, Beard.

The somewhat common ideology, however, hardly inhibited discussion. One historian remembers sitting directly across from Hesseltine's and Beale's offices, when he was a first-year graduate student, and watching the spectacle of these two learned scholars as they roared out of their offices—somewhat resembling the figures coming in doublestep out of two sides of an old-fashioned cuckoo clock—met halfway, screamed at each other about a point one of them had made in a lecture that morning, and then retreated into their respective rooms. The astonished student thus learned that some people at Wisconsin took the profession seriously. And perhaps in part because of that seriousness, as well as because of the Wisconsin Progressive tradition, students seemed to become politicized at Madison at a time when politicization was not the norm at other universities. A 1950s student at the University of Iowa, where much of the new social and political history was being born, later remarked that a major difference between the two schools seemed to be the greater extent of political commitment (and radicalization) that occurred at Madison. History, ideology, and politics were linked at Harrington's Wisconsin.

The graduate student watching the Beale-Hesseltine encounter also was reminded of something else: Fred Harrington was the person within the department to whom those two senior professors, and most others, looked as their mediator and power broker. He served as chair between 1952 and 1955 and was the power-behind-the-throne thereafter. Harrington, in turn, knew how to exploit the other faculty for the sake of his students. In the late 1940s his entering seminar numbered as many as ten first-year Master's candidates. "My working rule," he later wrote, "was that only one a year would be encouraged to go on toward the doctorate." Harrington most notably used Hesseltine's legendary seminar to "winnow the minnows and get the fish," as one of the fortunate fish recalled. Hesseltine brutally criticized sloppy research methods and loose writing style, but in a few brief years he had produced T. Harry Williams, Frank Freidel, Kenneth Stampp, Richard Current, and Samuel Merrill, so he was obviously doing something right. One survivor later wondered, however, whether it was really useful criticism to have written across your research paper in large red letters: "S-H-I-T."

Those who survived Hesseltine then confronted Harrington. Their styles were wholly different. As Harrington wrote in a personal letter to William Appleman Williams in early 1990:

I consciously tried to be severe—how else to make them see the difference between aiming to be an adequate college teacher and a publishing scholar? Early on I saw John D. Hicks, who was soft on his seminar people, and was unable to get them to make the most of their talents. While Hesseltine, who prided himself on being brutal, got better results. I learned a lot from Bill [Hesseltine] though I didn't try to duplicate his meatax tactic.

Or, as the most famous member of the so-called "Wisconsin School," William Appleman Williams, remembered, "Hesseltine came down on your first sentence like he was Darth Vader: have your laser sword in hand . . . Harrington came in with a 4″×6″ tear pad page," briefly introduced the topic, then sat "smoking" paperclips until the students exhausted their questions. "If we had done our work," Williams continued, "he'd say 'good seminar.' If we had not, he would work his ruthless way through the question . . . and leave us all *stunned."*

Harrington later believed that a key to the seminar's success was that "perhaps most major professions steer their students toward a particular point of view," but "my own approach was to let students find their own interpretations. No doubt I did insist that they look at the economic side, so often neglected by diplomatic historians. No doubt I was myself influenced by Beard and what the [1930s] depression did to historical thinking. But I did try to use the light rein." His students not usually categorized in the "Wisconsin School," such as Wayne Cole and David Healy, agree that, in Cole's words, Harrington never pressed "for conformity in points of view from us; instead, he drew out the best that each of us was capable of producing in our separate ways."

A "light rein," however, did not mean a light seminar. At the first meeting Harrington explained the facts of life: most books should have been articles, and most articles would better have been left unwritten. On the other hand, he expected his seminar's Masters theses to be published as articles and the seminar's dissertations as books. The best historian, he went on, probably had no business publishing more than three major books. Some well-known and often-cited national newspapers were to be viewed skeptically because they too often printed news that fit and did not keep their reporters in one place long enough to understand what was going on. The *Chicago Tribune*, on the other hand, he thought worthy of attention because its reporters were seasoned and the paper was not reluctant to think otherwise. Most books in the field, he casually informed the seminar, could be read in one hour.

With that comment he gave the class a list of fifteen books to be mastered for discussion the following week. The works of Hans Morgenthau, George Kennan, Dexter Perkins, Frank Tannenbaum, and Charles Beard were among those included on the list. After one week of sleepless nights the group emerged. The students were, as one later recalled, "a bunch of competitive, over-achieving self-starters," but in that respect no different from most other decent graduate seminars. The difference was Harrington. His "great virtue," one student recalled, "was not to get in the way," at least at the start. The discussion soon focused on what appeared to be a brilliant dichotomy: realism versus idealism. Realism, the students concluded, seemed preferable. Kennan's *American Diplomacy, 1900–1950* seemed to be the ultimate word on the subject. At that point Harrington gently suggested that it could be that Kennan took his pivotal material from A. Whitney Griswold's work of a generation earlier, it could be that Griswold was wrong, and it could be that realism versus idealism was far too simplistic. Why, for example, had the seminar not considered Beard more closely? So the group reread Beard and also the then-new accounts of ethnic and other interest groups. There is no recollection that the term "revisionist," not to mention "New Left," was ever uttered in the year-long seminar. Labels, including "Beardian," were usually floated, only to be shot down. Harrington seemed more interested in getting it right through intellectual pull and haul than in giving it a catchy label. As for "revisionism," he clearly believed that all historians worth much were automatically revisionist. Their job was not simply to rewrite the history of the past but to rethink it—and as fundamentally as possible.

After several such sessions, two students each week made their research presentations for their thesis projects. Another student led the criticism of each paper. Harrington also brought in advanced students whose purpose, in the view of the regular first-year seminarians, was to terrorize. Harrington usually prevented what Healy has nicely called "real bloodletting"—usually, but not always. When he incisively summarized each session, the students felt appropriately intimidated and ignorant. But he was never malicious, not even to those who deserved severe treatment, nor was he restrictive. He believed that "seminars are usually dull and thesis topics unimportant and uninteresting"; therefore, he let his students pick topics that interested them and held the possibility of publication. The topics were not limited to Harrington's own past, present, or planned research interests. There was, again to use a phrase of Carl Becker's, freedom and responsibility: the freedom to go out on one's own, the responsibility for doing fresh and well-substantiated work so one could simply survive the cross-examination in that seminar.

Sometime during the year the students would meet Nancy Harrington, and her warmth and concern (and her always surprising knowledge about what students and spouses were doing) would take much of the edge off any earlier fear. As a student began writing the dissertation, Harrington, moreover, was always available to help, but there was seldom—to use Williams's words—"I-wonder-what-if kind of conversation. Harrington wanted specific, Mafia-boots-in-concrete kind of questions." Graduate students, at least the more brave, came to call him "Mr. Fish-Eye" or "Mr. Cool" (and sometimes "Mr. Cold"). Harrington of course knew all this, and turned it to the student's advantage. "I have never been a mixer; I tend to be a bit formal, aloof, remote," he wrote in early 1990.

I deliberately kept my distance from undergraduates (after all I often had 1,000 course students at a time, and as many as 100 advisees). I did give good advice, very good, to course students and advisees, for I made a point of knowing the rules and angles; but I took care not to be cozy, chummy, lovable. (Not my way anyhow.) Graduate students: the seminar usually included beginners whom I had to tell not to go beyond the master's, easier if there was no close personal relationship. . . .

I guess Nancy and I did have a friendly relationship to my (and other) graduate students—she was better than I at that. But I mostly did separate home from office, natural probably with five children and two dogs and two cats most of the time; and I spent an incredible amount of time on faculty committees and campaigns, mostly to push social sciences and humanities against the dominant life-science administration. Of course we finally won and I became president; but probably I neglected my students sometimes. I made a virtue of this, saying I wanted them to find their own roads, though pressing them a bit on economic influences and skepticism toward policymakers, etc.; and they did make their own ways.

Several of Harrington's most productive seminars occurred when he served as Special Assistant to Wisconsin's President, 1956 to 1958, and as Vice President for Academic Affairs, 1958 to 1962 (when he became President). Harrington's advanced doctoral students knew his time was limited. David Healy remembered that they would rehearse privately until they could state their problem in less than fifteen minutes; it usually took far less. Then Harrington would pause and give a short response which, as Healy noted, "fully met the case." The short response was due in part to his administrative responsibilities, but the students became convinced that the manner also embodied his belief that history was a discipline, not free association, and that it was their job to be disciplined and succinct. The manner made an impact. A meeting with Harrington, like the possibility of hanging, concentrated the mind wonderfully, yet he seemed to devote endless time to criticizing chapters. Healy recalled that "the red circles" on "my first paper looked like the row of portholes on . . . an ocean liner."

Through it all, one consistent theme reappeared apart from the manner. That theme was the influence of Beard and the understanding and sensitivity with which Harrington and other Wisconsin faculty used Beard's work, especially *The Idea of National Interest*.[12] Analyses in the 1980s commented how "ideology" was a term of opprobrium in the 1950s, at least until a few social scientists began reinterpreting it.[13] There was even to be an "end of ideology," to use the title of a popular book of the time. No one who worked with Harrington took such ahistorical views. As Wayne Cole summarized, "Harrington's analysis emphasized the close relation between domestic . . . and foreign affairs, the continuity of expansion" in American history, "and the importance of economic bases for that expansion." Those were categories of analysis that had direct ideological implications, and all his students had to take them seriously. Harrington, it seems, largely ignored those who attacked Beard for his argument that Franklin D. Roosevelt misled the nation into World War II, even though those attacks were much in fashion during the 1950s. Instead, Harrington, with wider concerns, moved more from Louis Hartz's fascinating insight in *The Liberal Tradition in America*, a book that all serious students were then expected to know:

But after all is said and done Beard somehow stays alive, and the reason for this is that, as in the case of Marx, you merely demonstrate your subservience to a thinker when you spend your time attempting to disprove him. The way to fully refute a man is to ignore him for the most part, and the only way you can do this is to substitute new fundamental categories for his own, so that you are simply pursuing a different path.

It is not unreasonable to suspect that our own time will discover such categories and that they may well lie in the relation of America to other nations. Everyone knows the old saw [of Beard's and Becker's] about each age rewriting history from its own angle, and everyone agrees that the peculiar angle of our own age is the involvement of America with the world.[14]

Out of Harrington's understanding and teaching of that approach came his books on Horace Allen and, especially, Judge Parker; and, to a significant extent, out of it came Williams's development of an open-door ideology, McCormick's delineation of corporatism and a world-system approach, and Gardner's redefinition of Western liberalism in a revolutionary world—to cite three examples of the search for "new fundamental categories" by Harrington's students.

Harrington's personal ideology was thus framed much more by Beardian categories than by any New Left. McCormick, who now teaches Harrington's former courses at Madison, doubtless got it right when he said that Harrington is "a Jeffersonian Democrat." Resembling Henry Steele Commager, with whom he did his graduate work, Harrington has a gut faith in democracy, believes that a major responsibility of the state is to educate and to spread democracy, and assumes that anything that interferes with carrying out that responsibility—whether the interference is an irresponsible corporate structure or a dinosaur-like cold war mentality—deserves ruthless treatment. And Jeffersonian Democrats, as Beard demonstrated in his work, possessed a highly pitched sensitivity to power. McCormick believes that, when stripped to its essentials, the Harrington seminar was about "power. Who has it? Who has the will to use it? Who resists it? Accepts?" And why?

Harrington's views of power and faith in democracy also have had another impact. Jerald Combs has observed that, while some Harrington students have been outspokenly critical of capitalist development, and have used Marxist categories to evaluate that development, they—unlike leading Western European intellectuals who have used the same categories—have not called for change through violence. They instead believe in the system's ability to recognize its problems, debate the alternatives, peacefully construct other and better institutions, and thus rationally carry out needed reforms.[15] Such a belief is also evidence of an uncommon Jeffersonian faith in democracy and a replication of some of Beard's final thoughts, transmitted at least in part through the work of Fred Harrington.

His sensitivity to, and ability in wielding, power help explain as well why Harrington successfully cajoled other colleges in the 1950s to hire Wisconsin graduate students in a market that was nearly as difficult as the job situation of the 1980s. The so-called "Wisconsin Phalanx" (or "Big Red Machine," as it was referred to by those less enthralled by its successes) sought out jobs with great efficiency at historical association meetings, and Harrington was the point man who over time made an impact on the profession simply because of the role he played in appointing so many to its staff.

But one does not measure an impact such as Harrington's in quantitative terms of books published or the number of graduate students produced and placed. To see the evidence of his work, one can look to the superb network of higher education in the state of Wisconsin, the distinguished and international reputation of the Madison campus especially, and the tremendous influence of the University's history department over the past fifty years. One can also look to the students his seminar produced, and their students, who have done much to change the writing of American diplomatic history. A session at the Organization of American Historians' convention in 1985 focused on Harrington, along with Bemis and Bailey, as one of the century's most important and influential teachers of American foreign relations. In that sense, he has not only been the "father" of the so-called "Wisconsin School," but a father and grandfather of much of the significant writing in the field over the last half-century.

For him this book is written. To him this book is dedicated, with great affection—and thanks.

NOTES

1. Peter Novick, *That Noble Dream: The "Objectivity Question" and the American Historical Profession* (Cambridge: Cambridge University Press, 1988): 345.

2. Ibid., 346.

3. Bernard C. Cohen, *The Public's Impact on Foreign Policy* (Boston: Little, Brown, 1972).

4. Lloyd C. Gardner, "The Impact of the New Left," December 1984, manuscript copy, 1, in author's possession. In the following pages, all comments and quotations by Harrington's former students are found in personal letters written to Walter LaFeber during 1984 and early 1985, unless otherwise noted. As clearly demonstrated, the editors of this volume owe an immense debt of gratitude to these friends, and the same debt—as well as many others—to Fred Harrington for his willingness to write a candid letter on May 30, 1984 to LaFeber, and Harrington's agreement to use quotes from his long letter of March 1, 1990 to William Appleman Williams (a letter that was not sent because of Williams's final illness at the time).

5. This point is well made in Norman A. Graebner, "The State of Diplomatic History," manuscript copy, 5.

6. *Pacific Historical Review* 24 (November 1955):427.

7. Jerald Combs, *American Diplomatic History: Two Centuries of Changing Interpretations* (Berkeley: University of California Press, 1983):182.

8. *American Historical Review* 50 (October 1944):101.

9. *American Historical Review* 54 (April 1949):628–629.

10. Ibid., 57 (January 1952):552–553 has Rister's review; *Mississippi Valley Historical Review* 38 (March 1952):720–721 has Silver's comments; W. Eugene

Hollon of the University of Oklahoma also wrote an interesting review in *Pacific Historical Review* 21 (February 1952):79.

11. *Mississippi Valley Historical Review* 31 (June 1944):154–155.

12. Charles Beard and George H. E. Smith, *The Idea of National Interest: An Analytical Study in American Foreign Relations* (New York:The Macmillan Company, 1934).

13. Daniel Joseph Singal, "Beyond Consensus: Richard Hofstadter and American Historiography," *American Historical Review* 89 (October 1984): 997–998.

14. Louis Hartz, *The Liberal Tradition in America: An Interpretation of American Political Thought since the Revolution* (New York: Harcourt, Brace, 1955):28.

15. Combs, *American Diplomatic History,* 257.

CHAPTER 1

Brooks Adams and American Expansion

WILLIAM A. WILLIAMS

Long slighted as a somewhat eccentric brother of the more famous Henry Adams, Brooks Adams has received less attention than he deserves. Brooks Adams not only influenced Henry Adams; he also made a significant impression on such leading public figures as John Hay, Henry Cabot Lodge, and Theodore Roosevelt. Of particular consequence was Brooks's role in the development of United States foreign policy in Asia—and toward Russia in particular—from 1895 to 1908.

The Panic of 1893 brought Henry Adams into close and extended contact with his brother for the first time in several years. Henry, perplexed by the problems posed by the new industrialism, was quick to benefit from Brooks's researches and insight. By 1893 Brooks Adams had completed some ten years of exhaustive inquiry on which he had formulated a broad theory of history. And as the two brothers waited out their fortunes that summer, Brooks gave Henry the full argument of his thesis, which was shortly published as *The Law of Civilization and Decay.*[1]

In the course of this tutoring it is clear that Henry acquired from Brooks "certain fundamental conceptions of history, explicit in *The Law,* which subsequently bulked large" in his own writing.[2] By Henry's own admission it was Brooks who "discovered or developed" the law: "The book," Henry wrote, "is wholly, absolutely, and exclusively yours."[3] Of equal significance, however, is the fact that both Brooks and Henry Adams considered *The Law* to be the central problem of their life.

Brooks Adams sought a law of history but in effect rediscovered the sine curve. From the laws of mass, energy, and acceleration, he formulated a concept of society's oscillation between "barbarism and civilization." In the decentralization of the former, Brooks argued, fear bred imagination, which in turn begot the religious, artistic, and military types. But as the centralization of wealth (stored energy) proceeded, the "economic organism" tended to replace the emotional and martial man; and ultimately the pressure of economic competition reached a critical point, and the society either reverted to barbarism or collapsed—its energy exhausted.[4]

Brooks was appalled by his conclusions—that rational thought played "an exceedingly small part . . . in moulding the fate of men" and that a society's decline was marked by intense centralization and "economic competition." The first was personally unacceptable, but on every hand he saw evidence that such deadly concentration was well advanced in the United States. Desperate for a way out, Brooks brushed aside Henry's warning that he was beginning "to monkey with a dynamo" and from 1895 on primarily concerned himself with the search for a formula that would avert chaos.[5]

Brooks inclined to two conclusions: that the next concentration of economic power would occur in New York and that the expansion of the United States into Asia was the only technique by which *The Law* could, in effect, be repealed. The problem then became Russia, since in his view England was already becoming an economic vassal of the United States. But Brooks did not believe that Russia would acquiesce in American control of Asia; and so the key question was how to defeat St. Petersburg and take control of China. Well aware of his brother's new interest (Russia is mentioned but once in *The Law*), Henry's first reaction was one of fear and curiosity. "I fear Russia much!" he admitted to Brooks; and he concluded that "you ought to be,—like your grandfather,—minister to St. Petersburg."[6] As for Brooks's plan to preempt Asia as a colony, Henry was dubious. "Russia," he advised Brooks, "as yet seems too far to reach. We have not come to that point. Probably we shall never get there."[7]

For his part, Brooks proceeded to round out a detailed program for the repeal of *The Law*. That the job was completed during the winter of 1897–1898 is clear from Henry's correspondence. Henry wrote from Athens in April 1898 (where he was visiting the American minister to Greece, William Woodville Rockhill) to offer Brooks two jingles: one for the "wording of your Law" and the second for "your other formula." The latter documents Brooks's preoccupation with Asia.[8]

Under economical centralization, Asia is cheaper than Europe.
The World tends to economic centralization.
Therefore Asia tends to survive, and Europe to perish.

But Brooks was concerned with action, not jingles, and soon published a policy recommendation.

In February 1899—eight months before Washington enunciated the
Open Door in Asia—Brooks Adams presented his proposals in an
article in the *Fortnightly Review*. In the past, he began, American industry's "liberal margin of profit" had been "due to expansion" across
the continent. In the drive to control that market, however, industry
had been "stimulated" to produce a surplus. "The time has now
come," Brooks went on," when that surplus must be sold abroad, or
a glut must be risked." Those who failed to expand, he warned, were
"devoured by the gangrene which attacks every stagnant society and
from which no patient recovers." "Eastern Asia," he then pointed
out, "now appears to be the only district likely soon to be able to
absorb any great increase of manufactures." There was no choice,
Brooks Adams concluded, but to compete for that "seat of empire."[9]
This strident call for expansion fell on important ears.

Soon after his seminar with Brooks in 1893, Henry Adams became
obsessed with *The Law*. Not only did it arm him with a rational defense for his pessimism and disillusionment but it became the theme
of his endless discussions with John Hay, Henry Cabot Lodge, William Woodville Rockhill, and Theodore Roosevelt. As one witness recalled, "Henry sincerely admired his brother's intellect; he quoted
him the way Saint Augustine quoted Aristotle, only more frequently." As for the book itself, Henry took pains to see that it
reached "all the hands worth considering," including those "of the
Supreme Court and the Cabinet."[10] Henry's role in the propagation
of Brooks's ideas was particularly important prior to the date (September 1901) that Theodore Roosevelt became president. Those years
were especially significant because of Henry's intimate association
with Hay and Rockhill, who directed United States foreign policy
in Asia.

Henry Adams and John Hay had known each other since 1861, but
prior to Henry's summer with Brooks, their relationship was primarily of a gay social and intellectual nature. The character of the friendship changed noticeably, however, after Henry was apprised of *The
Law*. In 1891, for example, Henry complained that French "painting
and sculpture" made him "seasick." But in October 1893, Henry Adams suddenly began to discuss the fate of the world in terms of "uni-

versal bankruptcy," and by January 1898, he was "more immediately curious about Russia."[11] This new concern remained the central feature of their subsequent correspondence.[12] During these same years, moreover, Henry extended his friendship with William Woodville Rockhill.

Henry's acquaintance with Rockhill was of later origin because of the latter's duty as a State Department official in China and Korea and his subsequent expeditions to Mongolia and Tibet. But after 1890, their contacts were extended, and together with Hay they formed a seminar on foreign affairs. The group was temporarily disrupted, however, in 1897. First Hay was sent to London as United States ambassador. That left Henry "quite alone . . . except for Rockhill, in the atmosphere of foreign affairs."[13] A bit later Rockhill was again sent abroad, but this time Henry trailed along, and the two of them enjoyed a trip through the Balkans.[14] Not much later, however, Hay returned to take up his duties as secretary of state under President William McKinley, and these friendships took on added importance.

The first task which confronted Secretary Hay and Henry Adams was to get Rockhill home from Athens, where he was serving as United States minister to Greece. "Everything will be done," Henry assured him, "to bring you back." After some difficulty Hay secured Rockhill's appointment as director of the Bureau of American Republics, and the circle was again complete.[15] Hay had already "expressed a wish" to have Henry as "an associate in his responsibilities"; but Henry preferred to function in a more confidential manner. They began their routine of daily walks at four in the afternoon, time spent "discussing the day's work at home and abroad."[16]

These discussions, it is clear, were carried on within the frame of reference supplied by Brooks Adams. They "diagnosed the whole menagerie," as Henry recalled, and "killed and buried, in advance, half the world and the neighboring solar systems." But Russia plagued them constantly. "What *can* you do?" Henry challenged bluntly; and Hay confessed, in moments of despair, that the "only comfort after all is in your cheerless scheme of the correlation of forces."[17] But obviously, Hay did not really believe himself in such moments of fatalism, for all the while he actively sought to implement Brooks Adams's answer to the dilemma.

The remarkable correlation between Secretary of State Hay's "Open Door Notes" of September 1899 (and his later policy toward Russia) and Brooks Adams's detailed blueprint of the proper policy to be followed by the United States in Asia was not a coincidence. That is not to say that Brooks Adams was directly responsible for that policy. The secretary not only leaned heavily on Rockhill for advice concerning China but both of them were strong Anglophiles who lent a ready ear to British proposals to cooperate against Russia in the Far East.[18]

Most significant of all, of course, was the eager enthusiasm with which American economic interests responded to the lure of new markets in China. American capital, represented by the American Trading Company, the Bethlehem Iron Works, the Chase National Bank, other syndicates of American bankers, industrial corporations, and railroads, and the American China Development Company began to move into Asia as early as 1895.[19] The latter organization was one of the first to cross swords with the Russians, but of more immediate importance was the pressure exerted on the State Department by the Pepperell Manufacturing Company of Boston, cotton textile exporters. Their petition of January 1899 (endorsed by other business interests and supported by Senator Lodge) requested action to remove the "danger of being shut out from the markets of that portion of North China which is already occupied or threatened by Russia." A bit later the South Carolina mill owners declared that their "prosperity" depended "on the China trade."[20] This was the overseas economic expansion on which Brooks Adams based his analysis.

Yet these factors—vital as they were—do not fully explain the readiness with which Secretary Hay disregarded the advice of his representatives who warned that the English were America's "worst antagonists" in Asia and recommended that "our friendly relations with Russia should be enhanced."[21] Or, more significantly, his instructions to "act energetically" in behalf of those who signed the Pepperell petition.[22] It seems clear that he had been conditioned to an acceptance of Brooks Adams's broad analysis through his long and intimate association with Henry. Small wonder that Brooks Adams thought that "the only minister of foreign affairs in the whole world who grasped the situation was John Hay."[23] Nor did the influence of Brooks Adams decline in subsequent years.

Henry Adams, however, ultimately declined to support such vigorous expansion. True, for a time he thought "that the world has got to be run by us, or not at all"; but he soon changed his mind.[24] "I incline strongly now to anti-imperialism," he warned Brooks, "and very strongly to anti-militarism. . . . If we try to rule politically, we take the chances against us."[25] And as time went on, the old intimacy with Hay became "very awkward indeed," as Henry was "dead opposed to all his policy. . . . He is one wheel in the old machine of Hanna and Pierpont Morgan, and Root is the other." Not disposed to put his "fingers into the machinery," Henry Adams turned away to study the "dynamic theory of gases" and cultivate his "twelfth-century instincts."[26] But Brooks—who thought Henry (like his grandfather) only "disappointed because he was not supernatural"—stepped up the tempo of his campaign to repeal *The Law*.[27]

After 1901, Brooks Adams exerted his influence more directly—as adviser to President Theodore Roosevelt. Their intimate relationship was founded on a common determination to disprove the validity of *The Law*. They shared an incidental friendship prior to 1885, but during the following ten years the men developed a warm understanding. When Brooks married the sister of Henry Cabot Lodge's wife in September 1889, the friendship was further strengthened. A bit later, for example, Lodge and Brooks collaborated to organize the Commonwealth Club; and throughout the period, of course, Roosevelt was "always welcome" in the inner sanctum at 1603 H Street.[28] By 1895, Brooks and Roosevelt were not only cordial friends but the latter was well acquainted with the thesis of *The Law*.

That such was the case need not be doubted, for early in November 1896, Roosevelt acceded to Brooks's request to review the volume. Early that same spring, moreover, Roosevelt revealed that the study disturbed him considerably. He took particular care to advise Lodge that Gustave Le Bon was guilty of "fundamental errors . . . quite as vicious in their way as Brooks Adams'." Nor had he found solace in Le Bon's conclusions, which "contained a sweeping prophecy of evil quite as gloomy as Brooks'."[29] Roosevelt's review of *The Law* was written in the same vein.

"Few more powerful and . . . melancholy books have been written," declared Roosevelt; but though he picked at the thesis and its proof, his review is remarkable for its acceptance of much of Brooks's argument and phraseology. Friend Theodore considered Brooks "at his best in describing . . . the imaginative man whose energy manifests itself in the profession of arms." But TR, who had a "very firm faith" in the philosophy of steady progress, entered a strong dissent when Brooks denied that any individual or group could "influence the destiny of a race for good or bad." "All of us admit," Roosevelt conceded, "that it is very hard . . . but we do not think it is impossible."[30]

Other factors intensified Roosevelt's response to *The Law*. A practicing Social Darwinist, Roosevelt was also a close friend of Captain Alfred Thayer Mahan. And the captain's theory of an industrial mercantilism enforced by control of the sea not only influenced TR considerably but also supplemented the views of Brooks Adams. Likewise important is the fact that Roosevelt was a strong Anglophile.

These aspects of Roosevelt's personality and thought help explain his ready response to Brooks Adams's ideas and friendship.[31]

Roosevelt was one of the first to whom Brooks Adams revealed his own concern with *The Law*. "The whole world," he admitted early in 1896, "seems to be rotting, rotting." But at an early date Brooks recognized that Roosevelt was the perfect medium through which to act, and he began to play on TR's admiration for the military. "You are an adventurer," he wrote, "and you have but one thing to sell—your sword." Brooks went on to point out that the essence of life was to live and then bluntly challenged Roosevelt to join him in an assault on *The Law*. "Why not live," he asked, "and be hired by a force which masters you, rather than be crushed in a corner to no purpose?"[32]

Roosevelt gave ready assent to Brooks's plan to reemphasize the "martial man," who in turn would dominate the centralization and economic competition that threatened disintegration. "Peace is a goddess," TR declared in June 1897, "only when she comes with sword girt on thigh." Later, when Roosevelt became governor of New York, Brooks journeyed to Albany to warn TR of the dangers in militant trade unionism and the eight-hour day. But neither of the men ever lost sight of the real goal—to repeal *The Law*. On that occasion, as Roosevelt advised Hay, they discussed the possibility of "heading some great outburst of the emotional classes which should at least temporarily crush the Economic Man."[33] That Brooks had also briefed TR on his full program became apparent shortly thereafter.

The following year (1900) Brooks Adams published his detailed plan to destroy *The Law*. Entitled *America's Economic Supremacy*, it was merely an expansion of the article in the *Fortnightly Review*. From a careful review of the concentration and disintegration of England's economic power, Brooks drew one major conclusion: expansion into Asia must be pressed. The obvious enemy was Russia ("the vast monster"), but if Japan should prevail "the situation would remain substantially unaltered." Nor did the means pose any serious problem. Martial man was to be reinvigorated, and the United States, concluded Brooks, must "reduce" Asia "to a part of [its] economic system."[34] That the book was either ignored or misunderstood (and sold but a few copies) was unimportant; for Theodore Roosevelt became president of the United States less than a year later.

Roosevelt had already given the public a preview of what was to come. Writing in the *Independent* of December 21, 1899 (a mere six months after Brooks's summer visit), TR announced that "on the border between civilization and barbarism war is generally normal." It naturally followed, argued Roosevelt, that only "the mighty civilized

races which have not lost the fighting instinct" could, "by their expansion," gradually secure peace through the defeat of the "barbari-
ans." With reference to the Pacific, moreover, Roosevelt was careful
to note that "the great progressive colonizing nations are England and
Germany." The inference was clear: doubly so since Brooks declared
that Russia was "peopled by an archaic race."[35]

And Roosevelt's State of the Nation message on December 3, 1901,
must have sounded familiar to anyone who had read *The Law* and
America's Economic Supremacy. TR stressed two themes: military might
and the "permanent establishment of a wider market for American
products." With reference to China, he declared, the latter meant
"not merely the procurement of enlarged commercial opportunities
on the coasts, but access to the interior." For a summary, the president merely paraphrased Brooks (by whom, he took care to acknowledge, it had "been well said") in a categorical warning. "The American people," Roosevelt admonished, "must either build and maintain
an adequate navy or else make up their minds definitely to accept a
secondary position in international affairs, not merely in political, but
in commercial, matters."[36]

Despite such influence, Brooks Adams was impatient. Henry offered encouragement. "I rather incline," he wrote in April 1902, "to
suspect that, another year, your friend in the White House may feel
more grateful for your support than in the years now passing, even if
he is not more active in rewarding it. . . . Teddy's luck is not to be
forgotten."[37] Brooks, of course, had not long to wait. Senators Henry
Cabot Lodge and Jonathan P. Dolliver publicly acknowledged their
debt to Brooks Adams and urged the public to support both economic
expansion in Asia and opposition to Russia.[38] And Roosevelt soon
gave his undivided attention to China—for Brooks "the great problem of the future."[39]

The Far East was "uppermost" in Roosevelt's mind, and it was,
moreover, the "corrupt, tricky, and inefficient" Russians (Brooks
termed them "ignorant, uninventive, indolent, and improvident")
who early "aroused and irritated him."[40] This open and vigorous opposition to Russia, however, tends to obscure the fact that "at no
time" did TR favor Japan's complete ascendancy. In the struggle between those two nations his plan—in close harmony with Brooks's—
was "to exhaust both Russia and Japan" and thereby secure America's
supremacy in Asia.[41] But their undue emphasis on the Russian men-
ace caused Brooks and Theodore to lose the initiative to Japan.

Both men recognized their dilemma. What the Japanese "will do to
us hereafter," worried TR, "when intoxicated by their victory over

Russia, is another question."[42] Roosevelt was also ready to stop the whole affair on another count. Both Brooks Adams and TR's diplomatic troubleshooter, businessman George von Lengerke Meyer (the president, in his growing fear, had transferred him from Italy to St. Petersburg) warned that a revolution in Russia would be disastrous no matter what the final result.[43] A weakened Russia would further strengthen Japan while a reinvigorated Russia might threaten the Manchurian claims of all the interested powers. Yet either possibility seemed imminent as tsarist bureaucracy began to crack under the strain of war. Roosevelt confided his fears to some; to others his problem was obvious.

Henry Adams, for one, was near hysteria lest his brother ("who runs about and instructs the great") would precipitate a full-scale catastrophe. "We shall sink or swim" with the tsar, he cried, "half crazy" over the prospect of a revolution in Russia.[44] Roosevelt, too, was afraid. "I earnestly hope," he admitted to Meyer, that "the Tsar will see that he must at all hazards . . . make peace . . . and then turn his attention to internal affairs."[45] But Henry was not encouraged. Theodore, in his opinion, had "touched nothing which he has not deranged." It was not so much his fault, however, as it was "the rotten old machinery of society."[46]

Brooks Adams still argued, however, that the machinery "must be made to run"; a notion to which Henry replied that Brooks "had better just make his own, and the public's mind run, for the trouble is here."[47] And finally, his patience exhausted, Henry charged Brooks with full responsibility. "All you can do," he thundered, "is vapor like Theodore about honesty!—Damn your honesty! And law!—Damn your law! And decency!—Damn your decency! From top to bottom the whole system is a fraud—all of us know it, laborers and capitalists alike—and all of us are consenting parties to it."[48]

Clearly, the plan to repeal *The Law* had gone awry. But Brooks Adams and Theodore Roosevelt struggled on. The United States would be safe, TR assured Lodge, "if the Navy was strengthened." But "if as Brooks Adams says, we show ourselves 'opulent, aggressive and unarmed,'" a disaster might well occur. This phrase seems to have been a Roosevelt favorite, for he had also used it in his message of December 3, 1901. And after a guarantee for the Philippines had been negotiated (the Taft-Katsura Memorandum of July 29, 1905), Roosevelt staged a great show of force. The intent behind his dispatch of the fleet on a world cruise is clear: TR thought it "time for a showdown."[49] That the Japanese reaction might be something less than awe seems never to have been considered.

Brooks Adams and Theodore Roosevelt confessed their temporary failure but never abandoned their effort to get the world on a downhill pull. Both men blamed the public for their failure, saying that it lacked the strength to carry through.[50] But Henry Adams, among others, viewed the performance with grave misgivings. "I still see our Theodore," he confided to Elizabeth Cameron, "as before, in the guise of a rather droll Napoleon who thinks that the laws are not made for him."[51] And, in a moment of brilliant insight, he also rebuked Brooks. One of his own efforts, Henry found it necessary to explain to Brooks, was a joke; and then, almost as an afterthought, Henry added, "It can't help you in the least. Jokes never do."[52] For Brooks Adams, who thought his brother pathetic in that he was "disappointed because he was not supernatural," was even more so—Brooks thought himself to be just that.

NOTES

1. H. Adams, *The Education of Henry Adams: An Autobiography* (Boston: Houghton Mifflin, 1918), 337–339; compare H. Adams to E. Cameron of August 8, 1893, with same to same of September 15, 1893. *Letters of Henry Adams. Vol. II. 1892–1918*, edited by W. C. Ford (Boston: Houghton Mifflin, 1938; hereafter cited as *LHA*), 31, 33; B. Adams, "The Heritage of Henry Adams," in H. Adams, *The Degradation of the Democratic Dogma, with an Introduction by Brooks Adams* (New York: Harper, 1919), 88–90; B. Adams, *The Law of Civilization* (New York: Macmillan, 1896; New York, 1942, with C. A. Beard's suggestive essay as Introduction; citations from 1896 ed. unless otherwise noted).

2. C. Beard, Introduction, *The Law*, 24, 28.

3. H. Adams, *Education*, 360; H. Adams to B. Adams, June 5, 1895, *LHA*, 69–70; same to same, October 7, 1900, *Henry Adams and His Friends: A Collection of His Unpublished Letters*, compiled by H. D. Cater (Boston: Houghton Mifflin, 1947; hereafter cited as *HAF*), 499.

4. B. Adams, *The Law*, viii–xi.

5. B. Adams, *The Law*, vii, xi; H. Adams to B. Adams, June 5, 1895, *LHA*, 69–70; same to same, September [?], 1895, *LHA*, 82–84; same to same, December 27, 1895, *HAF*, 352–353; same to same, January 3, 1896, *HAF*, 354–355; same to same, April 2, 1898, *LHA*, 162–163; H. Adams to E. Cameron, August 21, 1905, *LHA*, 460.

6. B. Adams, *The Law*, 324–325; H. Adams to B. Adams, June 5, 1895, *LHA*, 69–70; H. Adams to Charles F. Gaskell, June 20, 1895, *LHA*, 72; H. Adams to B. Adams, February 18, 1896, *LHA*, 100; H. Adams to C. F. Gaskell, January 7, 1897, *LHA*, 119.

7. H. Adams to B. Adams, December 27, 1895, *HAF*, 353.

8. H. Adams to B. Adams, April 2, 1898, *LHA*, 162–163.

9. B. Adams, "Commercial Future: New Struggle for Life Among Nations," *Fortnightly Review* 71 (n.s. 65, February 1899), 274–283. This article became chapter 2 of *America's Economic Supremacy* (New York: Harper, 1900, 1947); H. Adams to B. Adams, August 20, 1899, *HAF*, 472–473.

10. H. D. Cater, Preface, *HAF*, lxxxiii, citing Mrs. Winthrop Chandler as his source; H. Adams to B. Adams, January 3, 1896, *HAF*, 354–355; same to same, January 24, 1896, *HAF*, 356–357; H. Adams to E. Cameron, February 26, 1900, *LHA*, 270, and H. Adams to C. F. Gaskell, December 20, 1895, *LHA*, 91, which call attention to Richard Olney's response to *The Law*.

11. H. Adams to Hay, June 18, 1892, November 7, 12, 1892, all in *LHA*, 11–12, 24–26; H. Adams to Hay, December 21, 1891, *HAF*, 259–260; same to same, October 18, 1893, *HAF*, 291–294; same to same, January 11, 1898, *HAF*, 143–144.

12. See, as representative, H. Adams to Hay, August 24, 1896, July 28, 1896, October 23, 1896, and October 28, 1896, all in *HAF*, 379, 390–393; and same to same, September 12, 1897, January 11, 1898, May 5, 1898, May 17, 1898, May 26, 1898, May 31, 1899, and December 15, 1899, all in *LHA*, 131–132, 143–145, 175–176, 179–181, 183–184, 230–232, 249–250.

13. H. Adams to Hay, January 4, 1894, *HAF*, 303; H. Adams to Rockhill, October 31, 1898, *HAF*, 451; H. Adams to B. Adams, February 7, 1900, *LHA*, 264.

14. H. Adams to B. Adams, April 2, 1898, *HAF*, 430–431; H. Adams to E. Cameron, April 10, 1898, *LHA*, 165; H. Adams to B. Adams, May 6, 1900, *HAF*, 461–462.

15. H. Adams to Rockhill, August 24, 1898, *LHA*, 187; the maneuvers that secured Rockhill's return can be followed in *HAF*, 452–460, and *LHA*, 207, 214, 218.

16. H. Adams to C. Gaskell, January 23, 1896, October 4, 1898, *LHA*, 93–94, 187; H. Adams to E. Cameron, November 15, 1898, November 21, 1898, February 26, 1900, April 6, 1902, all in *LHA*, 189, 190, 269, 394.

17. H. Adams to Hay, June 26, 1900, Hay to Adams, July 8, 1900, H. Adams to Hay, September 13, 1900, H. Adams to Hay, December 16, 1900, H. Adams to E. Cameron, February 18, 1901, H. Adams to E. Cameron, March 18, 1901, H. Adams to Cecil Spring Rice, February 8, 1901, all in *LHA*, 289–290, 292, 296–297, 305–308, 315, 316–317, 321–322, and note 10 above.

18. On British policy, see J. Chamberlain to Lord Arthur Balfour, February 3, 1898, quoted in B. E. C. Dugdale, *Arthur James Balfour* (2 vols., New York: Hutchinson & Co., 1936), I: 252–253; Hay's response to this proposal in Hay to Lodge, May 25, 1898: W. R. Thayer, *The Life and Letters of John Hay* (2 vols., Boston: Houghton Mifflin, 1915), II: 168, and Hay to C—S—H—, Oct. 29, 1900, *Letters and Diaries of John Hay* (3 vols., Washington, D.C., 1908), III: 199. On the influence of Lord Charles Beresford and Alfred E. Hippisley, see A. W. Griswold, *The Far Eastern Policy of the United States* (New York: Harcourt Brace, 1938): 48–49, 62–64.

19. C. Denby to R. Olney, February 25, 1895, quoted in E. H. Zabriskie,

American-Russian Rivalry in the Far East, 1895–1914 (Philadelphia: Greenwood, 1946): 33; B. A. Romanov, *Rossia v Manchzhurii, 1892–1906* (Moscow, 1928): 102–103; C. Cary, *China's Present and Prospective Railways* (New York: Lehmair: 1899): 14–17.

20. A. Vagts, *Deutschland und die Vereinigten Staaten in der Weltpolitik* (2 vols., New York: Winter, 1935), II: 1046–1047, 1040–1058; Griswold, *Far Eastern Policy*, 60, note 4.

21. Denby to Sherman, April 2, 1897, quoted in Vagts, *Weltpolitik*, II: 995–996; others pointed out that economic possibilities in Russia were far more important than St. Petersburg's threat to American trade in Manchuria, *Foreign Relations, 1899* (Washington, 1901): 594–599; Vagts, *Weltpolitik*, II: 1046–1047.

22. Adee to Tower, March 8, 1899, quoted in Vagts, *Weltpolitik*, II: 1047.

23. B. Adams, "John Hay," *McClure's Magazine* 20 (June 1902): 180; and see T. Dennett, *John Hay: From Poetry to Politics* (New York: Doubleday Page & Co., 1933): 289, where Dennett points out that Henry Adams may well have exercised such a critical influence. Dennett seems to have missed the fact that it was Brooks, not Henry, who developed the policy.

24. H. Adams to B. Adams, April 29, 1901, *LHA*, 330.

25. H. Adams to B. Adams, February 8, 1901; same to same, May 7, 1901, *HAF*, 504, 507–509.

26. H. Adams to E. Cameron, April 6, 1902, *LHA*, 383; H. Adams to B. Adams, May 7, 1901, same to same, May 2, 1903, same to same, March 4, 1900, all in *HAF*, 487, 508, 545.

27. B. Adams. "The Heritage of Henry Adams," *Degradation*, 35.

28. *The Letters and Friendships of Sir Cecil Spring Rice: A Record*, compiled by S. Gwynn (2 vols., Boston: Little, Brown, 1929), I: 52.

29. *Selections from the Correspondence of Theodore Roosevelt and Henry Cabot Lodge, 1884–1918*, edited by H. C. Lodge (2 vols., New York: Charles Scribner's Sons, 1925), I: 218, 239.

30. T. Roosevelt, "The Law of Civilization and Decay," *The Forum* 22 (January 1897): 575, 578, 579, 587; T. Roosevelt to Sir A. Balfour, March 5, 1908, quoted in J. B. Bishop, *Theodore Roosevelt and His Time* (2 vols., New York: Charles Scribner's Sons, 1920), II: 107.

31. H. Adams to E. Cameron, February 23, 1902, *LHA*, 374; T. Roosevelt to Mahan, March 18, 1901, quoted in H. F. Pringle, *Theodore Roosevelt* (New York: Harcourt Brace, 1931): 374, 171.

32. B. Adams to T. Roosevelt, February 25, 1896, and April 26, 1896, quoted in M. Josephson, *The President Makers, 1896–1919* (New York: Harcourt Brace, 1940): 27, 60–61; and see Beard's Introduction, *The Law* (1942).

33. T. Roosevelt, Speech at the Naval War College, June 2, 1897, quoted in *Works: National Edition* (20 vols., New York: Charles Scribner's Sons, 1925), XIV: 182–199; T. Roosevelt to Hay, June 17, 1899, in Josephson, *President Makers*, 98.

34. B. Adams, *America's Economic Supremacy* (New York, 1947): 63, 78, 96, 98, 132, 151, 153, 155, 157, 170, 179, 193, 194; Henry advised Brooks that the

reviews were "lumps of drivel," H. Adams to B. Adams, February 8, 1901, *HAF*, 504. Prior to the appearance of the volume, Brooks also published another excerpt, "Russia's Interest in China," *Atlantic Monthly* 86 (September 1900): 309–317.

35. T. Roosevelt, "Expansion and Peace," *The Independent* (December 21, 1899), and *The Strenuous Life* (New York: Century Co., 1904), 23–26; Adams, *Supremacy*, 179.

36. T. Roosevelt, "Message of the President of the United States to the First Session of the Fifty-Seventh Congress, December 3, 1901," *Congressional Record*, 57th Cong., 1st sess. (Washington, D.C., 1901), XXXV: 82–83, 84, 86, 88, 89, 92; for passages of striking similarity written by Brooks Adams at an earlier date, see "Russia's Interest in China," *Atlantic Monthly* 86 (September 1900): 310, 317; "The New Industrial Revolution," *Atlantic Monthly* 87 (February 1901): 165; "Reciprocity or the Alternative," *Atlantic Monthly* 88 (1901): 154, 155; *Supremacy*, 82, 103, 105, 131–132, 192, 194; and see Roosevelt to B. Adams, September 27, 1901, *The Letters of Theodore Roosevelt*, edited by E. E. Morison (Cambridge, 1951), III: 152–153.

37. H. Adams to B. Adams, April 21, 1902, *HAF*, 524–525.

38. H. C. Lodge, "Some Impressions of Russia," *Scribner's Magazine* 31 (1902): 571; J. P. Dolliver, "Significance of the Anglo-Japanese Alliance," *North American Review* 174 (1901–1902): 594.

39. B. Adams, *Supremacy*, 194.

40. Pringle, *Roosevelt*, 372; T. Roosevelt to L. C. Griscom, July 27, 1905, quoted in T. Dennett, *Roosevelt and the Russo-Japanese War* (New York: Doubleday Page & Co., 1925): 241; B. Adams, *Supremacy*, 179; T. Roosevelt to Hay, July 18, 1903; A. L. P. Dennis, *Adventures in American Diplomacy, 1896–1906* (New York: E. P. Dutton, 1928): 359.

41. T. Roosevelt, conversation with Speck von Sternberg, Mar. 21, 1904, quoted in *Die Grosse Politik der Europäischen Kabinette, 1871–1914* (Berlin, 1921–1927), XIX: I, no. 5992; L. Griscom, *Diplomatically Speaking* (New York: Little, Brown, 1940): 244–245; Zabriskie, *Rivalry*, 107.

42. T. Roosevelt to Sir G. Trevelyan, Mar. 9, 1905, quoted in Pringle, *Roosevelt*, 380; T. Roosevelt to Spring Rice, December 27, 1904; Dennett, *Roosevelt*, 47–50.

43. B. Adams, *Supremacy*, 191; T. Roosevelt to G. von L. Meyer, July 7, 1905: Bishop, *Roosevelt*, I: 399–400.

44. H. Adams to E. Cameron, February 7, 1904, January 10, 1904, Aug. 29, 1905, all in *LHA*, 423, 419, 461.

45. T. Roosevelt to Meyer, July 7, 1905; Bishop, *Roosevelt*, I: 399–400.

46. H. Adams to E. Cameron, August 21, 1905, *LHA*, 460.

47. H. Adams to E. Cameron, August 21, 1905, September 3, 1905, *LHA*, 460, 462.

48. H. Adams to B. Adams, September 20, 1910, *LHA*, 549.

49. Lodge, *Correspondence*, II: 135; T. Roosevelt, "Message of December 3, 1901," *Cong. Record*, 57th Cong., 1st sess., XXXV: 1, 89; T. Roosevelt to Sir G. Trevelyan: Bishop, *Roosevelt*, II: 249–250.

50. B. Adams, "A Problem in Civilization," *Atlantic Monthly* 106 (July 1910): 26–32; "The Collapse of Capitalistic Government," *Atlantic Monthly* 111 (April 1913): 433–443; "The American Democratic Ideal," *Yale Review* V (January 1916): 225–233; T. Roosevelt to William Howard Taft, December 12, 1910: Griswold, *Far Eastern Policy*, 132.

51. H. Adams to E. Cameron, September 13, 1912, *LHA*, 603.

52. H. Adams to B. Adams, January 30, 1910, *LHA*, 533.

CHAPTER 2

Charles A. Conant, Economic Crises and Foreign Policy, 1896–1903

CARL PARRINI

Charles Arthur Conant was one of the first American intellectuals to address systematically the social, economic, and political problems of modern industrial capitalist society that crystallized in the United States during the Great Depression of 1893–1897. In books and a series of articles published between 1896 and 1903, Conant analyzed the essential problem of industrial capitalism as recurrent crises rooted in "surplus capital," a condition that Karl Marx had earlier analyzed as "overaccumulation" and that John Maynard Keynes, more than thirty years later, analyzed as the tendency toward excess savings and the "declining marginal efficiency of capital."

Conant was born in Winchester, Massachusetts, on July 2, 1861. He had no formal education beyond high school but engaged in vigorous self-directed study. He began to make himself into an economic expert when in 1889 he became Washington, D.C., correspondent for both the *Springfield Republican* and the *New York Journal of Commerce*. During his Washington correspondent years, he attracted the attention of Lyman J. Gage, who was William McKinley's secretary of the treasury. Through Gage, he came to the attention of Hugh H. Hanna and Elihu Root, both of whom were prominent members of the U.S. banking community; the former served as executive director of the executive committee of the Indianapolis Monetary Convention, and the latter served as general counsel to the Morton Trust Company of New York. Conant worked closely with Hanna in the monetary convention movement to propagandize in favor of a central bank in the

United States. As McKinley's secretary of war, Root sent Conant to the Philippines to study the archipelago and recommend policies to make the islands safe outlets for capital investment. Subsequent to successfully completing that mission, Root had Conant added to the board of directors of the Morton Trust in early 1902. He then acted as agent for the House of Morgan as well as the Morton Trust in efforts to get U.S. government guarantees for risky foreign investment in the Philippines and China. Although he failed to obtain the agreement of the Roosevelt administration to such guarantees, he did become a member of the Commission on International Exchange (CIE), which Roosevelt instructed to work on monetary stabilization in China and Mexico as well as other areas of Latin America, such as Cuba and Nicaragua. On July 5, 1915, he died while on a mission in Cuba.

The first part of this essay examines Conant's understanding of the evolution of the capitalist investment system, the process of accumulation, and the capitalists' investment function, all of which led him to develop a critique of classical economic theory. From his studies and his experience as a financial journalist, Conant developed a theory of economic growth. The second part of the essay deals with the way in which Conant applied his theory to policy in the Philippine islands, which was then adapted to Chinese currency reform.

In the books and articles of 1896–1903, Conant urged policymakers in the government, industry, and banking to abandon the historic assumptions prevailing since Adam Smith and David Ricardo that the principal need of a developing society was to accumulate capital for investment in its own resources and enterprises. The title of one of his articles, "Crises and Their Management," indicated the extent to which he had departed theoretically from Smith, Ricardo, Jean Baptiste Say, and John Stuart Mill. The article—and the supporting model, demonstrated therein—asserted that crises were endogenous to modern capitalism, characterized as it was by mass production preceding market demand. It also asserted that crises could not be avoided but could be mitigated in their severity and could be skillfully managed; thus policymakers could help to shorten crisis periods. While Conant supported monetary policy as a tool available to central bankers to help ease the duration of crises, he did not believe that by itself, monetary policy could manage crises. One of his greatest theoretical innovations was his assertion that fiscal policy had to be combined with monetary policy to manage successfully the periodic crises of modern capitalism. It was these assumptions that led Conant to urge policymakers to reform the way in which the investment system had worked prior to the crisis of 1893.

Conant urged a historic reversal, arguing that the main problem for advanced industrial societies was not the accumulation of capital but the finding of outlets for "surplus capital," both at home and abroad. In this connection, his works constituted an argument for a "planned" domestic "fiscal policy" and a public policy designed to create investment opportunities in less-developed areas for the profitable investment of the surplus capital of all the industrial nations.

At the very time when the "new imperialism" was in its heyday he succeeded in convincing the political and economic leaders of the United States that they ought to pursue both an imperialist and a "postimperialist" international investment policy, combined with just enough fiscal policy at home to yield relatively high profits to capital and relatively full employment to labor in the United States and implicitly in the industrial capitalist community of nations generally. Between 1896 and 1903, Conant anticipated the various solutions to the problem of surplus capital that Keynes later suggested during the crisis of the 1930s. Consequently, Conant's pioneering work not only guided public policymaking on how to stabilize industrial capitalism in his own day but also provided an analysis of the problems that the modern industrial system still faces almost one hundred years later, and his work suggested the basic approach to the way in which modern policy since the end of World War II deals with the malfunctioning of the investment system today, both domestically and in international efforts.[1]

While Conant acknowledged that the period around the turn of the twentieth century was "not the first time that the supply of capital [had] outrun the limits of effective demand," he argued that the phenomenon had acquired an entirely new dimension because mass production had caused savings to increase geometrically, and consequently the problem of surplus capital was far more severe than it had ever been historically. To cope with the problem, Conant argued that it was appropriate and necessary to reassess classical economic theory and its central postulates, which tended to encourage society to subordinate almost all economic activity to the process of saving for investment. While he admitted that "classical economic theories are indisputably correct when applied to the relative poverty of society two or three generations ago when directed against a policy which handicaps competing power by taxing industry unduly," for wasteful government expenditure, he suggested that in modern times, expenditure by the state on nonmilitary goods and services, even those not directly productive, would be of social utility.[2]

He urged American business and political leaders to consider the fact that mercantilist political economists, such as William Petty and Dudley North, were trying to grapple with real problems in their own historical epoch and that therefore the assumptions they had made were in many cases appropriate to solving real problems. For instance, he argued that in a past time when there was insufficient respect for laws to protect contracts and there were few real protections for the profits, the goods, and even the lives of merchants in international trade, and when there were few satisfactory ways to store savings for future investment, the recommendation of the political economists to pile up gold was a most satisfactory way to secure and protect the accumulation and transferability of profits from commerce.[3] In the modern epoch, the relatively widespread respect for law and order, sanctity of contract, and free exchange of national currencies had now negated the rationality of holding all, or even most, of the profits of trade in gold. But what the critics of the mercantile system had called "gold fetishism" had not been irrational in the time of Petty and North. He acknowledged that some aspects of the mercantilist doctrine, such as state-sanctioned commercial monopoly, hobbled industry and that the classical or laissez-faire critique, as it gained wide acceptance, had helped to emancipate "industry from maedieval [sic] fetters." While he criticized the mercantilist tendency to create large war-making establishments, he noted that defense was sometimes necessary to the maintenance of an independent and vibrant national economy. Conant urged the public policymakers in his own day to treat the assumptions of laissez-faire as "historically determined"; by analogy with the mercantilist period, he argued that classical economic theory itself ought to be reassessed. Those portions of theory inappropriate to modern conditions ought to be discarded, and other portions ought to be adapted to modern conditions. He hastened to reassure his audience that the basic axioms of classical theory would "never lose their value as the fundamental principles of political economy," but he maintained that a strict adherence to them would not help much with adjusting the modern social system's "industrial and moral life so as to obtain the greatest result from the smallest expenditure of labor."[4]

Conant's conceptualization of the changed nature of the economic problem first crystallized when he noted, in examining the British economic crisis in the middle of the eighteenth century, that a decline in profit rates and rising unemployment had been preceded by investment in what we would call infrastructure, the building of canals, and loans to farmers for enclosure and irrigation, all of which turned out to be unprofitable. He also noted that these developments were accompanied by "fifteen years of the continuous waste of war." While orthodox economic theory would have suggested war and the associated "waste" of resources as the cause of the crisis, Conant's comparison of the data from the crises of 1837, 1847, 1857, 1866, 1873, and 1890 seemed to show that even when there was no war, if there was a relative decline in the profitability of investment, an economic crisis ensued. He also reasoned that the decline in profitability was a function of the fact that the goods and services produced by new investments could not be marketed. "The overproduction of commodities by means of machinery has been one of the recent forms of the sinking of capital. . . . This power of production has been carried to such a point that it has in many cases outrun the effective demand of the community."[5]

Conant noted a distinction between overproduction of services that infrastructure development created, such as canals, railroads, and means of communication, and investment to produce goods for final consumption. Conant argued that frequently investment in equipment to produce goods for final consumption was more likely to be "wasted," as lack of short-run effective demand for such goods would effectively reduce, if not totally eliminate, returns from such investment. However, investment in canals, railroads, communication, and power-generating capacity by reducing costs of inputs to industries producing for final consumption would tend to sustain or even raise the rate of profit on capital invested to produce goods for final consumption. Conant thus argued that of the two kinds of capital investment, the one in infrastructure provided more stability to the investment system than did the investment in equipment for the production of consumer goods.[6]

He then attempted to determine the factor that interfered with or restricted the rate of investment, especially in infrastructure and capital goods, such as steel rails, locomotives, rail cars, switching equipment, structural steel, and power plants. One of these inhibiting factors was the common practice of capitalists to operate their plants at full capacity. Even when capitalists knew that such a practice was counterproductive—in the sense that to market the production of full-capacity utilization, they had to cut their prices to unprofitable levels—they continued to do so because it earned some revenue to service-bonded debt *and* because the practice was less costly than closing the plant. Conant warned capitalists that such full-capacity utilization tended to shift income shares away from capital and toward labor by creating a kind of "overfull" employment, hence increasing wage levels due to labor scarcity. This provided an important reason for capitalists to take an immediate interest in Conant's analysis as well as in his suggestions that they reassess their traditional attachment to the axioms of classical economic theory.[7]

Having discovered that the source of crisis resided in misplaced investment, due to lack of sufficiently profitable investment opportunities, Conant located and then described secondary causes. For example, as some capitalists became unable to pay their commercial bills on time because of unsold goods in the market, the payments clearing system became disrupted. A crisis might further deepen as capital withdrew, first from the foreign bill market, then from the long-term capital (bond) market. And it might be exacerbated by foreign capitalists' fear that the U.S. Treasury would be unable, or unwilling, to tighten credit under pressure from Congress to encourage banks to extend credit to high-risk business. In the absence of an independent central banking system in the United States, foreign investors suspected that treasury policy would increase inflationary tendencies in the economy; there was no mechanism free of congressional pressure that could tighten credit and therefore reassure capitalists in the short-term bill and long-term bond market about the safety of the principal of their investment. To prevent such threatened disinvestment, Conant worked vigorously for a central bank in the United States. British and other foreign investors in U.S. government and corporation bonds feared that William Jennings Bryan and the "silver Democrats" might persuade Congress to include a larger silver share in the currency, threatening the gold value of these bonds. Conant observed that rising foreign demand for gold payments was symptomatic of incipient crisis conditions because it was a signal to the banks that the ratio of reserves to the volume of loans was insupportable, which led the banks to call their loans. This action, in turn, intensified the payments crisis.[8]

As a gold Democrat, Conant campaigned during the 1890s to limit silver coinage at levels far below those authorized by the Sherman Silver Purchase Act and after that act's repeal in 1893, below the levels advocated by pro-silver political leaders in the U.S. House and Senate. He attempted to determine "scientifically" what limits would be consistent with maintaining the gold content of the dollar. He found that if the monetary authorities discontinued coinage at the point when the supply of silver coins began to outrun demand, which would be indicated by the decline of the value of the silver dollar in relation to gold currency, this would do much to maintain at par the gold exchange value of the dollar.

His analysis of the causes and immediate consequences of economic crises—overaccumulation, or surplus capital—led Conant almost inexorably toward a critique of the "quantity theory of money." He became an advocate of the need for experts with a broad view of the economy to undertake the management of the money supply, in part because he believed that the overwhelming evidence indicated that immediately before an economic crisis, the money market gave incorrect signals to bankers and entrepreneurs, who thus tended to expand credit when they ought to be reducing it. This aspect of his crisis theory equipped him with a set of ideas that later became an important basis for the managed currency and banking system that he set up in the Philippine islands and that he subsequently hoped to establish in China.[9]

Convinced that overaccumulation, or surplus capital, was the cause of the crisis of 1893–1897, Conant attempted to spread this idea among the capitalists, although it went against received doctrine. Capitalists accepted, to a greater or lesser degree, the axiom that there never could be too much accumulation. Conant tried to convince them that to come to grips with the causes of crises and their remedies, they had to accept the idea that there was indeed surplus capital. He therefore concentrated on demonstrating both to government policymakers and to bankers in charge of private investment funds that the observed relative decline in effective demand for goods and services meant that the existing level of savings and hence accumulation of capital was too large.

As evidence of the existence of surplus capital, Conant pointed out that the value of "most of the obligations of solvent states and corporations had been reduced" and that their actual return to investors at market prices had "tended toward two and a half percent." These reduced rates of return in the United States were paralleled abroad, including the rates of the nearly completely secure British Government Consols. He also cited the fact that the substitution of machinery-driven mass production for hand labor had now so altered the accumulation process that the slow accumulations of early centuries were now "multiplied almost in a geometrical ratio as the increased savings of one year went to develop the capacity for savings by the growth of machine plants and means of communication in the years which followed."[10]

In explaining declining rates of return, Conant rejected the charges that (1) investors were simply making too many errors of judgment about what constituted productive investments, and (2) certain weaknesses in human nature, like greed, led to bad investments. Instead he ascribed declining rates of return to "the great excess of saved capital seeking investment" when measured against the relatively small number of safe and profitable outlets.[11]

Once accepted that not all the capital accumulating could be profitably and safely invested, the issue of the optimum size of the investment fund could be acknowledged. Conant attempted to fix this figure by asking what magnitude would "maintain a really healthy equilibrium between supply and demand." It seemed to Conant that three different but related private investment activities ought to determine the fund's size: (1) "an amount of savings sufficient to restore the wear and tear of the existing equipment of production and exchange"; (2) additional capital to "provide new equipment for the increase of population and business"; and (3) "a fund of free capital for investment in really profitable new devices for saving labor and increasing production." He further maintained that "when the amount of saved capital passes this point the result is disastrous to individuals" making the investments, "if not to the whole community." This was a complete reversal of previous accumulation theory, for it denied the axioms of "Say's Law" to the effect that savings not invested would automatically be converted into consumption.[12]

Capital that had been accumulated but not immediately invested, Conant explained, represented "the withdrawal of the purchasing power . . . from the field of demand for consumption goods." In accepted economic theory, according to Say's Law, depositors of money in banks would respond by simply using their savings to purchase consumer goods. But Conant pointed out that the primary purpose of savings deposits was to earn old age income to support middle-class income savers. He suggested as an alternative government spending to care for the aged, which would allow middle-income people to convert their savings in whole or in part into effective consumer demand.[13]

Old age insurance seemed to Conant a partial solution to the structural problem of surplus capital. "It is probable," he explained in 1900, "that the removal of the mass of laborers from the field of those saving for investment would diminish considerably the amount of capital seeking investment on the money market. It would, on the other hand, materially increase the demand for consumption goods." To the usual objections of Say's Law advocates that government taxation and spending to finance old age insurance would place U.S. industry at a competitive disadvantage with foreign producers by increasing real wage costs, Conant pointed out that among the United States' leading international market rivals, "Germany has already taken some long steps toward old age insurance, and Great Britain is seriously considering the subject." To those who objected that such policies would lead to "capital shortage," he responded that the social insurance was simply "the substitution of the direct method of taxation for the indirect method of saving," with current earnings of workers supporting those in old age retirement. In similar fashion, he maintained that current active laborers would "rely upon similar assessments upon the active laborers of the future to sustain them in their old age." Effective demand for consumption of goods would be increased from the income of the laborers themselves, leaving the savings of capital still free for investment.[14]

Conant went beyond advocating social insurance. He noted that there had already taken place a considerable increase in public expenditures, not simply in continental Europe and Britain but also in the United States. By analyzing the direction of those increased expenditures and assessing their social utility, he developed an appealing argument for increasing public expenditures while avoiding waste. He asserted that the pattern of such expenditure was in increasing public spending for sanitation, improved highways, public buildings, and, especially, improved education. In this connection, Conant cited Secretary of the Treasury Gage's statistics that showed salaries paid to schoolteachers in the United States rose by more than 300 percent between 1870 and 1899. He praised this sort of socially beneficial government spending because it helped both to utilize surplus capital and to increase the quality of education. However, he strongly opposed government spending for the military simply or mainly to consume surplus capital. But since he believed that the most important stimulus to the new imperialism was the economic pressure of surplus capital, he argued that under certain circumstances, an aggressive warlike foreign policy might be warranted if it yielded foreign investment outlets and the associated export markets.[15]

Conant did not favor unduly increased taxation to fund government social spending. He observed that capitalists became hesitant to invest in the face of rising taxes. Consequently, he advocated increased government borrowing at the national, state, and local levels to fund the increased spending. The increased issue of government bonds would attract funds from the otherwise uninvested surplus, with which the government could pay teachers' salaries and invest in the construction of school buildings and the like. Thus government borrowing would not discourage private investment but would sop up part of the surplus capital and increase the consumption of goods and services.[16]

Conant reasoned that society could obtain multiple benefits from expanded public employment, far beyond simply increasing the comfort of the community in consuming surplus capital. Such spending could assist in "developing the economic power of the community." In addition, society could "pay the added cost of a larger official class" as well as of the growth of the professional classes, including poets, singers, actors, and journalists; "with the growth of wealth all these occupations [had] become legitimate and honorable callings," and in Conant's view, society ought to encourage them.[17]

In addition to these changes in government fiscal policy, Conant argued for constructive "promotion" or corporate reorganization in the private sector. In his view, innovative corporate reorganization grew out of the accumulation of surplus capital. He explained that when one manufacturer bought out another, this was because there was plentiful money capital available to finance the process. The existence of surplus capital, he held, had led to ruinous competition that had two undesirable effects. On the one hand, it forced prices down to very near the cost of production; on the other hand, it stimulated the creation of production facilities that duplicated existing facilities. The result was that capitalists operated their plants at or near full capacity, dumping the surplus on national and world markets at prices below short-term variable costs.[18]

The creation of large integrated corporations required financial institutions that were capable of raising substantial capital on the security of attractive financial instruments and that employed personnel familiar with both business law and government practices. Conant noted that the banking trust companies, with their management personnel and legal staffs, provided these necessities of the corporate reorganization movement.[19]

Conant explained that even the most powerful and wealthy national banks could not by themselves perform this function. He attributed the promotion of most of the large corporations after the economic crisis of 1893–1897 to the activities of the specialized investment banking houses and the large trust companies, especially those located on Wall Street. He argued that in every significant aspect of corporate reorganization, they were more capable than the national banks. He pointed out, first, that the national banks were legally bound to help stabilize the currency under the National Banking Act and therefore needed to maintain large reserves to guard against the consequences of bank runs and panics. Second, they were bound by law not to allow more than 10 percent of their capital to be lent to any one borrower. Third, virtually all of their deposits were withdrawable on demand. The investment banks and the trust companies did not suffer from any of these disabilities: they could lend larger portions of their deposits than could national banks; they could lend as high a percentage of their deposits to a single borrower as they deemed prudent; and a large portion of their deposits were in the form of long-term and trust accounts, in which demand for withdrawals were at predetermined times. In addition, because trust companies had to meet periodic obligations under their trustee responsibilities, they were "very chary of committing themselves officially to new flotations." Indeed, according to Conant, "some of the most conservative make it a point not to float shares, however good, in common stocks, but limit themselves to bonds, which have priority of lien upon the property upon which they are secured." Their reputations for safety and the fact that much of the surplus capital to fund corporate reorganizations was lodged in their trust accounts made the large trust companies in New York indispensable to both the merger and corporate reorganization movements.

But perhaps as important as the other advantages, Conant explained, were the legal departments staffed by persons with knowledge of corporate law and with government political experience at the presidential cabinet level. For instance, Root had been general counsel to the Morton Trust Company before he became secretary of war, and after he left the War Department, he returned to doing legal work for Morton. Two secretaries of the treasury, Charles S. Fairchild and Gage, joined large New York City trust companies after leaving the Cabinet. The former became head of the New York Security and Trust Company and the latter, head of the United States Trust Company.[20]

Although Conant was fully familiar with advertising as a means of creating new wants that would expand effective demand and realized that technological innovation (highlighted in the economic literature later by Joseph Schumpeter) could consume some surplus capital, he did not expect either to grow so large as to consume most of the surplus capital accumulating in the foreseeable future. In addition, since Conant held that nondefense government spending tended to increase effective demand for goods and services without increasing the general rate of profit and that it, therefore, tended to redistribute national income from capital toward labor, he believed that government spending could reduce capitalists' investment proclivities (Keynes's "animal spirits"). He believed that some further stimulant to investment was needed to stabilize the capitalist social system.[21]

Since among the trust company executives were those who had exercised power over private investment decisions and government fiscal policy, Conant had to fashion techniques consistent with their conception of the national interest. While he did not oppose President McKinley's campaign for reciprocity treaties with developed as well as developing nations, Conant did not believe that tariff reductions, even to the point of relatively "free trade," would be sufficient to enlarge markets to the extent necessary to stimulate the full use of available investment funds. In this connection, he pointed out that both high tariff nations, such as the United States, and free trade nations, such as Great Britain, were suffering from the heavy burden of surplus capital.[22]

In part for these reasons, Conant turned to the idea of creating an international "investment empire," pointing to four different historical examples: (1) the development of the American west prior to 1893; (2) the recent development of Australia prior to the crisis of 1890; (3) the development of the less-developed areas of Eastern Europe, particularly tsarist Russia; and (4) the astounding growth of Japan in the very short period since the Sino-Japanese War of 1894–95.

With respect to the United States, Conant observed that the railroads had been the largest single consumers of capital investment. By 1893, almost two hundred thousand miles of railroad had been constructed, consisting of track, equipment (including rolling stock, switches, signals, and telegraph equipment), and structures such as bridges, terminals, and roundhouses. He also observed that this infrastructure (he liked the French term "installations") opened up new areas and the resources within the areas they served (such as farm, timber, and mineral lands) for additional capital investment. Although he was well aware that there were still many theoretical opportunities for further resource development in the advanced industrial countries, he argued that at the existing level of expected profits, capitalists believed that available outlets were too risky to be developed at that time. Conant believed that the practice of duplicating production facilities meant that capitalists tended to accept lower returns to avoid the high risk inherent in new domestic resource development.[23]

Because he was pessimistic about the possibility of sufficient investment outlets in the United States, he searched abroad for areas that were currently heavy borrowers of capital to collect data about what made such areas sufficiently low risk and sufficiently high profit yielding to overcome the fears of foreign capitalists. He examined areas undergoing modernization, such as Australia, Japan, and tsarist Russia, as well as some of the relatively "unprogressive" countries of Asia and the Pacific, such as China and the Philippine islands.

He found that Australia had experienced a period of development as an important outlet for European surplus capital and that between the years 1874 and 1898, the Australian people "were in the fortunate position of having an almost unlimited credit with their English and Scots countrymen, which enabled them to borrow more liberally and on better terms than any other people." In these years, they borrowed nearly $1.5 billion. The investment of this British capital in Australia resulted in the creation of a large government and private debt. The proceeds of the public debt were used by the Australian government for infrastructure projects, particularly a great railroad network, which, in turn, allowed private capital to penetrate and develop rich new grain-growing and sheep-producing lands and which also allowed private capital to open up new mineral lands, especially areas with rich veins of gold. Some of the capital was even applied to the development of manufactures. The gold, sheep, and grain provided exports to pay interest on the foreign loans. Conant further noted that without the creation and relatively smooth functioning of the global stock and produce exchanges, especially those in London, the "creation of debt in the form of negotiable securities" would be difficult, hence the confidence of investors necessary to allay the fear of the risk to their investment's principal as well as the potential loss of liquidity would have made transfer of capital from foreign nations to Australia—whether for the use by government or corporations—difficult, if not impossible.[24]

Basing his analysis on his examination of the role of British capital in Australian development up to the crisis of 1890, Conant offered a "model" of economic development and growth, which he applied as well to Japan, central and southeastern Europe, and Russia. It seemed to him that the key to growth in Russia and Japan, to the recent rapid development of their resources, their home markets, and their foreign trade, lay in their monetary reforms of the late 1890s, which placed their fluctuating silver currencies on a stable gold exchange basis. Their stable convertible currencies attracted foreign capital that went into developing their natural resources. Foreign investors felt assured that the principal of their capital would be safe and that they could repatriate profits without losses in exchange. Adapting the model to even less developed countries than Japan and Russia, Conant formulated rules of behavior for statesmen, bankers, and capitalists preparing countries such as China for the receipt of capital and consequent economic growth; the rules were designed to make these countries relatively lower-risk and higher-profit outlets for the surplus capital of industrial nations.[25]

Conant's essay, "The Economic Basis of Imperialism," published in

September 1898 in the *North American Review,* analyzed the Spanish American War as effectively putting the United States in the race for empire. He outlined the strategies the United States might follow in dealing with its own surplus capital problem: (1) it might seize colonies to administer, modernize, and invest in them; (2) it might develop markets and investment outlets in nominally independent countries but maintain effective control of them by projecting a naval power; or (3) it might develop a policy that insisted on the equal right of the United States to trade with and invest in the politically independent nations and colonies of the less-developed world.[26] Although Conant seemed to be presenting a choice to his audience, his economic theorizing up to this point, especially the first edition of his *History of Modern Banks of Issue* (New York: G. P. Putnam's, 1896), espoused a theory of economic development that stressed the general advantage of investment in developing areas without restriction. The third option, the generalization of the Open Door Policy encompassing an insistence by the United States on its right to invest in developing areas with no special privileges for the United States or any other industrial nation, was the option Conant actually supported.

Because he generally agreed with Conant's theoretical position and because he was impressed with Conant's work as a monetary expert with the Indianapolis Monetary Convention of 1898, Secretary of War Root selected Conant to go to the Philippine islands in 1901 as a special commissioner for the War Department to make a report on conditions there as they might relate to the possibility of modernizing the islands and making them an attractive target to U.S. investors.[27]

Conant solidified his position by proposing a gold exchange monetary system for the Philippines that contrasted with a system proposed by Paymaster General (of the U.S. Army) A. E. Bates. In an October 31, 1900, memorandum to Comptroller of the Currency Charles G. Dawes, Bates argued that the "chief object to be sought . . . is the improvement and development of trade and this object, in my opinion, will be best attained by not disturbing the existing system of currency." Bates acknowledged that the "ideal currency of the whole world is gold," but he believed that "the present use of gold over a larger territory than the supply justifies would lead to financial disturbances, distrust and disaster." Thus, he concluded that "it is expedient and conducive to the commercial interests of the Philippines that the currency should continue on a silver basis." But what Secretaries Root and Gage were interested in was a monetary and financial system that would encourage the investment of capital in the development of Philippine resources. Gage had already endorsed

Conant's plan for a gold exchange standard as "practical" before Conant departed on his banking mission to the Philippines.[28]

Before Root appointed him, Conant convinced Root that it would be insufficient for the president of the United States, through Civil Governor William Howard Taft and the Philippine Commission, to enact monetary, banking, and coinage rules for the islands, as they had the power to do under McKinley's executive order establishing the Philippine Commission as the executive as well as legislative colonial power. A stronger legal basis was needed. As Conant explained, to the extent that they were "prudent investors," "capitalists contemplating investing" would be "chary of venturing their capital largely in the islands" without congressional legislation. Even new action by President McKinley, in the form of an "executive order, except as it was regarded as the forerunner of similar action by the Congress of the United States," would not convey "the assurance to investors at home and abroad of that permanency of monetary conditions which is absolutely essential to invite large investments and the projections of railways, manufacturing enterprises and other measures for the rapid development of the islands." Such legislation "would fix the monetary system definitely in a manner which would enable capitalists to know in what form of money debts would be contracted and discharged in the Archipelago and under what conditions profitable banking investments could be made." Conant went on to advise that the Philippine currency unit be placed on a forced exchange ratio with the U.S. gold dollar. He opposed any U.S. action, executive or legislative, that would exclude or expel non-U.S. banking capital from the islands, as such a closed door investment policy "would be contrary also to that policy of equality towards all nations which was proclaimed by Judge [William R.] Day in the [peace] negotiations at Paris" establishing the peace treaty with Spain.[29]

As Conant conceived his mission, and as Root approved it, he planned to experiment with the Philippines by applying the specific policy implications of his theory of economic development, drawn in part from his study of events in Australia, Japan, Russia, and the United States. He also entered on his work in the Philippines with a view to applying the lessons learned there to reforming China so as to make it a secure outlet for the investment of the surplus capital of the industrial system. Before he had departed for the Philippines, he had already concluded that the Philippine monetary system should be changed by placing it on a gold exchange standard. Conant also went to the archipelago with the conviction that to attract American and other foreign capital, the U.S. government would have to guar-

anty interest payment on Philippine bonds issued to finance the
building of an economic infrastructure.

Conant concluded that institutions and practices had to be established in the islands which would preserve existing wage levels while
breaking down the patron-client labor relationship, which he regarded as amounting to virtual peonage. He also recommended government regulations to encourage investment by all interested capitalists—American and non-American.[30]

Two weeks later, on July 23, 1901, Root appointed Conant a special
commissioner for Philippine affairs. In a letter to Taft, the civil governor, he outlined the scope of Conant's mission in much the same
terms that Conant had formulated. Root explained to Taft that he
hoped to obtain the legislative results Conant had recommended. In
introducing Conant to Taft, Root praised him as the author of *A History of Modern Banks of Issue* and *The United States in the Orient* and for
his role in helping draft the Gold Standard Act of 1900. He also informed Taft that Conant was a close adviser to Treasury Secretary
Gage and was Gage's choice to undertake the mission.[31]

A monetary reform that would reassure potential foreign investors,
in Conant's view, must be so devised as to avoid disrupting the existing internal wage-price structure in the Philippine islands. "Silver,"
Conant noted, "is the natural money of undeveloped countries,
where the scale of wages is low, and such countries can only be given
the benefits of the gold standard, without detriment to their own interests, by some system which combines the large use of silver with
measures for linking it closely to gold values." Since the general purpose was to encourage investment abroad and since capitalists would
"be deterred from investments under the silver standard" and "attracted under the gold standard," Conant had to find a way by which
"the use of silver money [could] be continued while it [was] given a
fixed and unquestioned relation to gold." In this way, Conant argued,
"the double result will be accomplished of leaving undisturbed the
present customs of the people and of extending a tempting invitation
to American and foreign capital to enter and develop the islands."
In this general approach, Conant was also specifically suggesting
techniques to deal with the objections Paymaster General Bates and
others had raised against extending the gold standard to the
Philippines.[32]

Conant went on to observe that "all trade between silver countries
and gold standard countries is carried on under conditions which are
more or less speculative." This was the case, he explained, because
due to long-term silver depreciation since the 1870s, "the value of

silver as expressed in gold is subject to constant fluctuations." From the standpoint of capitalists residing in gold standard countries, rates of return paid in the currency of a silver standard country would have to be twice the face value of a dividend paid in a gold standard country. As Conant observed, this would be the case especially with "securities paying a fixed and low return if the dividends on such securities were payable in silver. A declared dividend of 3 percent in silver would [at current ratios] shrink to less than 1–1/2 percent when converted into gold." It was for this reason Conant noted, that "the accumulated capital in the great civilized countries has in recent years refused to seek investment in silver countries." He explained that "since it is in the gold standard countries that the great surplus of capital has been accumulated, which is now being offered in the world money markets for the development of the tropical countries, it is absolutely essential that monetary legislation as well as that regarding the sanctity of contracts and security of property should be such as to attract the investors of these countries." [33]

Two different groups raised objections to Conant's broad approach to preparing the Philippines for investment; but they did so from opposite directions. On the one hand, the advocates of a simple and direct extension of the U.S. gold standard currency into the Philippines argued that since gold currency gave foreign investors "confidence" and since the U.S. dollar was such a currency, applying it directly in the Philippines would be the best stimulus for investment of American surplus capital there. On the other hand, silverites argued that since silver was the natural money of less-developed areas, simply applying a silver standard would tend to stabilize wage and price relations in the archipelago. Conant had to fend off attacks from both directions to create a workable system. [34]

He centered his program for a gold exchange standard on a gold stabilization fund. He proposed that a silver peso be coined, in the first instance, from existing Mexican dollars, which were circulating as currency at their bullion value in the islands (and in the Far East generally). Conant would smelt them and recast them at a weight approximately 15 percent below their bullion value. This would yield a fund of approximately $3,000,000 (U.S.) as a gold reserve against a planned initial currency of $20,000,000 (U.S.). "It is probable that a gold reserve of this amount . . . would be sufficient to maintain the value of the silver coins at the parity established by law." If too much of such currency were in circulation, Conant explained, "demands would be made upon the gold reserve by the presentation of silver for exchange." The silver would be stored in the reserve fund, that is, taken out of circulation by fund managers; "the gold withdrawn would be exported from the country." "Thus," he continued, "by the decisive influence of foreign exchange, the currency in circulation would be reduced and would be kept adjusted." If business conditions changed and demand for currency expanded, the reserve fund authorities would import gold as additional reserves.[35]

Conant's plan implemented the principles underlying the War Department report on coinage for 1900. It had advocated finding "some substitute for the Mexican dollar, as well as for the Spanish-Filipino dollar," a substitute that would have a stable value in relation to the U.S. dollar but that would also appear to the general public in the islands to be "substantially what they have long been accustomed to." Conant proposed (1) the coinage of a Filipino peso, worth "legal tender for 50 cents in the gold money of the United States"; (2) that the "coin should be issued by the Government of the Philippine Islands in such quantities . . . as may be required by the needs of trade" in the view of the government; and (3) that the "coin should be maintained at par with gold by the limitation of the amount coined and by a gold reserve, to be constituted from the seigniorage derived from the coinage of silver bullion." He also proposed that in the interests of efficiency and equity, the managers of the gold exchange fund should have the discretion in domestic exchange operations to pay or not "to pay gold for silver at par." He recommended this measure because "gold is the most inviting form of wealth for hoarding, and its free issue in exchange for silver might stimulate hoarding instead of discouraging it." Although classical economic theory postulated that gold could only be obtained for some good or service, or a quantity of silver equivalent to the gold so surrendered, Conant had no qualms about rejecting received doctrine when it contradicted experience. Statistics for gold export and import into the archipelago showed him that "it seems to be the fact nearly all the gold sent from the United States to the Philippine Islands has disappeared. It is not now found in general circulation." Partly this was the case because Philippine merchants, many of whom were of Chinese origin, were in the habit of exporting gold to China, where "as a rule," according to the Schurman Commission, "gold in China commands a fairly good premium." However, to assure foreign capitalists, Conant advised freely exchanging gold at par for silver on demand of foreign investors and those merchants making external payments to gold standard suppliers. These arguments dealt rather effectively with the advocates of a uniform silver currency for the islands. Conant's refutation of the advocates of simply making the U.S. dollar the legal tender of the Philippine islands was more difficult.[36]

If the U.S. dollar was imposed on the islands as legal tender, it would make external payments of interest, dividends, and redemption of principal to foreign investors in stable gold standard currency simple. But it would disrupt domestic wage payments within the islands; "it would create great confusion in retail prices and in rates of wages." At least initially, Filipinos in the interior of the country would not recognize that a U.S. fifty-cent piece "possesses the same value in exchange as the Mexican coin of twice its size and weight." In American money, the laborers "would receive half as much silver as under existing conditions." Even if the laborers understood all this, Conant pointed out that Filipino petty capitalists would be sorely tempted to cheat the laborer by falsely claiming to him that goods now denominated in American dollars were the same price as goods previously denominated in Mexican dollars. Cutting the laborers' purchasing power by as much as 50 percent would, in Conant's view, be "politically disastrous by checking the growing contentment so necessary to the process of pacification."[37]

It was highly likely that cutting the wages of agricultural laborers in this way would impoverish them and thus lead many to join the insurgency. Conant also cited the evidence of what had transpired in Puerto Rico when the U.S. dollar was introduced as the major currency. "Leading bankers and businessmen" reported "that both prices and wages rose as expressed in American money, because of the attempt in many quarters [such as merchants in Puerto Rico] to create the impression that the American gold dollar was the exact equivalent of the silver peso which was converted into American money." Fortunately, there was no insurrection in Puerto Rico.

But even if an information campaign were waged to inform consumers about the real exchange value of U.S. money and thus prevent unscrupulous merchants from cheating their innocent customers, "the American currency would still be open to an important objection." This was so, Conant explained, because "wages are expressed in small amounts in the Philippine Islands, and many articles of necessity to the natives are sold for such trifling sums that for small transactions even the American cent is too large a unit." To remedy this, Conant recommended that the smallest Filipino coin be the *centavo*, which would be half of a U.S. cent (in exchange value). Many local laborers received about 20 centavos for a day's work (a *peseta*).[38]

For these reasons, both a single silver standard or a single U.S. gold dollar-based standard would be insufficient. Consequently, Conant supported a gold exchange standard in the Philippines with an internal silver circulation. In order not to disrupt the internal wage-price structure, he supported external gold payments to assure American (and other foreign) capitalists that investment of their surplus capital in the archipelago was absolutely secure with regard to exchange (as distinct from market or commercial) risks.

Conant argued that the gold exchange standard would also tend to prevent potential negative consequences of an unfavorable balance of payments. Indeed, the islands (really those overseeing economic development there) could import in excess of exports because exporters in the advanced capitalist countries would be accepting in payment for their exports the bonds of the Philippine government so long as they were certain that they would receive their interest in gold or gold exchange and so long as theoretical redemption in the long term of the bonds' principal was expected to be in gold. Even if the proverbial widow or orphan had to raise cash and sell the bonds, since they would have a gold guaranty under Conant's new gold exchange standard, they could raise the cash by selling their bonds on the global "bourses." While investors were thus assured of "fixed" exchange rates in terms of currency convertibility, President Theodore Roosevelt rejected Conant's suggestion that the U.S. Congress guaranty the actual rate of return on bonds issued by the Philippine Commission to finance Philippine infrastructure development in roads, canals, railways, bridges, water (flood control), and power systems. Conant had to resort then to the much less reassuring (to foreign capital) expedient of a guaranty that the Philippine Commission itself would issue. While the commission had such power, its guaranty could not prove as reassuring as one by the U.S. Congress because the latter possessed a much wider fiscal base and because that base was relatively secure against civil unrest (despite residual populist rhetoric). The fiscal base of the Philippine Commission was itself questionable due to the ongoing nature of the Philippine insurrection.[39]

Under the pre-Conant money and banking system, the silver currency in the islands was subject to continuous inflation, and both local and foreign bankers charged exorbitant rates of interest, sometimes as much as 25 to 40 percent per annum on short-term agricultural loans. Conant pointed out that a corporation on the island of Negros, which made small loans to small farmers while nominally charging 25 percent interest, "in effect collects from 30 to 40 percent on the value of the amount loaned, by requiring that the crop of the borrower shall be delivered at the price fixed by the company, that purchase of supplies shall be made from its stores, and that operations connected with the marketing of the crop shall be conducted under its charge and its profit." To Conant, it was "obvious that under favorable conditions a rich field lies open here for the loan of

American capital at rates which will greatly relieve the present condition of borrowers in the Philippines and yet afford profits far in
excess of those which are usually earned in enterprises at home." The
reason such lenders charged such high rates was, in Conant's view,
that using crops as security for such loans might present a situation
in which crop failure (due perhaps to drought or flood) would lead to
destruction of the security. If the land itself were pledged as security
and if modern methods of production were introduced, a market for
sugar (plantation) land could be created, and thus land as security
would justify lower lending rates.[40]

Conant suggested two things to reduce these credit costs and so
provide for an increase of agricultural production. First, he proposed
that the U.S. colonial administration (the Philippine Commission) encourage local "savers" to deposit their surplus cash (in the new gold
exchange currency) in local agricultural banks. This would increase
the supply of short-term capital for agricultural loans, and since the
exchange rate was now "stable," the Philippine branches of European
banks would have to lower their interest rates to compete with the
local bankers. By reducing costs, this would further tend to expand
agricultural production. Thus the internal agricultural economy as
well as the more export-oriented foreign enclave would both tend to
be developed. Second, he proposed that American banks be encouraged to enter the Philippine banking market to lend to U.S. capitalists
on the islands. Participation of American banks in supplying short-
term credit to Philippine agriculture and the much more important
and profitable task of supplying banking services to the foreign investment sector (particularly American capitalists) raised thorny issues. Although President McKinley had issued a set of instructions
for a Philippine Commission, in effect providing for a colonial government in the Philippines, under the Constitution of 1787, the regulation of the currency was a power of Congress, not the Executive Department. The president's colonial power was largely subsidiary to his
authority as commander in chief of the armed forces of the United
States. The Philippine Commission could itself issue regulations for
the establishment of U.S. banks in the islands. But Congress could
undo such presidential action by direct legislation or more surrepti-
tiously by exercise of its appropriation power in a manner so as to
undermine the executive's policy through the Philippine Commission. Conant had to deal with this possibility.[41]

In addition to land mortgage banking, which would increase the
productivity of agriculture and help to establish a market in land,
Conant argued that the provisions of the National Banking Act of the

United States be extended to the Philippines. This, he explained, "will facilitate trade between the islands and the United States to an extent which will not be possible under a system of purely local banking," that is to say, one conducted under the authority of the Philippine Commission. He maintained that the right of U.S. national banks to do business in the islands had to be given legal status by Congress and that such commercial banks had to be regulated by the comptroller of the currency of the United States. Specifically, Conant proposed that Congress give legal authority to national banks to establish branches in the Philippines. Up to that point (1901), "no national bank of the United States [could] lawfully maintain a branch," whether at home in the United States or in the colonies of the United States, such as the Philippine Islands, "under the interpretation given by every succeeding Comptroller of the Currency to the national banking law." Conant therefore proposed that the National Banking Act be modified to allow branches of national banks and to allow those branches to issue circulating bank notes. These were branching powers not enjoyed by national banks at home. Indeed, Conant proposed that restrictions on national bank branching in the United States be lifted; he suggested instead that "national banks established in the Philippine Islands and national banks of the United States should have authority, with the approval of the government of the Philippine Islands, to establish branches in any part of said islands and in the United States."[42]

Conant was proposing, in effect, that colonial law be used to change domestic banking laws. Undoubtedly, he was correctly assessing the economic efficiency of the proposed changes; these alterations in banking law would facilitate the concentration of capital in the hands of the controller-managers of the national banks, which were, in turn, much more able than local or most state banks to safely and profitably invest the accumulating (short-term) surplus capital of the United States both at home and abroad. But also such changes would decrease the weight of independent bankers in the investment system and so undoubtedly act to help concentrate control, if not ownership, of productive property in fewer, albeit more efficient, hands.

The McKinley-Roosevelt administration responded favorably to Conant's proposals on both money and banking, largely because those proposals were designed to facilitate the investment of surplus capital in the archipelago; they defined this investment problem as the obstacle to social and economic stability for the system. In this sense, they were acting as responsible statesmen. There is no evidence that they were seeking personal, social group, or social class profit in so acting.

When Conant submitted his report to Congress, it encountered strong opposition. Silverites insisted on a kind of free and unlimited silver coinage for the Philippines, on the grounds that silver was the natural money of less-developed nations. Many of these silver inflationists saw this as a way to "do something for silver," that is to say, to subsidize silver by creating an artificial demand for it. Gold monometalists advocated direct use of the U.S. dollar in the Philippines.[43]

Conant's experience with the Philippines made him the ideal person to undertake a leading part in the McKinley-Roosevelt administration's plan to prepare China for the receipt of the surplus capital of all the industrial capitalist states. Some time between November 1896 and March-April 1898, American leaders arrived at a consensus that surplus capital was accumulating in the United States and that makers of public policy had to find some means to utilize it in a way that did not decrease profit margins and/or seriously diminish employment opportunities in the domestic economy. McKinley ran for the presidency on a platform that called for enactment of a true gold standard, ending the "free and unlimited coinage of silver" (that is, monetarily excessive coinage of silver), and that advocated that the U.S. government negotiate reciprocity agreements with foreign countries, both with the "Third World" and, more significantly, with the other advanced industrial nations. Such mutual reductions of tariffs on lines of production in which each nation possessed "comparative advantage" would, American leaders rightly believed, stimulate world trade many times the rates of growth of domestic production. They expected that this, in turn, would encourage the domestic investment of the capital thus accumulating, because such a growth in exports would increase profit rates and improve expectations about the continuing increase in profit rates in the future. The McKinley-Roosevelt administration succeeded in getting Congress to pass the Gold Standard Act of 1900 but did not get Congress to agree to a system of reciprocity treaties with other industrial nations that might have stimulated this kind of interindustrial nation trade.

By and large, Congress rejected McKinley's reciprocity proposals, except as they would apply to noncompetitive Third World exports, because reciprocity with modernized nations would have required the surrender of the profit interests of some American capitalists and the existing employment opportunities of some American workers. Congress was authentically and almost immediately representative of local production interests. The president could attempt to convince and "wheedle" but not coerce Congress into making any important market concessions to other industrial countries. Hence, McKinley's effort to build on the principles of comparative advantage to stimulate the investment of surplus capital was a failure.[44]

On March 2, 1903, Congress accepted Conant's gold exchange standard for the Philippine islands, but it rejected his suggestion that the National Banking Act be applied to the islands. It also rejected Conant's proposal that national banks be allowed to branch abroad. When these congressional decisions are considered in combination with Theodore Roosevelt's refusal to allow the U.S. government to guaranty the interest on Philippine bonds, they go far to explain the slow rate of economic development of the Philippine islands and to some extent explain the modest degrees of success Conant attained in attempting to make the archipelago a much more significant outlet for the surplus capital of the United States than it did become. But on March 3, 1903, Congress passed a law establishing the Commission on International Exchange to undertake a program, which Conant largely originated, to establish a gold exchange standard in China as a means of making China the major outlet for the surplus capital of all the industrial capitalist nations. By that date, then, the McKinley-Roosevelt administration had implicitly accepted Conant's critique of Say's Law (or Say's identity) and explicitly followed its implications in foreign policy by attempting to create investment outlets in the Third World. It also followed Conant's technical advice for bringing that process to reality. Neither the administration nor Congress was yet ready to follow his suggestion that fiscal policy be utilized at home to consume surplus capital. That development awaited the depression of the 1930s. But Conant deserves acknowledgment and credit for his original contributions to the theory of fiscal policy and its relationship to the stabilization of modern capitalism.

It is widely recognized that the decade before and after 1900 was a watershed in U.S. foreign and domestic policy and, indeed, in international relations generally. To some students of the period, it was an epoch in which the new imperialism came to fruition; to others, it was the time in which the United States engaged in the "great aberration" of imperialism but, somewhat paradoxically, also the time in which Americans returned to their historic antiimperialist roots. Others have argued that subsequent to 1898, the United States never deviated from imperialist policies but passed to an essentially neocolonialist system of disguised indirect rule. Closely related to whether or not imperialism was a "great aberration" was the issue of the degree to which American foreign policy has been and/or is driven by either domestic or social and economic imperatives or is instead essentially a response to the policies of foreign nations. Both sides in the "aberration" and "neocolonialist" debate have collected so much evidence for their conflicting positions that they tend to cancel out one another. One actor in the drama who had an especially significant role in defining and implementing domestic financial *and* foreign policy in the years shortly before and subsequent to the turn of the century, Charles Arthur Conant, is proving especially useful in shedding light on and even resolving much of what is in dispute.

On the infrequent occasions when Conant is discussed in the scholarly literature, he is usually described as an "economist" or an "economic adviser"; this gives the innocent reader the impression that he operated largely at a technical, hence secondary, level of policymaking, both at home and abroad. Actually, Conant functioned as both a theoretician of the domestic corporate reorganization and as a theoretician and formulator of domestic banking and monetary policies appropriate to the crafting of the nation's foreign policy in the epoch of the new imperialism. Conant's role ought to be restored to our historical memory.

NOTES

1. The best work on the postimperialism phenomenon is in Richard L. Sklar, "Postimperialism: A Class Analysis of Multinational Corporate Expansion," *Comparative Politics* 9, 1 (October 1976): 75–92. See Martin J. Sklar, *The Corporate Reconstruction of American Capitalism, 1890–1916* (New York: Cambridge University Press, 1988): 61–69, 72–82. Also see Carl Parrini, "Theories of Imperialism," in Lloyd C. Gardner, ed., *Redefining the Past: Essays in Diplomatic History in Honor of William Appleman Williams* (Corvallis: Oregon State University Press, 1986): 68–74; and Carl P. Parrini and Martin J. Sklar, "New Thinking About the Market, 1896–1904: Some American Economists on Investment and the Theory of Surplus Capital," *Journal of Economic History* 43, 3 (September 1983): 559–578.

2. Charles Arthur Conant, "Can New Openings Be Found for Capital?" *Atlantic Monthly* 84 (November 1899): 600, and "Recent Economic Tendencies," *Atlantic Monthly* 85 (June 1900): 740.

3. Ibid., "Recent Economic Tendencies," 737, 746–747. Conant acknowledged that mercantilist thinkers sometimes argued that the acquisition of gold would lead to prosperity rather than that prosperous nations evidenced their prosperity by acquiring gold, but he also asserted that "it is doubtful if the more intelligent supporters of the theory took so crude a view."

4. Charles Arthur Conant, *A History of Modern Banks of Issue, with an Ac-*

count of the Economic Crises of the Present Century (New York: Putnam, 1896): 461–463.

5. Ibid., 461–463, and "Can New Openings Be Found?" 603.

6. Conant, *A History of Modern Banks of Issue*, 462–463. While acknowledging that there was no such thing as absolute overproduction, Conant did maintain that investment in means of production of consumption goods, the final product of which was not consumed, was more harmful to the (investment) system than investment in infrastructure. For instance, he argued, "But overproduction for all practical purposes is production beyond the effective demand of those who have the means and habit of using, and the capital employed in the production of goods which are not consumed is more hopelessly sunk than if devoted to railways or public works; for railways and public works may prove of value in the future, even if their production has outrun the necessities of the present."

7. Ibid., 464. In connection with the problem of high-capacity utilization in times of stagnant sales, Conant argued that "an industrial enterprise which continues to operate without profit or at a loss during a period of depression transfers all its benefits, therefore, to the wage earners, and their wealth is enhanced at the expense of the owners of inherited or accumulated capital."

8. Charles Arthur Conant, "Crises and Their Management," *Yale Review* 9 (February 1901). In this essay, Conant analyzes primary and secondary causes of crises. He continues to maintain his earlier position that surplus capital is the basic cause of crises and gives examples of how supply now precedes demand, hence how investment uncertainties increase and how and why the tendency toward overproduction grows and how fixed investment in capital goods ("mills and machinery") cannot be shifted to lines of production where demand is increasing. On p. 377, he explains that "capital once invested in the machinery of production cannot always be easily converted to other uses." Money capital can be moved, but physical capital cannot. "Arguments based upon this mobility refer to the loan fund of floating capital and are not applicable to capital which has been fixed in mills and machinery." To understand his crisis theory, one ought to read the whole of this article, pp. 374–398. As early as his first edition of *A History of Modern Banks of Issue*, in 1896, Conant theorized primary as against secondary causes of crises (i.e., independent as against dependent variables in the jargon of modern social science) as when he rejected, in the language of French economist Clement Jugular, the claim that "'wars, revolutions, tariff changes, loans, variations of fashion, new pathways opened to commerce are still accused' as the cause of crises." But to Conant, they were dependent variables, secondary causes. "These events," he said, "often come to precipitate the panic at a particular moment, like the match which causes the explosion when the powder train is fully laid" (461). Conant's first work for a central bank was when he served as executive secretary on the Indianapolis Monetary Commission in 1898. See n. 9, below, which discusses Conant's opposition to the quantity theory of money.

9. In Conant's view, a central bank, in the role of banker of last resort, could also encourage the extension of credit once a crisis had begun, to prevent failure of otherwise solvent institutions. On this, see his "Crises and Their Management," 389–391. Although he was not the first American critic of the "quantity theory of money," Conant did argue in his essay, "The Future of the Limping Standard," *Political Science Quarterly* 18 (June 1903): 221, that contrary to the claim of the silverites in the campaign of 1896 "that prices are regulated by nothing but the volume of the standard money," many other factors affected the prices of goods and services. Further, in his essay, "The Law of Value of Money," *Annals of the American Academy of Political and Social Science* 16 (September 1900): 14, he argued that "in the case of money changes in the demand have much more influence than changes in the supply."

10. Although Conant conceptualized "surplus capital" in the first edition of *A History of Modern Banks of Issue* (462), he waged his most intensive campaign to convince the business and government policymakers of this view in several articles. See, e.g., "Can New Openings Be Found for Capital?" 600–604, and "The Economic Basis of Imperialism," *North American Review* (September 1898), esp. 333–334.

11. Conant, "Can New Openings Be Found?" 603–604.

12. Conant, "Economic Basis," 328–330, and "Recent Economic Tendencies," 740–743.

13. Conant, "Recent Economic Tendencies," 742–743.

14. Ibid., 739–742.

15. Charles Arthur Conant, "The Growth of Public Expenditures," *Atlantic Monthly* 87 (January 1901): 51–53, and "Economic Basis," 339–340.

16. The increase in the public debt would provide secure financial instruments in which some of the surplus capital could be invested, virtually without risk. Hence such government borrowing would help to "manage," if not "solve," the surplus capital problem.

17. Conant, "Growth of Public Expenditures," 51–53; see also Conant, "Recent Economic Tendencies," 740–741.

18. Charles Arthur Conant, *Wall Street and the Country* (Westport, Conn.: Greenwood, 1968): 21–22, 37; Conant writes, "The work of the promoter in recent years has tended to increase the transferability of capital by providing a method for getting rid of useless plants without direct loss to their owners" (37). Here he was referring to the fact that when general corporations were formed by promoters, they generally took the least efficient plants out of production and decreased production levels so as to buoy profits, but those who had owned the least efficient plants prior to the promotion had received compensation for their marginal and usually unprofitable plants. In his first edition of *A History of Modern Banks of Issue* (463–464), Conant had explained that "an industrial enterprise which continues to operate without profit or at a loss during a period of depression transfers all its benefits, therefore, to the wage earners." Corporate mergers obviated this practice.

19. Conant, *Wall Street and the Country*, 214–215.

20. Ibid., 212–215, 223–228. The fact that the trust company personnel

administering the surplus capital were also the federal government officials most concerned with the investment of that capital in secure outlets made the trust companies societal intersections of public policy decision; this was not well understood by other intellectuals of the day, nor, one might add, is it understood by scholars of our own day.

21.   Conant made it clear as early as 1896, in *A History of Modern Banks of Issue* (464), that higher-capacity utilization, which would be a result of government fiscal policy to stimulate the economy, would increase consumption without increasing profit, hence redistribute income from capital to labor, while overseas investment activity in infrastructure would not have that effect, and since he rejected defense spending as a means to stimulate demand, this left only some sort of overseas economic activity.

22.   Ibid. Conant did not believe that tariff barrier removal would "solve" or deal adequately with the problem of surplus capital. He never departed from that position in his later publications. Also see "Economic Basis of Imperialism" (330), where he makes the point that "the convulsions attacking the great civilized countries" were taking place "without respect for their differences in tariff policies" but with a common phenomenon of "surplus capital" as an explanation of the various "convulsions" or "crises."

23.   In this connection, Conant argued that a "congestion of capital of serious proportions was threatening during the third and fourth decades of the [nineteenth] century. . . . There came suddenly, however, several great outlets for saved capital. The most conspicuous was the building of railways which demanded hundreds of millions, first in England and France, then in America, and finally in the countries of Eastern Europe, South America, Australia, and India." This raised the rate of interest (profit). See Conant's "Can New Openings Be Found for Capital?" 602; see also "Crises and Their Management," 382–383.

24.   Charles Arthur Conant, "A Special Report on Coinage and Banking in the Philippine Islands, Made to the Secretary of War by Charles A. Conant of Boston, November 25, 1901," in *Appendix G in Annual Report of the Secretary of War, 1901* (Washington, D.C., 1901): 190–191, on Russia and Japan. On Australia, see "Growth of Public Expenditures," 53–55.

25.   "Can New Openings Be Found?" 602–608. On the introduction of the gold (exchange) standard and consequent large-scale foreign investment and economic growth in Russia and Japan, see Conant "A Special Report on Coinage," 190–191.

26.   "Economic Basis," 339. Conant inaccurately implied that he did not think it particularly important exactly which means the United States selected as it entered on its campaign to obtain foreign investment outlets and related markets: "It need not be determined in just what manner that policy shall be worked out. Whether the United States shall actually acquire territorial possessions, shall set up captain generalships and garrisons, whether they shall adopt the middle ground of protecting sovereignties nominally independent, or whether they shall content themselves with naval stations and diplomatic

representations as the basis for asserting their right to the free commerce of the East, is a matter of detail."

27. Conant had no faith in efforts to monopolize investment outlets in the developing world as an ultimate solution to surplus capital. "Incidentally and for a time," he said, "political dependencies and 'spheres of influence' afford an enlarged market for finished goods." But it was law and order, respect for contract and a sound currency, not investment monopoly, that investors needed. See "Can New Openings Be Found for Capital?" 608.

28. National Archives Record Group 350 (hereafter referred to as NA RG 350). Conant to Lyman J. Gage, Oct. 16, 1900; Gage to Root, Nov. 8, 1900; also Paymaster General A. E. Bates to Lyman J. Gage, Nov. 1, 1900; Conant to Gage, July 9, 1901, and Root to Taft, July 23, 1901. Also see Paymaster General A. E. Bates to Comptroller of the Currency Charles G. Dawes, printed in *Annual Report 1900, Comptroller of the Currency*, p. 53.

29. NA RG 350, Conant to Colonel Clarence R. Edwards, Chief Bureau of Insular Affairs, War Dept., July 9, 1901 (Root MSS), and Root to Taft, July 23, 1901. Root described Conant in glowing terms to Taft, saying that Gage had consulted Conant when he (Root) asked Gage for advice on Philippine money and banking, and he also credited Conant with having much to do with the Gold Standard Act of 1900 through Conant's work for the Indianapolis Monetary Commission.

30. Conant outlined most of the specifics of the way in which he conceived his mission in a letter to Secretary of the Treasury Gage, which Gage in turn forwarded to Root with Gage's endorsement. On this, see NA RG 350, Conant to Gage, Oct. 16, 1900, and Gage to Secretary of War Elihu Root, Nov. 8, 1900. Also see Conant to Clarence R. Edwards, Chief of the Bureau of Insular Affairs, War Dept., July 9, 1901, and Root to William Howard Taft, July 23, 1901.

31. NA RG 350, Root to Taft, July 23, 1901.

32. Conant, "A Special Report on Coinage," 184, 190–194. Also see *Archivo Historico, Secretaria de Relaciones Exteriores de la Republica Mexicana*, "Comision de Cambios Internacionales de la Republica Mexicana: "Continuation of the Explanation given by Mr. Charles Conant on the 'Ratio' in the Conference of July 4, 1903," 6. I am grateful to Tom Passananti of the University of Chicago History Department for the material from the *Archivo Historico*, Mexico City.

33. Conant, "A Special Report on Coinage," 189–190.

34. On March 28, 1902, Conant wrote to Root about the problem with Senator Allison. But he was still hopeful. "I do not think that the attitude of Senator Allison should lead to the abandonment of the contest at the present time." Conant to Root, March 28, 1902, Root MSS, Library of Congress. This letter was on Morton Trust Co. stationery, which bank Conant had joined as treasurer the month before in February 1902.

35. Conant, "A Special Report on Coinage," 200–201.

36. Ibid., 181–194, 204.

37. Ibid., 182.

38. Ibid., 183.

39. Ibid., 239, 231; after speaking with Frank A. Vanderlip, vice-president of the National City Bank of New York, and other Wall Street bankers, Conant endorsed the idea that the U.S. Congress, through legislation, should guaranty bonds issued on behalf of the Philippine government. Indeed, Vanderlip even wrote a letter to appear in the record of the U.S. House of Representatives Committee on Insular Affairs advocating such a guaranty. Fortunately, Conant withheld it from the committee, although he showed it to the committee chair, Henry M. Cooper. Conant endorsed Vanderlip's guaranty proposal on Janaury 25, 1902, when he wrote to Colonel Clarence R. Edwards, Chief of the Division of Insular Affairs (Secretary of War Root's chief colonial officer), "I think that this is the best solution of the matter from a financial point of view, and stated my reason for this opinion to the House Committee when I was before them last week." NA RG 350, Conant to Edwards, Janaury 23, 1902. I have been unable to find Edwards's or Root's reply, but Congress extended no such guaranty, and when Conant made the same proposal of a guaranty on U.S. investment bankers' investment in China later in that year (1902), President Roosevelt rejected it.

40. "A Special Report on Coinage," 231–232. Conant also seemed to imply that should a crop fail and the land pass to an American bank, the bank could then engage American capitalists to manage the production process (production of sugar in this case); under such conditions, Conant said, "an enterprising American bank would probably find little difficulty in persuading American capitalists to undertake the management under conditions which would insure large profits and relieve the bank from serious risk." Hence while the cost of credit would go down, the risk to the Filipino peasant of losing his land would most certainly increase under Conant's reform plan.

41. Ibid., 232. In his report, Conant took note of the fact that the Philippine Commission could probably proscribe banking regulations for the islands. "Mortgage banking," he argued, "is a matter of local law in most of the states of the American Union," yet he wanted Congress to pass an act removing existing prohibitions of the granting of franchise (concessions) in the islands and also laying out some general guidelines "as an assurance to the investing public that such franchises will be granted only under sound conditions." But then he observed that "whatever the competence and knowledge of the local government, a legislative act by the law-making power of the United States will afford a more definite assurance of permanency of policy to the investing community at home and abroad." In his correspondence with the War Department, Conant was a good deal more candid; for instance, in Conant to Clarence R. Edwards (Chief Division of Insular Affairs), July 9, 1901, NA RG 350, Conant argued, "nothing less than legislation will give the assurance of stability. I do not think that great good will be accomplished by the adoption of the best possible system merely by executive order, except as it was regarded as the forerunner of similar action by the Congress of the United States. I doubt very much also whether legislation by

the authorities of the Archipelago would convey the assurance to investors at home and abroad of that permanency of monetary conditions which is absolutely essential to invite large investments and the projection of railways, manufacturing enterprises and other measures for the rapid development of the islands." Although Conant here refers to "monetary conditions," he is also referring to concessions or "franchises" and getting rid of existing prohibitions on franchises, allowing American banking capital to take agricultural land as security for loans to farmers (i.e., "peasants") and to market such land to American capitalists in the event of the small borrower's crops failing. But on February 13, 1903, fearful that Congress would not enact his Philippines currency bill, he wrote to Elihu Root, in frustration, asking "whether you did not believe the Philippine Commission has sufficient power to establish a gold standard by its own legislation, in the Philippines?" See Conant to Root, Feb. 13, 1903, Root MSS, Library of Congress.

42. Conant, "A Special Report on Coinage," 208–211.

43. Conant dealt with those who suggested simply imposing a gold dollar standard on the Philippines by pointing out that this would introduce U.S. coins that would be in denominations too large for practical use. Such coins would introduce uncertainty and lead to merchants cheating laborers as they had traditionally used Mexican silver coins. This, in turn, would tend to reduce labor's purchasing power and so cut living standards and thus create a fertile field for Filipino insurgent recruitment. In Conant's words, it would "introduce a new disturbing influence on a people already more or less irritated as to political and economic subjects." U.S. House of Representatives, Committee on Insular Affairs, *Hearings, "Coinage System in the Philippine Islands,"* 57th Cong., 1st and 2d sess., 1901–1903 (Washington, D.C.: GPO, 1903), Jan. 14, 1902–1903, 503–506, 600–616. On Conant's effort to refute the advocates of continuing some sort of (fluctuating) silver standard in the islands, see Conant to Root, March 28, 1902, Root MSS, Library of Congress. He told Root he did not think he had convinced the Senate Silverites against a silver standard, "but," he argued, "I think I shook them somewhat in regard to its merits and in regard to the objections made to the working of my plan. . . . One of the arguments I made to the Committee [of the Senate] on Tuesday I think I rather staggered them in their theory that the silver standard would promote trade with silver-using countries." He showed them that in the case of the Philippines, imports from gold standard countries were more than twice that from silver standard countries—$13,884,686 vs. $5,572,156. This, of course, cut the ground out from under them and ultimately told in the congressional acceptance of Conant's plan. The argument that silver promoted foreign trade was effectively refuted.

44. On reciprocity during the McKinley years, it is well known that the so-called Kasson treaties of reciprocity required two-thirds approval in the U.S. Senate as commercial treaties; it is equally well known that the Senate did not approve any such reciprocal concession treaties with any other major industrial nation competitor. A good and analytical discussion of U.S. tariff

policy can be found in F. W. Taussig, *The Tariff History of the United States* (New York, 1931). Theoretically, of course, other options were open to the administration. They could have encouraged corporate reorganization-consolidation. But this was already taking place and did not consume enough of the surplus capital. Exploiting technical innovation was proceeding apace; it also consumed some but not enough of the surplus capital. Increasing consumption levels via fiscal policy was already being done. Statesmen were also exploring consumption augmentation's militarist relative, increasing naval building, but none of this consumed enough of the surplus capital to relieve the problem. On this, see Conant, "Economic Basis," 337; also "Growth of Public Expenditures," 45–47.

CHAPTER 3

Admiral William B. Caperton
Proconsul and Diplomat

DAVID HEALY

Admiral William B. Caperton never witnessed a naval battle in his forty-four years of active service, yet his brief, intense career in gunboat diplomacy was unique in his time. From 1915 to 1919, Caperton led major Caribbean interventions in Haiti and the Dominican Republic, helped to decide an election in Nicaragua, and spent two years in South America firming up support for the United States during the First World War. The scope and variety of his pseudo-diplomatic activities make him an exemplar of the role of the armed forces in American foreign relations.

Caperton was born in Spring Hill, Tennessee, in 1855 and graduated from the United States Naval Academy in 1875. In a period of neglect and retrenchment for the armed forces, it took him twenty-four years to rise above the rank of lieutenant and then another fourteen to become an admiral. This glacial rate of promotion was accompanied by a series of humdrum assignments; promotion was by seniority, and high rank went to those willing to wait for it. In addition to normal sea duty, Caperton served with the Coast and Geodetic Survey and as a steel inspector, an ordnance inspector, a lighthouse inspector, on an officers' retiring board, and as a naval base commander. He took command of a modern cruiser in 1907 and a battleship in 1908, finally rising to flag rank in 1913. His only war service came during the Spanish-American War, when he served aboard a gunboat patrolling the Cuban coast. In 1915, Caperton was known in the navy as a quietly competent officer who enjoyed dancing and social life. His career to date had given him no particular preparation for the special duties on which he was to embark.[1]

In December 1914, Rear Admiral Caperton took command of the Cruiser Squadron of the North Atlantic Fleet. Created in 1902 specifically for Caribbean service, the squadron was normally composed of some half-dozen small cruisers and gunboats whose mission it was to patrol the region, monitor trouble spots, and provide a measure of readily available force when necessary. The several vessels of the squadron would usually be dispersed widely about the region, answering to the demands of both the Navy and State departments. Caperton's new command was created mainly for diplomatic purposes, and he himself began his diplomatic functions almost immediately.[2]

During most of 1915, Caperton was concerned largely with affairs in Haiti. That small and poor country, the world's first black republic, seemed to have fallen into permanent political upheaval at a time when regional stability was the ultimate goal of U.S. policy in the Caribbean. In Washington's eyes, endemic revolution there slowed economic development, discouraged foreign investment, and blocked progress toward constitutional democracy. Worst of all, it gave occasion for Europe's great powers to involve themselves in Caribbean affairs, potentially challenging American hegemony. Germany aroused the worst fears and was long assumed to want a naval base that could threaten U.S. access to the Panama Canal. A disorderly Caribbean, with frequent revolutions and bankrupt governments, was an invitation to outsiders to fish in troubled waters. Political stability, could it be imposed, would presumably bring security, prosperity, even democracy. Thus, Washington labored for years to check revolutions in the region but with less than complete success.[3]

In 1915, Haiti was the worst case of Caribbean disorder. Of six presidents since the end of 1908, three were deposed by revolution, one blown up in his residence, and one allegedly poisoned, while the incumbent clung only shakily to office. Three different men headed the government in 1914 alone, as the revolutionary cycle spun ever faster, and Washington decided it was time to take a hand. In July 1914, the State Department proposed a treaty giving the United States control of Haitian customs collection and thus of their government finances. Based on a similar arrangement with the Dominican Republic established in 1905, the draft treaty represented an attempt by Washington to begin stabilizing the Haitian scene, but the idea was angrily rejected in Port-au-Prince. The United States nevertheless had some input into Haitian finances through the National City Bank of New York, which by 1915 controlled the National Bank of Haiti, a foreign-owned corporation invested by contract with the functions of a national treasury. Conflict between the bank and the government grew intense in 1914, arousing further concern in the State Department. By the end of the year, Washington was on the verge of intervention; eight hundred marines went to Port-au-Prince aboard a transport, but another change of government just as they arrived persuaded policy-makers to wait and observe events.[4]

When Admiral Caperton steamed south on his flagship in January 1915, it was to Haiti that he went first. Another revolution had al-ready begun there, and by the end of February yet another president, Vilbrun Guillaume Sam, had come to power. Caperton forbade both sides in the brief civil war to loot or burn cities or harm foreign life and property and closely patrolled the fighting areas with his ships but had not otherwise interfered. Leaders on both sides had re-spected his orders, while the new president promised to be a stronger leader than his predecessors; perhaps the revolutionary cycle was checked.

For a time, Guillaume Sam prevailed. Ruling with an iron hand, he repelled a new revolutionary movement at Cap Haitien, and five months after taking office he seemed firmly in command. Suddenly, however, late in July 1915, a group of conspirators in the capital staged a successful coup. Guillaume Sam had jailed all known politi-cal opponents, and in a last act of revenge he ordered their mass mur-der. Almost 170 leading Haitians, including two former presidents, died in this massacre, word of which aroused the people of the capital to an unprecedented fury. The fallen president, wounded in the leg, escaped to the French embassy for refuge but was discovered there by a mob and quite literally torn to pieces. Meanwhile, other vigilante groups hunted down and killed those who had actually carried out the slaughter of the political prisoners.[5]

Caperton had been policing the conflict between government and rebel forces around Cap Haitien, on Haiti's north coast, when he got word of these events at the capital. He arrived at Port-au-Prince on July 28, 1915, just as the mobs were lynching Guillaume Sam and his henchmen. Ironically, Caperton's approach gave the final signal for mob violence; when his flagship *Washington* came in sight out at sea, someone shouted that the Americans would protect the French em-bassy and its hated refugee and urged action before they could land. The response was instant and deadly, and the admiral arrived in the midst of events of a savagery that horrified responsible Haitians as much as foreigners. As the *Washington* anchored off Port-au-Prince, the diplomatic corps came out en masse to demand that Caperton land a force to keep order and protect foreigners. They found a land-ing party already mustered on the *Washington*'s deck, and by nightfall some 330 sailors and marines patrolled the city. A few hours after ordering the landing, the admiral received radioed instructions from his government to do so. The U.S. occupation of Haiti had begun.[6]

At first Caperton worked with a committee of safety of the sort traditionally formed in such emergencies by local notables. The capital swarmed with armed men of varying political persuasions, and the Americans of the landing party felt distinctly insecure, especially in light of the violence that had just ended. In response to Caperton's urgent request, the battleship *Connecticut* arrived with five hundred more marines a week later. The admiral had already laid his plans, and the very night the fresh marines arrived saw the beginning of a more decisive takeover of the city. On August 5 and 6, the marines seized without warning all of the city's forts and barracks and disarmed and disbanded their garrisons. When the Committee of Safety, now politically active and renamed the Revolutionary Committee, objected to this violation of Haitian sovereignty, Caperton first disavowed the committee and then dissolved it. Clearly, more was involved in the American landings than the protection of foreign life and property.[7]

Since factional fighting continued in the north around Cap Haitien, Caperton sent a vessel there to round up the opposing leaders. The USS *Nashville* landed 250 men to occupy the town, while the chief Haitian presidential contenders were packed off to the capital. The principal rebel chief, Rosalvo Bobo, had claimed to be the rightful successor to Guillaume Sam, but Caperton had him brought aboard the *Washington* for a conference. There, among the ship's big guns and armed men, Bobo was forced to accept the status of a mere presidential candidate, while Caperton and the *Washington*'s captain, Edward Beach, pondered the political situation. It was customary when a government had failed to hand over power to whomever had overthrown it, after the national legislature had formally voted to do so. The legislature did the electing, but normally it simply ratified the victory of the latest revolutionary winner. The coup that toppled Guillaume Sam, however, was carried out by a small group that merely wished the removal of the dictator and did not represent any particular presidential aspirant. Furthermore, it was Caperton and the Americans who now held armed control in the capital, and many began to look to them for guidance in the choice of a new leader. Beach and Caperton canvassed the available candidates.[8]

They soon decided on Philippe Sudre Dartiguenave, the president of the Senate. Dignified and middle-aged, Dartiguenave was also tractable, promising to accept long-term controls by the United States which included supervision of the customs and a continued military presence. Caperton recommended him to Washington and asked permission to allow a presidential election. The State Department agreed to these proposals on August 10, at the same time ordering the admiral to tell the Haitians two things: no candidate would be acceptable who might resume the factional disorders that had plagued Haiti (this was clearly meant to rule out Bobo); and "the United States expects to be entrusted with the practical control of the customs, and such financial control over the affairs of the Republic of Haiti as the United States may deem necessary for an efficient administration."[9] Captain Beach duly delivered this message to an informal meeting of the Haitian Congress hastily called in a downtown theater on August 11. At another meeting on the same day with the former Revolutionary Committee, whose members now backed Bobo, Beach threatened death to any who fomented violence on election day.

On the following day, the Haitian legislature, now well prepared for its duty, elected Dartiguenave president by a solid 94 votes out of 116 cast. The new chief executive was promptly inaugurated, and the American occupation rested on a firmer base, a constitutional president having filled the power vacuum that existed on Caperton's arrival. U.S. troops occupied Haiti's two chief towns, Port-au-Prince and Cap Haitien, the new president gave every sign of docility, and a second marine regiment, this time 850 strong, arrived on August 11 aboard the *Tennessee*. Everything seemed to be falling into place.[10]

Up to this time, Admiral Caperton had largely improvised policy as he went along, receiving State Department approval after the event. On August 14, however, just seventeen days after American troops first landed at Port-au-Prince, the admiral received detailed instructions for a draft treaty to be presented to the Haitians. It provided for a general receiver of customs, to be named by the president of the United States, who would collect and disburse the customs receipts that made up most of Haiti's government revenues. A financial adviser, similarly appointed, would supervise the Haitian government's fiscal operations. In addition, both the army and the civil police of Haiti were to be replaced by a single national constabulary, whose commanders would also be named in Washington. All of these new officials would be citizens of the United States, not Haitians. Thus, in a single document, the U.S. government sought control of Haiti's finances, law enforcement, and military power. The treaty was to be in force for ten years, after which it could be renewed for another decade at the option of *either* party.[11]

Not surprisingly, these demands aroused widespread Haitian opposition, reaching even within President Dartiguenave's new cabinet. When this became evident, Caperton called together the president, the cabinet, and congressional leaders and told them that the treaty must be approved quickly and exactly as presented; no modifications would be tolerated. Speedy approval of the treaty, however, was impossible in the face of public disapproval, and Dartiguenave made it clear that he could not capitulate at once without losing all support. The Haitians responded with a revised draft treaty that reversed or watered down each of the U.S. terms but that the State Department rejected out of hand.[12]

In the midst of such tensions, Caperton was shocked to receive orders to seize the remaining Haitian customshouses, located in eight coastal towns not yet occupied by U.S. forces. This expanded military takeover would force the admiral to further disperse his modest forces, while making an already tense political situation even more dangerous. Protesting to Washington, Caperton obeyed his orders; the barely two thousand marines under his command now occupied ten towns spanning the entire Haitian coast. At this, even the pliant Dartiguenave protested, in response to which Caperton declared martial law in the capital and its vicinity on September 3, 1915. Shortly afterward, this order was extended to cover the entire country. Some years afterward, Caperton wrote a revealing comment on the rise of Haitian opposition at this time: "Such unreadiness to accept the inevitable showed again the total unfitness of most Haitians for representative government."[13]

The concentration of forces in Port-au-Prince had ensured firm control there, but the American incursion had inspired rising resistance in the countryside. This was especially true in the north, where the so-called *cacos*, armed hill clans loosely organized under local leaders, held the balance of political power. In August, Caperton offered to buy up caco rifles with dollars, and although some were forthcoming, the threat continued. In September, scattered fighting occurred, beginning a small-scale war between cacos and U.S. marines. Aggressive marine patrols penetrated the cacos' country and attacked their camps. The cacos suffered severe losses in two major clashes on September 26, and most of them came to terms a few days later. The remainder retreated far into the hills, where the marines found and stormed their last stronghold in November.

The cacos lost almost two hundred dead in the fighting, plus scores of wounded; the marines' loss was one dead and one wounded. Secretary of the Navy Josephus Daniels called a halt to the campaign after the November fighting, believing the resistance crushed and unwilling to see more Haitians die, though Caperton would have preferred to continue the campaign. Daniels's judgment soon proved correct: the cacos had had enough. Nevertheless, Caperton's aggressiveness was understandable. His relatively small force, deployed over an entire country, could retain control only by moving fast and hitting hard. As he had reported in August, "Serious hostile contacts have only been avoided by prompt and rapid military action which has given United States control before resistance has had time to organize." A large force might overawe the Haitians, but a small one must demonstrate its strength through action. He believed he must crush centers of resistance as fast as they formed or face a general uprising involving major slaughter. Caperton's fears were prophetic: in 1918–19, some years after his departure, American forces put down a massive caco uprising at a cost of some three thousand Haitian dead.[14]

The imposition of martial law and the defeat of the cacos strengthened Caperton's hand. On September 16, 1915, the Haitian government signed the treaty, and on November 11, after prolonged debate, the Haitian Senate approved it by a vote of twenty-six to seven. This Senate approval reflected a combination of persuasion, coercion, and some bribery on Caperton's part, in a campaign of unremitting pressure and a flow of mixed promises and threats. With the treaty in place, the U.S. military occupation had a legal basis, though occupation measures soon stretched far beyond the treaty's terms. The U.S. marines, a client president, and the Haitian-American treaty created a framework of power that was to control Haiti for nineteen years, until 1934.[15]

Since the treaty conflicted with the Haitian constitution in some respects, President Dartiguenave proposed to draft a new constitution. The move crystallized congressional opposition stronger than any yet seen, with congressional leaders threatening to impeach Dartiguenave. The president responded by dissolving the legislature and recalling its lower house, the Chamber of Deputies, to act as a constituent assembly. When both houses defied him, Dartiguenave turned to Caperton, who reluctantly enforced his dissolution decree in May 1916. For many years to come, there would be no national legislature, only a rump client state headed by a president and kept in power by the marines.[16]

In imposing this new power structure on a foreign country, on short notice, with limited forces and relatively little bloodshed, Caperton displayed toughness, flexibility, and political skills. An energetic and decisive commander, he quickly grasped the applications of force to politics. To heighten the sense of his power, he deliberately maintained a splendid isolation aboard his flagship, delegating most contacts ashore to the *Washington*'s able, French-speaking Captain Beach. The admiral nevertheless cultivated close personal relations with a number of the Haitian elite and never drew the social "color line" later imposed by occupation personnel. On occasion, he made public appearances at social functions, especially balls, where he was attentive to the local young women. According to one Haitian, "He was a tireless dancer . . . ; one found him, after a waltz, with the buttons of his uniform remaining imprinted on the breast of his partner, so tightly did he hold her in his arms."[17] Caperton shared much of the racial prejudice of his nation and time and was skeptical of Haitian capabilities, once calling Haiti a "land of seething discontent, professional revolutionaries, and a national and ingrained political dishonesty." Yet he made an effort to know the Haitian upper class and even to understand their country's problems. He took his consultations with the Haitians seriously. One of his local advisers was an elderly former president, François Legitime. By his own account, "When I became discouraged, I usually went to see the old man, and through an interpreter, frequently his good looking Daughter, I managed to get a good deal of consolation and encouragement."[18]

The admiral took the 1915 treaty at face value, expecting it to provide for U.S. supervision over an essentially Haitian administration. He was thus surprised and displeased when, shortly after his departure, the marine occupation forces and new treaty officials took over virtually the entire operation of the government, and he promptly indicated his disapproval to Washington. Confident that American hegemony would bring Haiti peace and prosperity, the admiral also thought he had assurances that the State Department would promote the country's economic development once the treaty was approved, and he was sorely disappointed at the continuing lack of action in this regard. He was nevertheless still convinced of the benefits of U.S. control and ready to use both ruthless and devious means to make it effective.[19]

In guiding the intervention and its political development, Caperton exercised large powers of decision. The State Department's representative in Port-au-Prince, the young charge d'affaire, Robert Beale Davis, Jr., was virtually put under Caperton's orders and comported himself throughout as a loyal subordinate.[20] U.S. policy over the recent past had clearly moved toward intervention in Haiti, but Caperton was left to make the crucial early moves on his own. Once he had developed a political solution for Haiti, Washington approved it and then, at last, revealed its own further policies, most notably, in the terms of the 1915 treaty.

This early freedom of action was later to cause the admiral trouble. In 1921, the U.S. Senate began a yearlong investigation of the Haitian intervention and a subsequent parallel action in the Dominican Republic, both of which had involved Caperton. Voicing an emerging antiimperialism, some senators asked who was responsible for launching the Haitian intervention. By then retired, the admiral was called before a Senate committee to explain why he had begun the military occupation. The senators quickly brushed aside his references to protecting life and property, correctly perceiving them as mere excuses. Unable to cite specific orders for some of his most significant actions, Caperton found himself for a time in danger of being charged with beginning the occupation on his own personal initiative. Unable to satisfy his inquisitors, he simply outlasted them, using delay and evasion as tactics.[21]

At the time, however, Caperton's performance in Haiti earned him the approval of both the Navy and the State departments and propelled him into new chapters of gunboat diplomacy. The next episode, in fact, began before his Haitian duties had ended, in the neighboring Dominican Republic. Another Caribbean government was collapsing, and the Wilson administration was once again determined to resolve the crisis on its own terms.

The United States had been involved in the internal affairs of the Dominican Republic since 1905, when Theodore Roosevelt had instituted a customs receivership later regularized in a 1907 treaty. At first, all had gone relatively well under the new arrangement, but the assassination in 1911 of a strong and popular president marked the end of political stability. After repeated efforts by the Taft and Wilson administrations failed to restore lasting order, President Wilson himself had dictated the terms of a final truce and a new national election. These measures, along with a ban on future revolution, comprised his "Wilson Plan" of 1914. The victorious candidate in this election, Juan Isidro Jimenez, was installed in power with public warnings that the United States would meet any future attempt at armed revolt by force if necessary. Jimenez was the fourth Dominican president in three years, and the Washington authorities were determined to stop the chaotic rotation of regimes and revolutions.

Instead of preventing new cabals against the president, however, the American assurances merely involved the United States in the mounting vicissitudes of the new regime. Except for the backing of

Washington, Jimenez had few political assets. Long a dominant figure in Dominican politics, he was now old and in poor health, while many former followers had been drawn off to new factional leaders. He had won the election narrowly, only after making a bargain to share power with the leaders of two rival factions. This shaky coalition showed cracks almost immediately, while new U.S. demands put further pressure on President Jimenez.[22]

Amid growing concern about the Dominican situation, Washington pressed ever harder for a full-scale protectorate there. An ultimatum delivered to Santo Domingo in November 1915 required the Dominicans to accept not only a financial controller but an American-led constabulary, as in Haiti, that would replace the existing national forces. Trapped between a host of domestic enemies and the politically impossible American demands, Jimenez vacillated until pushed by his few followers into a decisive move. In April 1916, he attempted to arrest his strongest opponent, Secretary of War Desiderio Arias. The attempt failed, and Jimenez fled to the countryside to become little more than a fugitive. Under Arias's leadership, the Dominican Congress declared Jimenez impeached and deposed, but the president challenged the legality of the action. The U.S. minister, William W. Russell, who had attempted to mediate the dispute, had to choose between the sides. Guided by the Wilson Plan, he gave his approval to Jimenez as the constitutionally elected president. The U.S. government now had to put up or shut up, but its position was complicated by the refusal of Jimenez to sanction the use of force against his countrymen. When pressed by Russell to do so, the president simply resigned.[23]

Left with a power vacuum, the ingenious Russell elevated the four remaining cabinet ministers to the status of a collective executive and appealed to Washington. There was no thought in the State Department of recognizing the Arias movement as a legitimate government. To do so would mean abandoning the Wilson Plan's ban on forcible overthrows and presumably giving up any hope of political stability in the Dominican Republic. The obvious alternative was to use force, and on May 5, 1916, three hundred U.S. sailors and marines landed on the coast near the capital to uphold Russell and his newly minted "Council of Ministers." A week later, on May 12, Admiral Caperton arrived from Port-au-Prince to take charge.

As he had confessed before leaving Haiti, Caperton had only a "smattering idea" of conditions in the Dominican Republic or of U.S. policy there. He found a thoroughly confused situation, which Russell explained to him in detail. Arias held the capital with over a thousand men; he controlled the army and the Congress and was popularly regarded as the head of the government. Virtually no one accepted the authority of Russell's Council of Ministers, which was as lacking in armed forces as in popular support. Caperton had brought with him three hundred more men for the landing party, which swelled his force ashore to six hundred. In dealing with the locals, Russell and Caperton were on their own.

On the day after his arrival, Caperton went with Russell into Santo Domingo to meet Arias. After an unsatisfactory conference, the two handed Arias an ultimatum signed by both of them: the "rebels" must disband and turn over their arms and ammunition to the Americans by 6:00 A.M. on May 15 or Caperton's forces would enter the city and forcibly disarm them. Never replying to this ultimatum, Arias simply abandoned the city before the deadline, while Caperton's force moved in to occupy it at the stated time.[24]

As in Haiti, Caperton now controlled a national capital but was faced with a power vacuum. He and Russell had refused to accept Arias as president but lacked their own candidate, while everyone looked toward the action of the Dominican Congress in choosing a new executive. As occupation chief, Caperton publicly proclaimed that he had taken control of the city in response to its seizure by armed rebels. He forbade citizens to carry arms and asked public officials to remain at their posts and cooperate with U.S. authorities. However, he found it harder to find collaborators in Santo Domingo than in Port-au-Prince. "We seem to have no friends here whatever among the Dominicans. . . . Even the women and children almost turn up their noses as we pass by and treat us with silent contempt," Caperton reported. Although Arias had lost considerable prestige by fleeing from an American force much smaller than his own, his decreased popularity was not matched by any increase in that of the Americans'. The air was heavy with hostility; local newspapers described the public mood as one of "silent protest" against the occupation. There was, however, no overt resistance.[25]

For the moment, political problems were more pressing than purely military considerations. Control over the Congress and its choice of a president was the first objective of Russell and the admiral, but they found the going difficult. From the beginning, the Dominican Congress resisted the Americans' request to defer the presidential election. On the day after the American occupation of Santo Domingo, the Chamber of Deputies nominated Dr. Federico Henriquez y Carvajal, president of the Supreme Court. Under Dominican law, the deputies nominated a single candidate, whose name was then sent to the Senate for approval. If the Senate did not concur by a majority vote on three succeeding days, a new name had to be sent to the Senate for approval.

Since Henriquez was a compromise candidate rather than a factional choice, Russell and Caperton were uncertain how to react to his nomination. In some puzzlement, they radioed Washington for a statement of future U.S. policy in the Dominican Republic. The State Department instructed them to examine the archives of the legation, where U.S. policy could be found. This somewhat cryptic response appeared to mean that they were to interpret the situation for themselves in the light of declared U.S. goals in the country.[26]

Under the circumstances, exploration seemed in order, and the admiral and the American minister decided to interview Henriquez, who initially made a favorable impression. He had not sought the presidency, he declared. He judged the people weary of revolution and believed that most revolutionists would turn in their arms for five dollars per rifle. The two Americans were reassured, but their satisfaction was soon dispelled by rumors that Henriquez had moved into the Arias camp. Next Caperton learned with consternation that the Senate had approved Henriquez for the first of the three required times. After conferring with Russell, the admiral sent a warning to the Congress that persistence in its "open disobedience" would result in a declaration of martial law. The threat gave the Senate pause, and Russell soon received unofficial assurances that the electoral process would go no further for the time being.[27]

While the situation remained delicate, Caperton felt his hand was strengthened by the arrival of more marines, some taken from the Haitian occupation force. By the end of May, he had under his command the USS *Memphis,* a large armored cruiser, and more than a dozen lighter naval craft. Over eight hundred marines and sailors occupied Santo Domingo, while perhaps as many were present aboard ship at the capital and other coastal points around the country. Caperton was determined to use a firm hand: "We will have to take charge of matters here and deal with them pretty much as we did in Haiti." "Revolutions must be wiped off the calendar," he reported, ". . . and it is a pity that we cannot attend to the disbursing as well as the collection of the revenues of this country." The admiral had already lost patience with the Dominican leadership. "These politicians seem to be, if possible, more untruthful, more unreliable, and greater schemers, than our friends, the Haitians," he asserted. The instant transition from a Haitian to a Dominican political crisis had exhausted the admiral's forbearance; he had left Port-au-Prince with president and legislature locked in a struggle terminated only by his own intervention, only to find a similar contest awaiting him in Santo Domingo.[28]

The Americans' problems were further complicated by the highly regional nature of Dominican politics. The president appointed twelve provincial governors who were in theory responsible to him, but in fact they ruled like petty princes. An incoming president often had to give governorships to unfriendly local bosses who were simply too strong to defy. Even in normal times, the central government in Santo Domingo had at best only partial control of the country, and there was usually an open revolt in progress somewhere. Thus, effective control of Santo Domingo would not ensure American mastery of the country, even if they achieved mastery over the president and Congress. The hostility of some of the northern governors to American power led Caperton to order the occupation of Montecristi and Puerto Plata, the principal north coast ports. The landing of U.S. troops at the two northern towns on June 1, 1916, brought small-scale fighting but few casualties. Two days later, a skirmish at Montecristi left an estimated seven Dominicans dead and many wounded, after which forcible resistance lapsed.[29]

Meanwhile, the Dominican Senate threatened once more to elect Judge Henriquez president. Again, Caperton and Russell visited Henriquez, attempting to secure advance assurance that he would accept the American scheme for a protectorate. Henriquez would promise nothing, however, and appeared to be definitely in Arias's camp. At this point, guidance finally appeared from Washington. Neither Arias nor Henriquez nor any Arias supporter should become president, the State Department announced. If possible, Russell and Caperton should delay the election; otherwise, the successful candidate must be informed of American plans and promise to support them. "Impress on all factions that this Govt. will not recognize any Govt. in Santo Domingo not satisfactory to it and as this Govt. intends to maintain financial control such recognition will be absolutely necessary."[30]

On June 9, the Senate gave Henriquez a unanimous second vote for the presidency. Since one more such vote would elect him, the matter was nearing a climax. Caperton and Russell almost despaired of getting satisfactory preelection promises from presidential candidates but still believed that they could force the selection of someone acceptable to the United States. They warned congressional leaders that American troops would remain in the country until the required concessions had been made, while an unsatisfactory presidential choice would receive neither recognition nor revenue until he did what was demanded of him. This threat, plus growing division among his countrymen, led Henriquez to withdraw his candidacy on June 12. The Americans had again bought some time.[31]

Caperton still believed that the Dominicans would ultimately capitulate to his demands to restore their own government and avoid direct U.S. rule. The trouble was, he complained, that the Dominicans were so hostile and so deceitful that he could never predict their actions. "I have never seen such hatred displayed by one people for another as I notice and feel here," he reported. "We positively have not a friend in the land. . . . The only way to handle them is by force and the big stick."[32]

The big stick soon came into play. General Arias had retreated to Santiago in the northern interior, where he was reported to have a thousand men under arms. The arrival of a fresh marine regiment on June 19 convinced Caperton that it was time to remove the Arias threat. This new force was sent to Montecristi with orders to move on Arias at Santiago. On the second day of their advance inland, the marines met resistance from a small force entrenched in a position long regarded as impregnable, but concentrated machine gun fire and a frontal attack quickly routed the defenders. Other skirmishes followed, including a stiffer one early in July in which the Dominicans lost twenty-seven killed, five captured, and many more wounded. This discouraged further resistance, as the marines approached Santiago on July 5. Arias then surrendered without a fight, ending the active campaigning.[33]

The northern military campaign increased the pressure on the Dominicans in the capital, as did the American assumption of financial control. A stalemate ensued: the Dominican Congress would elect no one who was unacceptable to Arias, while the Americans rejected anyone whom he favored. Various candidates tested the winds, but none could break the deadlock. And so matters stood on July 7 when Caperton received instructions to leave Santo Domingo as soon as possible, to take command of the Pacific Fleet. A week later, he departed, leaving the country firmly in the grip of an American military occupation, without yet having resolved its political status.[34]

In reality, Caperton's relief came just in time to save him from sharing in the ultimate failure to create a Haiti-style protectorate in the Dominican Republic. Just after his departure, the Dominican Congress tried once more to fill the presidency. Its abandoned candidate, Federico Henriquez y Carvajal, had a brother, Francisco, who had lived for the previous twelve years in Cuba. All factions now united suddenly around Francisco Henriquez, electing him president before the Americans could react. Because of his long absence from the country, the new president could not be blamed for past events, nor could he be approached in advance by the Americans with demands for prior pledges; thus, he had made no promises and subsequently refused to do so. The aim was to secure a Dominican chief executive who still had freedom of action but had not yet incurred the enmity of the United States.

In fact, Russell refused to recognize the new regime, demanding first the usual assurances from Henriquez. When the president failed to give them, Russell impounded all government funds. Henriquez offered counterproposals designed to soften Washington's terms, but the State Department made no concessions. After weeks of deadlock, Russell was recalled to Washington for consultation, and on November 19, 1916, Capt. Harry S. Knapp of the U.S. Navy proclaimed the establishment of a military government in the Dominican Republic. The attempt to erect a client government had failed.[35]

While Admiral Caperton played a major role in Dominican events during a critical period in their development, he was considerably less important in the Dominican story than in the Haitian one. He arrived on the scene only after an American intervention had already begun and left before its final resolution. It was he who established American military control, through the seizure of Santo Domingo and the northern ports and the march on Santiago, but this was his principal contribution to the situation. Equally significant, he did not exercise total control in Santo Domingo but shared it with Russell. In Haiti, the diplomat had been subordinated to the admiral; Caperton made the decisions on the spot, and it was his information and advice that guided his superiors in Washington. Russell, in contrast, was the more important figure in Santo Domingo. Carefully selected to replace a failed predecessor, Russell had years of experience in his post and the full confidence of the State Department. His advice was most valued in political affairs, and he had already made key decisions before Caperton arrived. However, the two men worked smoothly together, and virtually all decisions during Caperton's tenure were made through the joint consultation and mutual agreement of the admiral and the minister.

Admiral Caperton had seen many of his hopes dashed in Haiti, where after initially ordering affairs as he desired, he had found himself unable to achieve the more constructive goals he sought for that country. The Dominican case was even less encouraging, as a universal popular hostility blocked his efforts to work through local collaborators. Far from questioning the utility of such interventions, however, Caperton's belief in their necessity seemed merely to grow stronger. A few months after leaving Santo Domingo, he reaffirmed his faith.

Now is the time for us to tighten the grasp on these wavering Southern Republics, and the sooner we take a firm, positive, and honest stand with them, the better for all hands. We have no one to interfere at present, and by the time the World is at peace again, we should have firmly established our position, and our connections with these Countries.

From a military point of view, we can hold them in Status Quo, but, to my mind, now is the time to encourage, and, I might say, force, them to help themselves, and by a proper means, to induce them to cooperate with us and allow us to establish good, strong, and firm governments for them.[36]

The admiral was to carry these convictions into the further responsibilities that awaited him in his next assignment.

Admiral Caperton's appointment to command the U.S. Pacific Fleet marked the pinnacle of his naval career. He was now a full admiral; although rear admiral was then the navy's highest permanent rank, the three major fleet commanders carried the higher rank ex officio. As organized in 1916, the seagoing navy was divided into three fleets, the Atlantic, Pacific, and Asiatic, plus detached vessels. The Atlantic Fleet was much the largest, containing all of the battleships and most of the navy's fighting strength, while the other two were made up mostly of older or lighter vessels or half-manned ships in reserve status. In theory, however, the three fleets were coordinate commands, and in any case, Caperton had gained a post that placed him well within the inner circle of the navy's "top brass."[37]

As in his former command, Caperton found that his new duties included an element of gunboat diplomacy. Revolutionary disorders in Mexico were still a major concern. In addition to watching Mexico's west coast, the Pacific Fleet maintained at least one vessel at Corinto, Nicaragua, to support a U.S. protectorate recently established in that country. Even as Caperton took over his new command in July 1916, the political pot was beginning to boil in Nicaragua. A presidential election was slated for October 1, 1916, and the resulting tensions attracted notice in Washington. "We had better henceforth keep the navy as closely in touch with the Nicaraguan situation as we have heretofore in the Haitian and Dominican matters," the chief of the State Department's Division of Latin American Affairs noted in August.[38]

The events that made the government of the United States so deeply interested in Nicaraguan elections had originated some half-dozen years earlier, when Nicaraguan President José Santos Zelaya had faced a revolt against his long domination of the country. The dictator had regularly agitated Central America with his international intrigues, jeopardizing the stability so sought after by the Americans in the regions bordering their cherished Panama Canal project. Actively resisting the growing U.S. influence in the area, the Nicaraguan had emerged as a prime target for the wrath of the northern Colossus. The administration of President William Howard Taft had therefore seized on the uprising in Nicaragua to support the rebels and employed both diplomatic and military means to force Zelaya from power. When the president resigned in favor of a chosen successor, U.S. authorities refused to accept his replacement. Washington wished not only to be rid of Zelaya but to oust the entire surviving oligarchy of Zelayista officials, whom it thought as bad as their chief. The sustained pressure told, and in August 1910, the ruling Liberal party was plucked from power root and branch.

The next two years witnessed an intricate contest between the chief elements of the curious coalition of politicos who, with American help, had united to overthrow the Liberals. With Washington acting as power broker, Adolfo Díaz emerged as president early in 1911, restoring the Conservative party to power for the first time in a generation. In 1912, however, the minister of war rebelled against Díaz, who had little chance of survival without American support. Intolerant as usual of Caribbean instability, the State Department ended the rebellion by sending in some two thousand marines. From then on, a marine legation guard of one hundred men remained permanently in Managua, to signify that Nicaragua's politics would henceforth be controlled from Washington.[39]

Nicaragua had become a client state, and the State Department was inevitably involved in settling who would succeed Díaz, whose term of office was drawing to a close. Since the succession threatened to bring on an open struggle, Washington thought it prudent to have naval and marine forces at hand. Admiral Caperton's first official notice of this situation came in mid-August 1916, in the form of a dispatch from the Navy Department: "About September 15th desire additional vessel at Corinto, Nicaragua, also yourself in Flagship in Gulf of Fonseca, ostensibly making investigation regarding Nicaraguan waters for naval station." The admiral went down at the appointed time, stationing three cruisers in or near Corinto and organizing the marines aboard them into a provisional regiment in preparation for a possible landing.[40]

Caperton had been ordered to consult with the U.S. minister to

Nicaragua, Benjamin L. Jefferson, and to offer him the navy's fullest cooperation. On anchoring in the Gulf of Fonseca, he received a request from Jefferson to come at once to the capital. "Presence of naval forces here very effective in causing tranquillity," Jefferson notified the State Department on the same day; now the minister wanted to show off the American admiral to the local politicos for further pacifying effect. Caperton's reputation as a tamer of revolutionaries had spread across the entire Caribbean area and would doubtless enhance the impact of his presence.[41]

The admiral had come at a time of crisis for Jefferson, whose problems had begun to multiply. Washington favored General Emiliano Chamorro, currently Nicaraguan minister to the United States, as the next president. President Diaz, however, opposed Chamorro, his bitter rival for control of the Conservative party. Furthermore, the Conservatives were a minority party. The Liberals commanded the support of the majority of voters and were united behind Dr. Julian Irias, who had been Zelaya's right-hand man. Shortly before Caperton's arrival, Díaz had moved to make a deal with Irias. Rumor had it that Irias was to receive a cabinet post and other favors in return for throwing his support to Díaz's own candidate, Carlos Cuadra Pasos. As Jefferson reported, "Everyone expects the Legation to settle the election question," but the minister needed Caperton to enforce his edicts.[42]

Pressed by events, Jefferson lost no time in making the capital aware of Caperton's presence. On the day he arrived, Caperton went with Jefferson to meet President Díaz. The following day, they conferred at the legation with both Irias and Chamorro. From everyone alike, and apparently without difficulty, Jefferson extracted pledges of a peaceful election. The American minister felt his hand so strengthened by Caperton's presence that he asked him to stay on at the legation until the situation cleared. As Caperton informed his superiors, "With the advent of a squadron of American ships, political leaders are again giving the usual weight to the Minister's words and are less inclined to fractiousness."[43]

Since things were quiet in Mexico, the admiral saw no reason not to stay as Jefferson requested. "He says my presence is having a wonderful effect towards bringing these people together, and also towards quieting any revolutionary feelings that may have existed among the people." Caperton and Jefferson hit it off from the first, with Caperton soon praising the tact and firmness of his diplomatic colleague. Jefferson seemed remarkably successful in maintaining an urbane outward tone during tense and heated negotiations, Caperton thought. "I mix and mingle with the leaders of the various parties nearly every night at some reception," he wrote, "so that I am on very friendly and cordial relations, apparently with all hands." The high point of this social campaign came when Jefferson managed to corral all of the rival leaders in the legation at the same time for an evening reception, a feat almost unprecedented in Nicaraguan politics.[44]

It was not his social charm, however, that made the admiral important. As he noted, "We have our landing force on the three ships thoroughly organized and all arrangements made with the railroads for immediate transportation." As an inland capital, Managua was beyond the reach of the fleet but not of the marines. The country's main railroad line ran parallel to the Pacific coast, connecting the port of Corinto directly with the major cities of Leon, Managua, and Granada, which lay in a line along it. The population, economic development, and political centers of Nicaragua were concentrated in this coastal strip and about Lakes Managua and Nicaragua, which lay just inland from it. In the 1912 intervention, the marines had simply seized the railroad line to gain effective occupation of the country, and Caperton planned to do this again if intervention should be required. As he wrote the Navy Department, "I do not expect to be called upon to land, but am taking all precautionary measures, so that I will not be caught napping in case of a sudden call."[45]

Jefferson cleared his first big hurdle within two days of Caperton's arrival, when President Díaz agreed at last to back Chamorro. There was a price for this surrender: Cuadra Pasos, Díaz's candidate, would go to Washington as the new minister to the United States, while a Cuadrista would become vice-president and others would gain cabinet posts. And there remained the problem of Irias and his popular Liberal majority. Irias had, it was true, visited Washington in summer 1915 in an attempt to make his peace with the State Department. Asking for a free election in which he could compete, he offered in turn to pledge his cooperation with the United States. To the State Department heads, however, the election of Irias would mean the restoration of the "Zelaya system" and was therefore unacceptable on any terms.[46]

During the summer, Jefferson had suggested to the State Department the plan that was ultimately to overcome this problem: the United States should declare itself neutral between factions but announce as a general principle that it could not recognize any candidate who represented a return to the evils of Zelayaism. Washington approved this approach, and by September 20, Jefferson felt his position strong enough to bring matters to a head. On that day, the candidates were summoned to the U.S. Legation, where Jefferson, with Caperton at his elbow, laid down the American terms. To secure U.S. approval, the next president must fully accept the entire system of treaties and financial arrangements existing between Nicaragua and the United States. He must further promise to maintain peace and order in the country, with or without the presence of legation marines. Since Irias had earlier indicated his willingness to accept these terms, they had in themselves no invidious effect. The remaining conditions, however, definitely ruled out the Liberal candidate. The successful aspirant, Jefferson said, must be free of any taint of revolutionary activity and, most pointed of all, "must give satisfactory proof of not having taken an active and objectionable part in the administration of President Zelaya."[47]

Although this meeting was the decisive point of the entire electoral campaign, it was almost totally lacking in outward drama. Jefferson read his fatal announcement in an impersonal tone, denying that it was aimed at any one candidate, and no one chose to challenge the fiction of American neutrality. Irias simply thanked the minister for his frankness and promised to announce his intentions in a few days. In the event of his withdrawal, he would leave the country and practice law abroad, the Liberal leader declared quietly, but he would make no breach of the peace. Up to the last possible moment, Irias avoided an open break with the Americans, probably for fear of wrecking his political hopes. "He was always very polite and agreeable in his conversations with me, as was his bearing toward other American officials," Caperton recalled.[48]

Five days after this crucial meeting, Irias withdrew as a candidate and issued a manifesto revealing the American demands that had ruled him out of contention. All Liberal voters should boycott the election, Irias urged, so that it would have no color of legitimacy. Feeling among his supporters ran high. That afternoon a mob at Leon, the Liberal stronghold, threw fruit and dirt at seven American naval officers who stopped there on a train. On September 29, Irias departed the capital in an emotional scene witnessed by hundreds of cheering Liberals. To lessen the impact of this occasion, Caperton had arranged competing entertainment. He had previously summoned the band from his flagship to Managua, and while the Liberals gathered at the railroad station, another large crowd heard the navy's music and watched a parade of the legation marines. On the next day, however, the Liberals came to the legation some four hundred strong to protest. "A great deal of language was used which could not be translated in respectable English," Caperton noted, "but, in general, the crowd was very orderly."[49]

When voting began on October 1, the usual election brawls developed; several people were killed in Managua, but there was no general breakdown of order. Most Liberals refused to vote, so that Chamorro was virtually unopposed. It soon became apparent, however, that the final act of the election would be played out in Washington, not in Nicaragua. The Executive Committee of the Liberal party cabled Woodrow Wilson to protest "the unexpected and tardy declarations of Minister Jefferson which owing to their far-reaching significance absolutely exclude Liberal party from government of country." Meanwhile, Irias went north to pursue the matter in person, and by the end of October, he had attracted the attention of the New York press. The *New York Herald,* which had reported the Nicaraguan election in some detail, both printed and supported Irias's claims. "American Minister Controlled Nicaraguan Election, Leader of Liberal Party Charges," read one headline, while the accompanying story asserted that the *Herald*'s own information was in accord with the Liberals' version of events. The story also noted Caperton's part in the election manipulations, thrusting the admiral squarely into the ensuing debate.[50]

In defending himself to his superiors, Caperton was vigorous, if not convincing. Irias had reported Jefferson's terms inaccurately, he claimed; the ban against former Zelayistas was not universal but affected only those who had played an "active and objectionable role" under Zelaya. Furthermore, the Liberals' refusal to vote showed that they feared the verdict of a free election. "Our Minister's activities were absolutely proper," Caperton wrote later. "He made no interference, whatever, with the election." He had, it was true, "informed leaders that any candidate who was elected must fulfill certain requirements, in order to be satisfactory to the United States." But the votes were accurately counted, and all the voters were free to participate.[51]

Rather than feeling apologetic, the admiral considered the whole exercise a distinct success. Chamorro, he thought, was the proper choice for president and would do well if supported by the United States and closely guided by the American minister. Furthermore, the Nicaraguan people did not seem excessively dissatisfied with the outcome, at any rate to an observer who measured their relatively easygoing attitude against the implacable hostility encountered in the Dominican Republic. Caperton commented repeatedly on the courtesy and good order he found in Nicaragua, reporting at one point that the "populace seems decidedly friendly toward Americans." It had not been necessary to use force, or even to land the shipboard marines, while the various negotiations had been conducted without overt unpleasantness. All in all, the admiral was very pleased with the way things had gone.[52]

Caperton was not likely to develop qualms about controlling an election by removing the front-runner, for he had tried that very tactic himself in both Haiti and the Dominican Republic. Long since calloused to the ways of intervention, Caperton still believed firmly in the ends involved while refusing to worry much about the means. "Our Government has taken the proper stand, I think, in Nicaragua," he declared, "and it is necessary that we stand firmly and squarely for our position, as by so-doing the other Central American Countries will be induced and influenced to change their modes of Government along the lines of those we are helping Nicaragua to enforce. . . . They are all watching closely . . . , and the better classes of them will be only too ready to take advantage of the beneficial reforms which we are bringing about in Nicaragua."[53]

From autumn 1916 to spring 1917, Admiral Caperton was free of any significant diplomatic tasks, and as the United States went to war with Germany in April 1917, he concentrated on preparing his Pacific Fleet for wartime duties. To his surprise, however, he was destined to spend the war not in the Pacific but in the Atlantic, where his chief mission would again be diplomatic. Within a few months, he had become the United States' best-known representative in South America, working closely with civilian diplomats to maximize U.S. influence in the area.

In May 1917, Caperton received orders at San Diego to take four big armored cruisers from his Pacific Fleet into the Atlantic for wartime service. At the request of the British and French naval authorities, the United States had agreed to establish a South Atlantic patrol force based in Brazil and to patrol some two thousand miles of Brazilian coastal waters. Caperton's chief subordinate would take over the remaining naval forces in the Pacific, but Caperton would keep his rank and title as commander-in-chief of the Pacific Fleet, in spite of having moved to the Atlantic. This would make him the highest-ranking Allied naval officer in South American waters, which may have been the reason for the unusual arrangement.[54]

Caperton came to South America at a critical time. The German resumption of unrestricted submarine warfare and the subsequent

U.S. entry into the war had set off a wave of excitement, particularly in Brazil, which had also suffered from U-boat sinkings of its merchant ships. Brazilian public opinion was strongly pro-Allies, and the government there had close ties to the United States. After the Americans went to war in April, Brazil broke relations with Germany. Notice from Washington of the dispatch of Caperton's squadron to Brazilian waters brought further steps. In May, Brazil's President Wenceslau Braz asked his Congress to revoke Brazilian neutrality for the specific purpose of allowing the belligerent United States continued free use of Brazil's ports and facilities. The president justified this action on the grounds that the United States formed "an integral part of the American continent," declaring, "To this belligerent we are bound by a traditional friendship and by a similarity of political opinion in the defense of the vital interests of America." Later in May, the Brazilians seized over thirty German ships lying in their ports. Brazil was clearly in the Allied camp; the question was whether she would actually declare war on Germany.[55]

In mid-June, Admiral Caperton's squadron reached Bahia, a prospective patrol base. It was welcomed effusively by the Brazilians and almost immediately invited to visit Rio de Janeiro. The admiral hesitated to postpone his patrolling for a goodwill visit but agreed to it on the urging of the American embassy. The Brazilian government was somewhat nervous about the course of their neighbors, the Argentines, who pursued a policy of strict neutrality. The two were South America's natural leaders and rivals; the Rio government hoped that the presence of the American squadron might strengthen Brazil's hand against Argentina while generating support at home. Caperton's force accordingly proceeded to Rio.[56]

The four gray sister ships, each five hundred feet long and bristling with guns, made an impressive display as they anchored in line off the city. Much too large for routine antisubmarine patrolling, their speed and cruising range alone justified the assignment, but for parade and show purposes they were ideal. For the next two weeks, the squadron weathered an almost unbroken tide of receptions, parades, banquets, and ceremonies, as the people of Rio turned out in huge numbers to fete their visitors. Midway in the visit, Caperton urgently requested five thousand dollars from the Navy Department for entertaining expenses. It was quickly forthcoming, and he was able to match Rio's hospitality with his own. A highlight of his efforts was the Fourth of July festivities, featuring a parade of seamen ashore and a luncheon aboard the flagship for President Braz and a horde of Brazilian notables. The day ended with the navy giving a ball on shore, which Caperton breathlessly reported as "the Success of the Season, or any other Season. . . . It was a glorious day for the United States." [57]

The effort brought some results. On June 29, the Brazilians extended their revocation of neutrality from the United States alone to all of the Entente Allies, while after the squadron's departure, they consulted the American embassy about naval measures they might take to protect their own waters against U-boats. The embassy gave high marks to Caperton's public relations campaign but was unable to say when or whether Brazil would actually declare war. [58]

Even before Caperton left Rio, Washington had projected similar visits by his squadron to Montevideo and Buenos Aires. The middle two weeks of July it visited in Montevideo, the capital of Uruguay. The Uruguayan government had also protested the German resumption of U-boat warfare and had followed Brazil's lead in revoking neutrality in favor of the United States. Rather incongruously, they maintained diplomatic relations with Germany, however, and while pro-Allies in sentiment were wary of their neutralist Argentine neighbor. Again Caperton hoped to overcome the Uruguayans' caution by his display of American power and by reinforcing local enthusiasm for the Allies.

His reception was all that he could desire, for on arrival, an enormous crowd jammed the streets and brought the city to a halt. The admiral found "balconies crowded, banners waving, bands playing and continuous cheering and applause going on," so that it took the official caravan an hour to cover the mile from the waterfront to the U.S. Legation. Its prestige enhanced by its success in Brazil, the squadron found itself the height of chic in Montevideo, and another exhausting social schedule quickly developed. The official reaction was more restrained; Uruguay's president and minister of foreign affairs were demonstratively friendly, but in private conversations, they indicated limits to their pro-American stance. Uruguay's government normally took its cue in foreign affairs from the government of Argentina; having moved well beyond the Argentines already, they would go no further unless the latter country broke relations with Germany. [59]

This put the vital center in Buenos Aires, the site of the squadron's next visit. In summer 1917, the political balance there seemed to teeter on a knife edge. Public opinion expressed in mass meetings and demonstrations when German submarines sank Argentine ships, was strongly pro-Allies. Shortly before Caperton's visit, such public pressure had forced the government to present the Germans with a near-ultimatum on the subject. Offsetting the public's anger at Germany, however, was the determined neutralism of President Hipolito Irigoyen. Immensely popular with the common people, Irigoyen set his face against involvement in the European war and labored behind the scenes to head off an open break with Berlin. Even as Caperton's force arrived, the president was secretly negotiating a settlement that he would announce as a diplomatic triumph after the squadron had left. In the public part of this agreement, the German government solemnly pledged to respect Argentina's ships in the future; a secret annex contained Irigoyen's promise to keep his country's vessels out of the danger zone, a condition that his government had just publicly refused to accept. Caperton's visit, therefore, was a major test of President Irigoyen's ability to hold his country in line with his own neutralist policy, and Caperton hoped to arouse enough pro-Allied enthusiasm to stampede the government into the American camp. Even a small departure from Irigoyen's rigid neutrality would encourage Brazil and Uruguay to go further in their own movement toward belligerency.[60]

The Argentines initially received the squadron with every courtesy but with nothing like the wild excitement shown in Rio and Montevideo. Irigoyen himself was cautious and reserved, though several cabinet members and representatives of the Argentine navy were avowedly pro-Allies. The inevitable parades, banquets, and ceremonies seemed to generate an increasing warmth among the people, and at the end of the five-day visit, an estimated fifty thousand people marched in a torchlight parade in honor of the Americans, despite the steady cold rain of the Argentine winter. Final interviews with the ministers of foreign affairs and of the marines seemed highly promising, while Irigoyen grew warmly cordial but carefully avoided specifics in his conversations with the admiral.[61]

At the end of five weeks of goodwill visiting and attempted diplomatic pressure, Caperton found himself famous throughout South America, with instant access to important people everywhere. He had helped to improve his country's image and to popularize its cause. Embassy reports from all three capitals praised his effectiveness and charm; no man, they agreed, could have done better as a propagandist and advocate. The substantive results, however, were limited. Argentina remained determinedly neutral to the end of the war, though at one point in autumn 1917 it seemed doubtful that Irigoyen could stem a wave of anti-German fury. Brazil entered the war in October after additional sinkings of her ships by submarines, and Uruguay broke diplomatic relations with Germany and seized eight German ships lying in her ports. But both countries had been pro-Allies before Caperton's appearance, and while his visits may have helped to confirm the policy directions in Rio and Montevideo, they were hardly the root cause of them. The American squadron's visits probably made it easier for the two governments to pursue courses that they already preferred; beyond this, it is difficult to go.[62]

Caperton himself took his diplomatic mission with the utmost seriousness. On the eve of the squadron's arrival in Buenos Aires in July 1917, for example, he had a special order read on each of his ships, emphasizing the need for good behavior on the part of the sailors and the importance of making a favorable impression. "Each man must feel that he is playing a great game for his country," the order read; "I know that I can count upon every single man standing by our government in the wonderful chance we have of serving our country, a little different perhaps than we would do in battle, but nevertheless a means to an end."[63]

At the end of his extraordinary goodwill tour, the admiral was ready at last to take up his original mission of antisubmarine patrolling. By that time, however, it was becoming clear that Germany's U-boats would remain concentrated in the North Atlantic, with little threat to shipping south of there. Patrol vessels were needed where the real danger lay, while Caperton's big cruisers ate up appalling amounts of coal in a region where that fuel was acutely scarce. The Navy Department grew restive, and after Brazil's declaration of war in October, it moved to recover its ships. In the closing months of 1917, three of the four sisters of the squadron were withdrawn, to be replaced by two small, ancient relics of the Spanish-American War.[64]

Nevertheless, Caperton was left on the South American station with his flagship and continued until the end of the war to cultivate good relations in the region. During 1918, he shifted his diplomatic aim from the Germans to the British, whose commercial resurgence he feared once the war had ended. The voracious wartime demand for military supplies at the fighting front kept British factories fully occupied and ended Great Britain's long-held dominance of the Latin American market, while the British blockade entirely stopped Germany's overseas exports. The United States had inherited the market by default, and Caperton hoped to see this gain made permanent. He helped to secure a contract to overhaul two Brazilian battleships in a New York shipyard, working hard to wean Brazil's navy from its traditional British ties, and tried in other ways to consolidate the American hold on the local market. Such activities were his chief focus when the war ended in November 1918, and in April of the following year, he sailed home to retirement.[65]

Caperton was very disappointed that the Navy Department had first decimated his South American squadron, then eliminated it altogether when he himself left the scene. As he wrote shortly afterward,

> The sudden change in the Department's plans came as a blow to me for I had always been keenly interested in the diplomatic side of our naval endeavors. . . . And I believed that our influence had been for the direct benefit of American trade in South America . . . and of our friendship with countries south of the equator. Then suddenly, the beneficial influence was withdrawn, and at a time when South America demanded our coal, our ships, our materials and our manufactures. Never had a better trade opportunity been offered any nation. But we had sowed seed in fertile ground and had increased in South America a budding confidence in the United States and its people.[66]

The admiral exaggerated his own role in the pursuit of postwar trade, as he had earlier overestimated his effect on the area's wartime diplomacy. He nonetheless believed firmly in the importance of naval diplomacy, a natural result of the diplomatic focus of his own flag career. His fellow admirals disagreed; it was they who had pressed the Office of Naval Operations to abolish the South American squadron. The end of the European war would bring a general redeployment of naval forces, and the seagoing admirals feared any tendencies toward dispersion of the fleet to scattered geographic stations. They demanded that the navy's ships be largely concentrated in a single fighting force and dedicated to preparation for war. On returning to Washington, Caperton attempted to convert his colleagues to his own concept of a dual-purpose navy organized for diplomacy as well as fighting.[67]

In May 1919, Caperton submitted his plan for postwar naval deployment to the Office of Naval Operations, in a document entitled "The Diplomatic Mission of the Navy." In it, he proposed a global system of geographic stations, to which all but the major fighting ships could be assigned. In justification, he claimed that "the net result of maintaining squadrons on foreign stations in the way of cultivating national friendships cannot be over-estimated and, in both diplomatic and trade relations, is great and out of all proportion with the cost." In the coming postwar era, it was "vital to the country's interests that this means of keeping and increasing our friendship and prestige be not neglected." The nation must extend its foreign trade;

"the Navy can render enormous aid in this work by creating and developing a feeling of liking and trust for the United States." It could also bolster Pan-Americanism in the same way, the admiral asserted.[68]

As for the military function of the navy, this could be assured by creating a single fighting fleet containing the modern battleships and their essential consorts and auxilliaries, prepared at all times for war. The remainder of the ships should be distributed among six permanent stations abroad: the Asiatic, European, South Atlantic, South Pacific, North Atlantic, and North Pacific. Those vessels not permanently attached to the battle fleet could be rotated between that unit and the geographic stations, thereby maintaining their combat readiness. Thus, Caperton hoped to meet the demands of his fellow admirals while at the same time securing their recognition of the importance of the navy's diplomatic work.[69]

The response was not long in coming: the Navy Planning Committee considered the Caperton proposal and flatly rejected it. The peacetime mission of the navy, said the committee's report, was to prepare for war. Effective fighting ships should be integrated into the battle fleet and obsolete ones scrapped. Foreign port visits could best be made by the navy's newest ships, which would enhance the nation's prestige; divisions of the battle fleet could make such visits occasionally. At any rate, diplomacy was the business of the State Department, not the navy, while expanding foreign trade was a task for private banking and commercial interests. Ignoring the long record of the navy's involvement in diplomatic activities, the Planning Committee simply denied that such concerns were legitimate.[70]

It was not surprising that Caperton saw it otherwise. Few American naval commanders had been so deeply involved in such a wide variety of diplomatic functions or contributed so directly to shaping U.S. foreign policy. While seeing himself always as an implementer rather than maker of policy, Caperton placed himself solidly within the circle of diplomats. The State Department had been quick to understand this and to use Caperton regularly as a part of its diplomatic apparatus. Like many of his naval colleagues, the admiral was an imperialist; unlike them, he fully understood the navy's importance in erecting a Caribbean imperium and was willing to accept gunboat diplomacy as one of the navy's ongoing functions, much more a part of navy routine than those great battles of which other commanders dreamed. His imperialism rested on the widest possible theoretical basis; he thought U.S. hegemony was needed, in the Caribbean and elsewhere, to enhance the national security, promote economic expansion abroad, and spread the benefits of constitutional democracy. He firmly grasped the interplay of power and politics and was adept in the political use of armed force. Never devoid of idealism, his ideals were increasingly blurred by his belief that the end justified the means.

NOTES

1. "Tennessean Center of Eyes," *Nashville Banner*, Oct. 9, 1915; Caperton obituary, *Nashville Tennessean*, Dec. 22, 1941; "William Banks Caperton," *The National Cyclopaedia of American Biography* (New York: James T. White and Co., 1950), 36; 30–31.

2. Richard D. Challener, *Admirals, Generals, and American Foreign Policy, 1898–1914* (Princeton: Princeton University Press, 1973), 152–153; Richard W. Turk, "Strategy and Foreign Policy: The United States Navy in the Caribbean, 1865–1913" (Ph.D. diss., Fletcher School of Law and Diplomacy, 1968): 153.

3. For the development of U.S. Caribbean policy, see Lester D. Langley, *The United States and the Caribbean, 1900–1970* (Athens: University of Georgia Press, 1980); Dana G. Munro, *Intervention and Dollar Diplomacy in the Caribbean, 1900–1921* (Princeton: Princeton University Press, 1964); David Healy, *Drive to Hegemony: The United States in the Caribbean, 1898–1917* (Madison: University of Wisconsin Press, 1988); and Whitney Perkins, *Constraint of Empire: The United States and Caribbean Interventions* (Westport, Conn., Greenwood Press, 1981).

4. Hans Schmidt, *The United States Occupation of Haiti, 1915–1934* (New Brunswick: Rutgers University Press, 1971): 37–41, 50–52; Dana G. Munro, *The United States and the Caribbean Area* (Boston: World Peace Foundation, 1934): 150–153; Arthur S. Link, *Wilson: The Struggle for Neutrality, 1914–1915* (Princeton: Princeton University Press, 1960), 518–519, 526–532; David Healy, *Gunboat Diplomacy in the Wilson Era: The United States Navy in Haiti, 1915–1916* (Madison: University of Wisconsin Press, 1976), 27–33.

5. William B. Caperton, "History of U.S. Naval Operations Under Command of Rear Admiral W. B. Caperton, USN, Commencing January 15, 1915, Ending April 30, 1919," in Subject File ZN (Personnel), 1911–1927, Record Group 45, Naval Records Collection of the Office of Naval Records and Library, National Archives, Washington, D.C. (cited hereafter as Caperton, "History of Flag Career"): 1–14, 34–37. See also Schmidt, *The U.S. Occupation of Haiti*, 37–41, 50–52; Healy, *Gunboat Diplomacy*, 17–58; and Harold P. Davis, *Black Democracy: The Story of Haiti* (New York: Dodge Publishing Company, 1936): 155–156, 304–307.

6. Caperton, "History of Flag Career," 45–49; Captain Edward L. Beach, USN, "Admiral Caperton in Haiti," Subject File ZWA-7 (Haiti), Record Group 45, National Archives, Washington, D.C., 98–104.

7. Caperton, "History of Flag Career," 48–61; Beach, "Caperton in

Haiti," 106–124 ff., 131–133; *New York Herald*, July 30, July 31, and August 3, 1915; Healy, *Gunboat Diplomacy*, 62–72, 77–80.

8. Caperton, "History of Flag Career," 56–61, 64–72, 76; Beach, "Caperton in Haiti," 118–120, 128–129, 133–144 ff.; *New York Herald*, Aug. 5 and Aug. 7, 1915; Healy, *Gunboat Diplomacy*, 82–98.

9. Lansing to AmLegation Port-au-Prince, August 10, 1915, in Decimal Files, Haiti, Internal.

10. Caperton, "History of Flag Career," 62, 75–88; Beach, "Caperton in Haiti," 112, 116–117, 133–134, 145–163; *New York Herald*, August 11, 13, and 18, 1915; Ludwell Lee Montague, *Haiti and the United States, 1714–1938* (New York: Russell and Russell, 1966): 213–214; Healy, *Gunboat Diplomacy*, 71, 82–84, 99–117.

11. Lansing to AmLegation Port-au-Prince, August 14, 1915, in Records of the Department of State relating to the Internal Affairs of Haiti, 1910–1929, Record Group 59, General Records of the Department of State, National Archives, Washington, D.C. (cited hereafter as Decimal Files, Haiti).

12. Caperton, "History of Flag Career," 95, 102–104, 117, 133; Beach, "Caperton in Haiti," 166; *New York Herald*, August 25 and September 9, 1915; Healy, *Gunboat Diplomacy*, 134–137, 144, 152–154.

13. Lansing to AmLegation Port-au-Prince, August 18, 1915, and Caperton to SecNavy, August 19, 1915, both in Decimal Files, Haiti; Caperton, "History of Flag Career," 99, 111–115, 120–126, 151, 154 (quote is on 154); Healy, *Gunboat Diplomacy*, 138–140, 148–151.

14. Caperton, "History of Flag Career," 63–108 ff., 116–119, 129–141, 143–218 ff.; quote is from Caperton to SecNavy, August 19, 1915, in Decimal Files, Haiti. See also *New York Herald*, August 31, September 7, September 14, and October 7, 1915; and Healy, *Gunboat Diplomacy*, 145–148, 159–170, 181–184.

15. Caperton, "History of Flag Career," 144, 148, 169, 180–181, 196–213 ff.; Beach, "Caperton in Haiti," 168, 184–185; *New York Herald*, September 9 and November 2, 1915; B. Danache, *Le President Dartiguenave et les Americaines* (Port-au-Prince: Imprimerie de l'Etat, 1950): 47, 49–50; Healy, *Gunboat Diplomacy*, 154–158, 170–171, 175–181.

16. Caperton, "History of Flag Career," 246–251; *New York Herald*, April 11, 1916; Healy, *Gunboat Diplomacy*, 202–205.

17. The quote is from Danache, *Le President Dartiguenave et les Americaines*, 45.

18. The quotations are to be found in Caperton, "History of Flag Career," 3; and Caperton to Rear Admiral William S. Benson, Chief of Naval Operations, October 30, 1916, in William B. Caperton Papers, Library of Congress.

19. Caperton, "History of Flag Career," 250–251, 253–254; Caperton to Benson, June 26 and July 20, 1916, in Caperton Papers, Library of Congress; Schmidt, *The U.S. Occupation of Haiti*, 79.

20. Caperton, "History of Flag Career," 200, 203, 212; Beach, "Caperton in Haiti," 108–109; James A. Padgett, "Diplomats to Haiti and Their Diplomacy," *Journal of Negro History* 25 (July 1940): 315.

21. See U.S. Senate, *Inquiry into the occupation and administration of Haiti and Santo Domingo. Hearings before a select committee on Haiti and Santo Domingo, pursuant to Senate Resolution 112, 67th Cong., 1st and 2d sess.* 2 vols. (Washington, D.C., 1922). Caperton's testimony appears on 285–421.

22. See Sumner Welles, *Naboth's Vineyard: The Dominican Republic, 1844–1924.* 2 vols. (New York: Payson and Clark, 1928, reprinted by Savile Books, 1966), 2: 601–748; Luis F. Mejia, *De Lilis a Trujillo: Historia contemporanea de la Republica Dominica* (Caracas: Editorial Elite, 1944): 1–36, 44–46; Link, *Wilson: The Struggle for Neutrality,* 500, 503–515, 538–539; and Munro, *Intervention and Dollar Diplomacy in the Caribbean,* 103–106, 274–298.

23. Lansing to Wilson, November 24, 1915; Russell to Lansing, December 27, 1915, and April 15, 16, 27, 29, and May 1, 6, 7, and 10, 1916; all in Records relating to Internal Affairs of the Dominican Republic, 1910–1929, Record Group 59, National Archives, Washington, D.C. (cited hereafter as Decimal Files, Dominican Republic). See also Welles, *Naboth's Vineyard,* 2:748–766; Link, *Wilson: The Struggle for Neutrality,* 538–543; Munro, *Intervention and Dollar Diplomacy in the Caribbean,* 296–304; and Frederick May Wise, *A Marine Tells It to You* (New York: J. H. Sears and Co., 1929): 138–143.

24. Russell to Lansing, May 7 and May 10, 1916; Lansing to Russell, May 7, 1916; all in Decimal Files, Dominican Republic. See also Caperton, "History of Flag Career," 258–259.

25. Caperton, Report of Operations dated May 17, 1916, in Decimal Files, Dominican Republic; Caperton, "History of Flag Career," 258–259. Quotations are from Vice-Consul Carl M. J. von Zislinsky to SecState, May 17, 1916, in Decimal Files, Dominican Republic; and Caperton to Benson, May 18, 1916, in Caperton Papers, Library of Congress.

26. Russell to SecState, May 18, 1916, and Caperton, Report of Operations dated May 25, 1916, both in Decimal Files, Dominican Republic; Caperton, "History of Flag Career," 258.

27. Caperton, Report of Operations dated May 25, 1916, in Decimal Files, Dominican Republic; Russell to SecState, May 25, 1916, ibid.; Caperton, "History of Flag Career," 258–259.

28. Caperton, Report of Operations dated May 25, 1916, in Decimal Files, Dominican Republic; quotations are from Caperton to Benson, May 18 and 19, 1916, in Caperton Papers, Library of Congress.

29. Caperton, "History of Flag Career," 261–262, 425–437; Carl Kelsey, "The American Intervention in Haiti and the Dominican Republic," *Annals of the Academy of Political and Social Science* 100 (March 1922): 174–175.

30. Russell to SecState, June 2, 1916; Acting SecState Polk to Russell, June 3, 1916; both in Decimal Files, Dominican Republic.

31. Caperton to Benson, June 7 and 12, 1916, in Caperton Papers, Library of Congress; Russell to SecState, June 6, 1916, in Decimal Files, Dominican Republic; Caperton, "History of Flag Career," 266.

32. Caperton to Benson, June 15, 1916, in Caperton Papers, Library of Congress.

33. Caperton, Reports of Operations dated June 22 and July 8, 1916, in

Decimal Files, Dominican Republic; Caperton to Benson, June 7 and June 26, 1916, in Caperton Papers, Library of Congress; Caperton, "History of Flag Career," 270–271; Clyde H. Metcalf, *A History of the United States Marines* (New York: Putnam's, 1939): 348–349.

34.   Russell to SecState, July 13, 1916, in Decimal Files, Dominican Republic; Caperton to Benson, July 20, 1916, in Caperton Papers, Library of Congress; Caperton, "History of Flag Career," 272.

35.   See Welles, *Naboth's Vineyard*, 2:777–790; and Link, *Wilson: The Struggle for Neutrality*, 545–547.

36.   Caperton to Benson, October 30, 1916, in Caperton Papers, Library of Congress.

37.   See "The War Chiefs of the Navy," *World's Work* 30 (August 1915): 409–410. For periodic breakdowns of the disposition of all naval units, see contemporary issues of *The Army and Navy Journal*.

38.   J. B. Wright to Jordan Stabler, August 12, 1916, in Records of the Department of State relating to Internal Affairs of Nicaragua, 1910–1929, Record Group 59, National Archives (cited hereafter as Decimal Files, Nicaragua).

39.   See Munro, *Intervention and Dollar Diplomacy in the Caribbean*, 160–216, 388–406; Walter V. Scholes and Marie V. Scholes, *The Foreign Policies of the Taft Administration* (Columbia, Mo., University of Missouri Press, 1970): 45–67; and Arthur S. Link, *Wilson: The New Freedom* (Princeton: Princeton University Press, 1956): 331–341.

40.   Caperton, "History of Flag Career," 277–279.

41.   Ibid., 279; Jefferson to SecState, September 15, 1916, in Decimal Files, Nicaragua.

42.   Jefferson to SecState, July 18 and September 6, 1916, in Decimal Files, Nicaragua; Lansing to Jefferson, September 12, 1916, ibid.; Caperton, "History of Flag Career," 278, 281; Munro, *Intervention and Dollar Diplomacy in the Caribbean*, 406–413.

43.   Caperton, Report of Operations dated September 24, 1916, in Decimal Files, Nicaragua; Caperton to Benson, September 21, 1916, in Caperton Papers, Library of Congress; Caperton, "History of Flag Career," 282.

44.   Caperton to Benson, September 21, 1916, Caperton Papers, Library of Congress.

45.   Ibid.

46.   Jefferson to SecState, September 17 and 21, 1916; Caperton, Report of Operations dated September 24, 1916; all in Decimal Files, Nicaragua. See also, Munro, *Intervention and Dollar Diplomacy in the Caribbean*, 411.

47.   Jefferson to SecState, September 21, 1916, in Decimal Files, Nicaragua; Caperton, "History of Flag Career," 282.

48.   Caperton to Benson, October 28, 1916, in Caperton Papers, Library of Congress; Caperton, "History of Flag Career," 282, 286–287; Caperton, Report of Operations dated September 24, 1916, in Decimal Files, Nicaragua.

49.   Jefferson to SecState, September 26, 1916, in Decimal Files, Nicaragua; Caperton, "History of Flag Career," 283–285.

50.   Caperton, "History of Flag Career," 285–286, 288; Enoc Aguarde,

Secretary of the Executive Committee of the Liberal Party of Nicaragua, to Woodrow Wilson, October 21, 1916, in Decimal Files, Nicaragua; *New York Herald,* November 2, 1916.

51. Caperton, Report of Operations dated October 30, 1916, in Decimal Files, Nicaragua.

52. Caperton, "History of Flag Career," 291–292; Caperton, Report of Operations dated September 24, 1916, in Decimal Files, Nicaragua; Caperton to Benson, October 28, 1916, Caperton Papers, Library of Congress.

53. Caperton to Benson, October 28, 1916, Caperton Papers, Library of Congress.

54. Operations to *Pittsburgh* flag, April 28, 1917, in Subject File ZOX, Pacific Fleet, 1911–1927; SecNavy to C-in-C Pacific Fleet, May 9, 1917, in Area File, South Atlantic; both in Record Group 45, Naval Records Collection of the Office of Naval Records and Library, National Archives, Washington, D.C. See also Caperton, "History of Flag Career," 296, 302.

55. See Percy A. Martin, *Latin America and the War* (Baltimore: Johns Hopkins University Press, 1925): 33–36, 52–63, for an account of these events. Quotations are on 48–59.

56. Caperton, "History of Flag Career," 305–307.

57. Caperton to SecNavy, June 28, 1917, in Area File, South Atlantic; Captain F. K. Hill, U.S. Naval Attaché at Rio, to Office of Naval Intelligence, July 6, 1917, in Subject File WA-7, Brazil, 1911–1927, Record Group 45; Edwin V. Morgan, U.S. Ambassador to Brazil, to SecState, July 11, 1917, in Subject File ZOX; Caperton to Benson, July 6, 1917, in Caperton Papers, Library of Congress (quote is from the latter). See also Caperton, "History of Flag Career," 306–308, 311–312.

58. Hill to Office of Naval Intelligence, July 6 and 19, 1917, in Subject File WA-7; Morgan to SecState, July 11, 1917, in Subject File ZOX; Caperton, Report of Operations dated July 5, 1917, ibid.

59. Caperton, Report of Operations dated July 22, 1917; Robert E. Jeffery, U.S. Ambassador to Uruguay, to SecState, July 16, 1917; William Dawson, U.S. Consul at Montevideo, to SecState, November 5, 1917; all in Subject File ZOX. See also Caperton, "History of Flag Career," 307–309, 313–318; and Martin, *Latin America and the War,* 351–366.

60. Acting SecState to SecNavy, July 20, 1917; Caperton, Report of Operations dated July 5, 1917; both in Subject File ZOX. See also Glen Barclay, *Struggle for a Continent* (New York: New York University Press, 1972): 16–17.

61. Caperton to SecNavy, July 28, 1917, in Area File, South Atlantic; Caperton, Report of Operations dated August 5, 1917, in Subject File ZOX; Caperton, "History of Flag Career," 319–324.

62. For a narrative of these events, see Martin, *Latin America and the War,* 67–68, 215–224, 237–250, 367–372.

63. C-in-C Pacific to Commanding Officers, USS *Pittsburgh, Frederick, Pueblo,* and *South Dakota,* July 23, 1917, in Subject File ZOX.

64. Caperton, Report of Operations dated September 18, 1917, in Subject File ZOX; Pacific Fleet Flag, Fleet Order No. 4, December 19, 1917, in Area

File, South Atlantic; Caperton, "History of Flag Career," 309–310, 325, 334–336, 343–346.

65.   Caperton to Benson, January 29 and November 12, 1918, in Caperton Papers, Library of Congress; Caperton, Report of Operations dated May 31, 1918, in Subject File ZOX; Morgan to SecState, November 13, 1917, in Records of the Department of State relating to Internal Affairs of Brazil, 1910–1929, Record Group 59, National Archives, Washington, D.C.; Caperton, "History of Flag Career," 344–345. See also Joseph S. Tulchin, *The Aftermath of War: World War I and United States Policy Toward Latin America* (New York: New York University Press, 1917): 23–61.

66.   Caperton, "History of Flag Career," 397.

67.   See Admiral J. S. McKean, Acting Chief of Naval Operations, to Benson, Apr. 8, 1919, and Benson to McKean, May 24, 1919, in CNO File, Record Group 80, General Records of the Navy, National Archives, Washington, D.C.

68.   Caperton to Chief of Naval Operations, May 12, 1919, in CNO File.

69.   Ibid.

70.   Navy Planning Committee to Chief of Naval Operations, May 29, 1919, ibid.

CHAPTER 4

Thomas W. Lamont
International Banker as Diplomat

ROBERT FREEMAN SMITH

Alvaro Obregon, the president of Mexico, was puzzled. Although the year was 1921 and the United States had outlawed alcoholic beverages, he still wondered why his distinguished guest had suddenly requested a special train to take a "mixed party" down to the Isthmus of Tehuantepec. The president asked the man claiming to represent Thomas W. Lamont, senior partner of J. P. Morgan and Company, "Won't Lamont be satisfied with a special car?" The man replied, "Oh no no, he's a big man and insists on a special train." Obregon authorized a special train and undoubtedly wondered at how fast the banker had gone native. Perhaps he recalled his first meeting with Lamont, when he had come to the presidential office and Obregon called out to his attendant, "Bring some champagne, whiskeys, and liqueurs. I want you to know, Mr. Lamont, that you are at last in a free country." Lamont found out about the attempt to use his name to obtain a special train from the president of Mexico and stopped the train with its cargo of "fancy" women and gringo adventurers just as it was about to leave the station in Mexico City.[1]

What kind of person on a private mission, with no rank or title, could merit such special consideration from the head of a country that had not had very friendly relations with its neighbor to the north? Lamont was such a person—a born diplomat. Raised in the Hudson Valley of New York in the 1860s, he spent his youth in a less-than-affluent Methodist parsonage. In later years, he would become a Presbyterian, thus giving some credence to the old saw, "A Methodist is a Baptist who wears shoes and has learned to read and write; a Presbyterian is a Methodist who went to college."

101

Lamont graduated from Harvard University in 1892. Years later, he still remembered with intellectual excitement the classes he had taken from William James, Josiah Royce, Charles Eliot Norton, and George Lyman Kittredge. During his college years, he studied philosophy, the classics, history, and art—but not international relations. As he later wrote, "But as for any thought of war, or foreign aggression, or even serious study of current foreign affairs—none of that was within our ken."[2]

After graduation, Lamont went to work for the *New York Tribune* and then for Cushman Brothers (an agent for manufacturers, later reorganized as Lamont, Corliss & Co.), the Bankers Trust Company, and the First National Bank of New York. He was persuaded to join the firm of J. P. Morgan and Company in 1911, and he moved up rapidly until he eventually became chairman of the board. In spite of his immense success with the firm, Lamont would state in 1946, "I did not know then, nor do I know to this day, the techniques of banking."[3] But his primary role in the firm was that of diplomat and spokesman. This was not just public relations. Lamont represented and defended the company's broad interests not only in the business world but also in the arena of politics and international relations. In 1914, a writer described him "as a good mixer, unassuming, unpretentious, unconventional" and noted his "engaging personality."[4]

By 1914, Lamont had developed into an urbane, reasonable, and undogmatic businessman. This enabled him to negotiate quietly with foreign leaders on an informal, unofficial basis. He understood the role that economics played in promoting international stability, and time after time he used both his diplomatic skills and his ties to J. P. Morgan and Company to keep the lines of communication open between various foreign groups and the U.S. government. All too often, difficult circumstances created by nationalism and cultural differences, on both sides, complicated his efforts, but he did enjoy a fair amount of success during his career. He did experience some failures, but compromise is not always possible. And, to Lamont, compromise was the essence of negotiation.

Lamont was drawn into the arena of international relations more by foreign policy considerations than by pure banking matters. The House of Morgan had interests in both the Chinese and the Mexican foreign debt. In the case of China, the Morgan firm became part of the four-power banking consortium in 1910 (which became a six-power group in 1912). It had also participated in the Mexican loans of 1899, 1910, and 1913, but the bank held very few of the Mexican notes.

Lamont, however, became directly involved with the problem of Mexican finances when, in January 1917, President Venustiano Carranza's brother-in-law, General Zambrano, came to New York to request a loan of $10 million from the Morgan bank and to discuss possible U.S. investment in a "national Mexican bank." Lamont informed the Mexican representatives that "it was impossible that anything could be done until the Mexicans had composed their own political differences and had manifested some disposition to protect foreigners in their persons and in their property and there could be devised a general plan of refinancing which would embrace all Mexican obligations and necessities."[5] But Lamont assured the Mexicans that J. P. Morgan and Company was not hostile toward the Mexican government and hoped to be able to loan money to Mexico in the future.

In May 1917, Agustín Legorreta, head of Banco Nacional de Mexico, a private firm, visited the Morgan bank, and Martin Egan gave him a letter of introduction to Secretary of the Interior Franklin K. Lane. The secretary gave Legorreta some encouragement concerning a plan "to have the Mexican government raise or mobilize a large quantity of food products for the United States and allied governments, the project to be financed by American bankers." The U.S. government would participate "indirectly." Egan believed that at least "the bare possibility" existed that something might be done for Mexico. Legorreta departed before his scheduled, private conference with Secretary of State Robert Lansing, and these negotiations lapsed.[6]

During his visit to the United States in July 1917, Ambassador Henry P. Fletcher also made inquiries about the possibility of a Mexican loan from private sources. Fletcher had already been in touch with J. P. Morgan and Company, and it soon became apparent that while the bank officials had serious reservations about any sizable loan, they were not so dogmatic as the mining and agricultural corporations. Lamont suggested to Fletcher the possibility of a short-term loan guaranteed by the U.S. government. The intent of such a five- or ten-year loan would be to enable Mexico to "rehabilitate itself and make good the defaults on its outstanding obligations with the idea, prior to the maturity of this short-term loan, of consolidating its debt and refunding the present outstanding bonds with a new loan."[7] To J. P. Morgan and Company, the first priority was the refunding of the defaulted bond issues, and, to achieve this, company officials preferred less dogmatic tactics than those proposed by other business groups.

World War I brought Lamont into a working relationship with the

U.S. government. In fall 1917, he accompanied Col. Edward House on a trip to England to work out details for Allied cooperation. When the war ended, the secretary of the treasury requested that he represent that department on the American Commission to negotiate the peace, and in that capacity, he served on the Supreme Economic Council. Indeed, the New York banker tried to persuade Lloyd George and Woodrow Wilson to work with the leaders of revolutionary Russia. As a firm advocate of international cooperation and conciliation, he also became an advocate for the proposed League of Nations. Officials in the Wilson administration found in Lamont a man who shared many of their views and ideals.

Thus, it was logical that the State Department brought Lamont into the government's efforts to straighten out the finances of Mexico and China. During summer 1918, the State Department sent information about a proposed loan to Mexico to the president and requested authorization to try to induce the bankers to initiate loan negotiations. Wilson immediately approved the project and asked to see a more detailed plan. This was sent to Wilson on August 15, 1918, and it called in essence for the refunding of the Mexican debt and the establishment of a joint commission to supervise the finances of Mexico. The granting of any loan, however, would be based on the settlement of "all major questions of an economic and diplomatic character." [8]

Several conferences were then held between State Department officials and Lamont. At this point, the problems of loans and guarantees merged with the specific interest of the investment bankers in the foreign bonds of Mexico. The Morgan company had been under pressure from various European banks to take the lead in organizing a committee to represent the holders of Mexican bonds, and early in October, the State Department approved the Morgan proposal to organize the International Committee of Bankers on Mexico. Later, Lamont would reminisce about the informality of the proceedings: "The whole suggestion was sort of a spontaneous combustion arising from a lot of us fellows sitting around over there [at the State Department] one day and talking over the situation." [9] This committee, however, was to have the broad function of dealing with Mexican finances "as a whole." The specific instructions of the State Department spelled out the role of the committee in these words:

. . . that any group formed shall be under the leadership of American bankers and that the policy of the United States Government regarding Mexico be the dominating influence in the operations of this group. At the same time, the United States Government believes that all negotiations respecting investments under consideration should be carried on exclusively by the private bankers and not through the instrumentality of agencies of this government.[10]

The formation of such an "omnibus" committee, as Lamont called it, had several advantages: (1) all questions involving loans, bonds, reorganization of Mexican finances, and even the National Railways of Mexico would be handled in an integrated manner by one authoritative group; (2) the leading investment banks of Europe and the United States would have to deal with Mexico through an American-dominated committee that would take its directions from the U.S. government; (3) Carranza would be faced with a common bloc but not one involving official diplomatic representatives; and (4) a common front of the major investment banks would render more difficult any attempts by individual promoters to gain special advantages. In addition, the U.S. government would be in a position to control the lending of money to Mexico. Officials believed that a U.S.-controlled committee would counter pressure from European financial interests that might force European governments to settle matters independently and thus weaken the ability of the United States to achieve guarantees from Mexico.

Working through the Morgan branches in London and Paris, Lamont reached the major British and French financial interests. These interests saw some advantages in a common-front approach and raised very few objections to the Lamont plan. The British group inquired about the committee's plans for dealing with railroad, oil, and electrical interests, and Lamont replied that the committee would deal with all of these, probably in the form of subcommittees. The French were concerned about the number of representatives they would have on the committee, but this was settled by a formula apportioning 50 percent of the committee seats to the United States and 25 percent each to Britain and France. In August 1919, the Netherlands and Switzerland pressed for membership on the committee, and after some exchange of correspondence between Lamont and the State Department, the decision was made to give each country one seat. The decision was based on the stated necessity for maintaining the unity of creditor nations, provided that American control would be ensured.[11]

By summer 1920, however, the British and French sections of the International Committee were beginning to show signs of impatience.

Lamont informed the State Department of this "considerable pressure" and warned, "My private opinion to you is that we ought, within a reasonable time, find a *modus vivendi* or else we shall not be able to hold our five-power team in hand to the end." President Wilson did not like the proposal for Lamont and Sir William Wiseman to visit Mexico and recommended that it be "discouraged." [12] He did not want the loan question discussed prior to recognition because he believed that such a display of eagerness would make the Mexican government less conciliatory.

In spite of these doubts, tentative approval for the Lamont trip was given with the understanding that the mission would only be exploratory in nature. Shortly thereafter, the negotiations were terminated, and the State Department now advised Lamont not to make the trip. Wiseman went to Mexico as a private citizen and returned with a letter from the minister of finance formally inviting the committee to open negotiations in 1921. Earlier in the month, the minister of foreign relations had extended such an invitation to Lamont. He considered it "a little queer to decline," but the State Department officials made it very clear that they did not want him to go under any circumstances. The invitation was declined. Thus, the Wilson administration came to an end with an almost complete deadlock in negotiations with Mexico. The president's intransigence had blocked any efforts by the bankers to work with the Mexican government.

Prior to its involvement in the Mexican financial situation, in June 1918, the Wilson administration decided to create a new banking consortium for China, and Lamont was given the job of obtaining the cooperation of the banking groups and the governments of Britain, France, and Japan in the creation of a new China consortium on American terms. [13] Although not seriously interested in China, Lamont did what he could to organize the new group. Japan proved to be the sticking point due to its insistence that all concerned recognize that country's preeminent interests in Manchuria. State Department officials pleaded with him to negotiate with the Japanese, and in February 1920, Lamont went to that country. To the banker, the economic reality of the situation was the Japanese sphere of influence, and he worked for a compromise. Both the Japanese and U.S. governments played the role of intransigent, but Lamont finally obtained an agreement that practically recognized the Japanese position in Manchuria without spelling out the details. In May 1920, Japan joined the Consortium, and the *New York Times* stated that the agreement ranked second only to the one signed at Paris. [14]

One of the primary results of Lamont's negotiations was the close relationship he established with the Japanese bankers. For the next decade, they would consider him to be their main contact in the United States, and he would work with the bankers to try to keep the Japanese government on a course of moderation and conciliation. The Consortium actually produced nothing for China, but as Warren Cohen notes, "giving nothing to the Chinese was soon described as the Consortium's most valuable contribution to China."[15]

The Republicans returned to the White House in 1921 with the election of Warren G. Harding, and Lamont quickly established a close relationship with the new secretary of state, Charles Evans Hughes. The International Committee continued to act as an unofficial instrument of U.S. policy, especially in its efforts to keep the major European banking interests unified behind a common policy. But the activities of the committee entered a new phase after March 1921. Lamont believed that the Wilson administration had not given the committee enough freedom of action in its dealings with Mexico. He told Hughes,

I, myself, have some doubts as to the complete wisdom of judgment expressed by Mr. Norman Davis in the matter. . . . In other words, I think it inexpedient that too much of an official cast should be given to the committee. It should never fail to work in harmony with the Department but should not be the creature of the Department, for it if is its usefulness is destroyed.[16]

Lamont and other committee members believed that making any debt negotiations contingent on the settlement of the Article 27 controversy, particularly in regard to the issue of ownership of subsurface deposits of oil, created a major problem for continued unified action of all the banking interests. The Obregon administration had openly stated its desire to negotiate a settlement with the foreign bondholders, and European bankers were clearly impatient with the "no negotiation" policy. Lamont wanted more flexibility, but he did agree with the continuation of the policy that no loan should be made to Mexico until after recognition. The State Department viewed the integration of private loans with recognition as an important tool for achieving its goals in Mexico.

The role played by Lamont cannot be characterized as lobbying or pressuring either for or against recognition. Perhaps it can best be described as a quiet process of trying to induce both sides to be less dogmatic and ideological in their approach to the issues. In a letter to Judge E. H. Gary, Lamont said that his attitude on recognition was "absolutely neutral," and he discussed his activities in the United States in these words:

I have felt that it [recognition] was such an important question that it would be unfortunate for the financial interest to take sides upon. On the other hand I have made every possible effort to make known my opinion that conditions in Mexico were on a stabler basis and that in general the government there was endeavoring to do the right thing. I have endeavored to build up the general standing of the Obregon government.[17]

In speeches and private conversations, Lamont stressed the point that disagreements between Mexico and the United States were over practical, economic problems and not over ideological differences. He had been informed by the British Intelligence Office that the present cabinet of the Mexican government was composed of members of the Third International, "but when I got down there, while I found them somewhat radical, they were not at all Bolshevistic or anarchistic."[18] To the American Bankers Association meeting in October 1922, Lamont presented a justification for the Mexican revolution and said that the Constitution of 1917 could be criticized more for its "unworkableness" than for its radicalism. In addition, he urged the bankers to have patience and sympathy for a neighbor that was slowly trying to solve its problems.

Lamont was concerned over the effects of harsh rhetoric on relations between Mexico and the United States. In the first draft of a letter to Secretary of State Hughes, he wrote,

I am much disturbed over this writ of attachment against the Mexican government and [I am] against the attempt to class that government with the Soviets. The logical conclusion, if such attachments are to be permitted, is to nullify all the work we have been building up for months past, with such Mexican government as exists today, which, on the whole, in my opinion (when its difficult political position is recalled) has done pretty well and made progress.[19]

Since that statement was a rather blunt criticism of some State Department pronouncements, Lamont eliminated it in the final draft. He did, however, incorporate the basic idea into other sections of the letter.

In spite of his concern over the tactics and rhetoric of the State Department, Lamont was in agreement with the basic goal of the department's Mexican policy. This was to obtain from the Mexican government a "fundamental declaration [embodied in some kind of official document] to the effect that property rights acquired under the law shall not be subject to confiscation." To achieve such a declaration, Lamont and Hughes agreed that the governments and bankers of creditor nations should present an "undivided front." When rifts in the front began to appear in 1921, Lamont went to England "for the purpose of coordinating the foreign interests," both for this reason and for the purpose of negotiating a settlement of Mexico's external debt. Leading exporters and bankers in London had prepared a memorial calling for the recognition of the Obregon government which they intended to present to the British Foreign Office. Lamont helped to rewrite this memorial so that the second draft was less insistent in its "tone." He also suggested that the presentation of the memorial be delayed. Not only was this advice followed but the British interests finally decided not to present the memorial at all.[20]

On the other side of the Rio Grande, Lamont urged Mexican officials to take a more pragmatic position on the issues involved in the recognition controversy and tried to convince them of the friendly sentiment of the State Department. In 1921, W. P. Hobby, former governor of Texas and a personal friend of President Obregon, was working for the unqualified recognition of Mexico. D. E. Pomeroy, of the Bankers Trust Company (New York), sent Lamont a copy of a letter from Hobby which stated that it was impossible for Obregon to sign a treaty to gain recognition. Lamont's reply—which was obviously intended for Hobby—said that the Treaty of Amity and Commerce proposed by Secretary of State Hughes was not a sine qua non. "Now," Lamont continued, "if Obregon says it is politically very hard for him to adopt this course, but he can adjust the matter with his Congress or Supreme Court, I should think that that would make no difference to the State Department." Pomeroy was additionally informed that any such action by Obregon would accomplish an "immense step in the rebuilding" of Mexico since this would be of major importance in convincing the great investment interests of the world of the viability of future credits and loans.[21]

Although Lamont was in basic agreement with the goals of the State Department, he took a less dogmatic and legalistic position concerning the kind of "declaration" (or "course of action") Obregon should adopt. The bankers wanted the Obregon government to survive, and Lamont's decision in 1921 to accept Obregon's invitation to come to Mexico for discussion of the external debt was largely based on his—and other committee members'—evaluation that such action would help to strengthen Obregon's position vis-à-vis possible rivals.[22] The visit would also provide an opportunity for Lamont to "make very clear to the Mexican authorities that there is an earnest desire on the part of the Committee to be of service to Mexico."[23] He hoped this would also encourage Obregon to move closer to the State Department's concept of international economic relations.

In the course of the negotiation over the external debt during 1921–22, Lamont established a friendly relationship with several officials; the most significant such contact was with Adolfo de la Huerta, the secretary of finance. The fact that Lamont was able to negotiate a formal agreement for the settlement of the external debt and that this agreement was accepted in toto by President Obregon is an indication of the nature of these relationships. In mid-1922, when de la Huerta was invited to visit Washington to meet with President Harding and Hughes, he informed several people that he regarded Lamont "as a prophet." As General J. A. Ryan, of the Texas Company, expressed it, "I have the highest respect for your splendid work with Secretary de la Huerta and I know that he has the highest esteem for you; and your efforts in New York will have a far-reaching effect upon the ultimate recognition of Mexico."[24]

Lamont and the Morgan firm were indirectly involved in the preliminary talks that led to the Bucareli Conference of 1923. While they were not involved in this conference, which produced recognition, it is evident that Lamont had helped to smooth the path for diplomacy.

The relationship between de la Huerta and the International Committee of Bankers on Mexico provided the background for Lamont's near-involvement as a mediator of rebellion. In fall 1923, de la Huerta resigned from Obregon's cabinet, and after a series of verbal attacks and exchanges of charges, the former official became the titular head of a rebellion organized by disgruntled generals. Lamont supported Hughes's policy of sending arms to the government of Obregon and refused to meet with the de la Huerta agent who was trying to raise money in New York.

Lamont was quite upset over the rebellion and feared that it might "unsettle conditions in Mexico for years."[25] Members of the International Committee of Bankers suggested that the group consider some possible means of mediation. As a result, Lamont went to Washington to confer with Hughes on January 30, 1924. Hughes stated that the U.S. government could not become involved in such a project but went on to say that "the International Committee strikes me as the only possible vehicle of mediation." Lamont then related the general outline of a rather complex, undercover plan to maneuver de la Huerta into asking for the mediation of the International Committee. A representative of one of the oil companies could be sent to Vera Cruz to talk to de la Huerta about the oil situation. In the course of the conversation, the representative would link the oil problem to the

Lamont–de la Huerta Agreement of 1922 and urge that de la Huerta meet with Lamont and a representative of the Obregon government to discuss ways of carrying out this agreement. It was hoped this conference would quickly move from discussion of the Bankers Agreement to the issue of the rebellion. As Lamont expressed it,

> I should expect to take de la Huerta aside and try to throw the fear of God into him, demanding to know why he had ever been such a fool as to break away from the government and then to turn traitor, giving him ample chance to answer back, to blow off steam, to say what a martyr he was, etc., but gradually getting him into a conciliatory mood, especially if between now and then some more of his forces get licked up.[26]

Lamont was not overly optimistic about the success of the plan, but he thought it was worth a try, and Hughes agreed. The secretary asked Lamont to go at once to the Mexican embassy and discuss the plan with the minister, Manuel C. Tellez, and Ramon Ross. After listening to Lamont, these officials commented that it was worth trying even though they shared Lamont's doubts concerning its eventual success. The next day, Tellez and Ross met with Hughes and Lamont at the State Department, and that evening (January 31, 1924) Ross departed for Mexico to communicate the plan to the government.

At this point, the written record ends, and there is no material in the Lamont papers concerning the reaction of the Mexican government. By the time the mediation proposal reached Mexico, it was already apparent that the government forces had the upper hand. They had won a major victory at Esperanza on January 28, and on February 12, Vera Cruz was occupied. After this, the conflict was largely a matter of mopping up the remaining pockets of resistance, and this was generally completed by early March. If the struggle had been prolonged, however, the Mexican government might have accepted the plan on the recommendation of Minister Tellez, and Lamont could have added another episode to his career as a diplomat without portfolio.

Lamont's relationship with the British Foreign Office enabled him to serve as such a diplomat and to repair a breakdown in communications between Hughes and the British ambassador, Sir Auckland Geddes, which threatened to disrupt United States–British cooperation on Mexican policy. The problem developed when Hughes did not find out about the arrangements that the former secretary, Bainbridge Colby, and Norman H. Davis had made with the British Foreign Office in 1920. The British had decided to extend recognition to Obregon but changed this decision at the request of Colby and Davis.

At that time, the British ambassador and Davis agreed on a policy of complete reciprocity of information and "cordial cooperation" on matters concerning Mexico. Davis informed Lamont that he had prepared a memorandum on these arrangements and called it to Fletcher's attention when the State Department changed hands in March 1921. Hughes, however, did not see the memorandum and formulated his recognition plan—the signing of a Treaty of Amity and Commerce—without consulting the British ambassador. Geddes read about the proposal in the newspaper and immediately went to see the secretary of state. According to Geddes, Hughes was "not particularly communicative"[27] and would not show him a copy of the note that had been sent to the Mexican government.

The ambassador was quite upset and mentioned the cooperative arrangement. After the conference, Hughes communicated with Davis and was fully informed of the earlier understanding. Then the secretary arranged for another conference with Geddes. During this conversation, he gave more information to the ambassador, but Geddes was still not satisfied. Hughes still would not show the note to the British ambassador.

Geddes then contacted Lamont and told him this was the "gravest thing that had happened in the last two years between the United States and Great Britain." As Lamont described the conversation,

He felt sure that his government was equally upset and would immediately recognize Mexico. I responded by expressing the earnest hope that no such rift would be allowed to come just on account of what was manifestly a fall down between the two administrations, our old and our new, and I pointed out to Geddes that a little allowance must be made for what looked like bad manners but was not intended as such. Geddes expressed the hope that I might be able to get the thing righted.[28]

Lamont had a "good frank talk" with Secretary Hughes. The secretary agreed to talk over the matter with Geddes, and Lamont gained the impression that he would try to soothe the ambassador's feelings and get back to a basis of cooperation. As Lamont noted in his letter to Vivian Smith, "The situation called for good nature and pleasantry on both sides."[29]

Hughes must have done a skillful job of soothing, since Geddes later told Lamont that "the atmosphere had been very much cleared up and everything was going very smoothly." Once again, Lamont had helped to smooth the paths of diplomacy and had helped to maintain the common front that he believed was vital for the settlement of Mexico's problems with foreign interests.

This was another example of Lamont's belief that issues between nations should be kept out of the arena of internal politics. He constantly advocated the use of the "discreet person" who could privately and quietly negotiate disputes. As he advised Sir William Tyrrell, in 1925, "Send down to Mexico some discreet, tactful person who will form friendly contacts with the Mexican Government and trade out your situation with the Government *prior* to your recognition."[30]

In spite of the deterioration in official relations during 1925, Lamont and his colleagues reached an agreement with the Mexican government and preserved relatively open communications. The bankers desperately wanted to preserve the debt agreement and avoid repudiation. Members of the International Committee of Bankers on Mexico repeatedly communicated with the new minister of finance, Alberto J. Pani, during 1925. But Mexican officials believed that de la Huerta had accepted excessively stiff terms in 1922, and they were in no hurry to rush into a new agreement or resume payments under the old agreement. The bankers even offered to try to raise a $20 million loan in return for resumption of the debt service and return of the railroads to private ownership.

Negotiations began in September 1925, and the next month the Pani-Lamont agreement was completed. Pani agreed that the National Railways would be returned "in such condition and under such terms as will yield net earnings sufficient to meet all the fixed charges" and that until December 31, 1929, the government would not permit any changes in rates or wages that would affect earnings adversely.[31] The debt included in the new agreement was as follows:

Principal $302,500,000
Interest $132,500,000
Total $435,000,000

Formal payments to the committee would begin in 1926.

During his stay in New York, Pani's extramarital sexual activities added spice to the negotiations and became a political issue in Mexico when the agrarian party used it to attack the administration of President Plutarco Elias Calles. In New York, the ultra-hardliners had hired a private detective to shadow the finance minister. The reports of his comings and goings with Gloria Faure, daughter of the sixth president of the third French republic, Felix Faure, were sent to Lamont by the group. The bankers did not believe in letting scandal interfere with financial negotiations, and the reports were ignored. But they were leaked to the newspapers, and the front page of the October 14 edition of the *New York Daily Mirror* prominently featured a photograph of a raven-haired beauty, posed with a dress provocatively raised above her knees, under a banner headline, "Señor Pani Is a Wonderful Lover."[32]

The young lady was rushed out of the country, and there were rumblings about prosecution under the Mann Act. Nothing developed in the United States, but Pani was bitterly attacked in the Mexican Chamber of Deputies. In a stormy session, the agrarians linked the minister's love life to the question of land reform and charged that Pani was selling out to Wall Street. A special committee went to see President Calles, who defended his minister and asked if it would please them to have "a cabinet of eunuchs." The committee reported back, and the session ended amid catcalls and general uproar. The turmoil did not last long, and the Pani–Lamont agreement was approved in December 1925.[33] The new agreement removed one basic issue complicating U.S.–Mexican relations and helped to maintain a bridge of relatively harmonious communication during a period of deteriorating official relations between mid-1925 and late 1927. This situation was caused by several factors including the Calles administration's renewed efforts to implement the retroactive interpretation of Article 27 and the hostile attitude (and actions) of the racist ambassador, James Rockwell Sheffield. By early 1927, some on both sides of the border were even talking about the possibility of military action.

When Dwight Morrow's appointment as ambassador to Mexico was announced in September 1927, a Mexican newspaper commented, "After Morrow comes the marines."[34] To some contemporary observers, this may have seemed to present a logical progression of events, but in reality the Morrow appointment was a distinct move in the opposite direction. Top-level Mexican officials knew this, since they had been involved for several years in negotiations with Lamont and the International Committee. Lamont and Morrow were colleagues in J. P. Morgan and Company and close friends. Lamont regularly supplied Morrow with information about the activities of the International Committee, and during 1926, Morrow began to work closely with Lamont on the Mexican question.

Prior to 1927, the attitudes and actions of Lamont, Morrow, and some of their colleagues had made a positive impression on several key Mexican officials. Feelings of trust, respect, and even friendship developed on both sides. Lamont and the Morgan company established a working relationship with Pani, Obregon, Legorreta, and Tellez. Most of these officials were identified with the national development wing of the "revolutionary family." This group generally stressed economic development based on some degree of national control over the economy, especially natural resources. They were willing to listen to, and even solicit, advice from the outside, provided it came from persons who treated them with respect and displayed some understanding of their national aspirations. Such was the basis of the rapport that developed between these officials and representatives of the Morgan bank. Disagreements and arguments did take place. At times the relationship was strained because of actions of other groups. In Mexico, the national development faction had to compete with other elements for influence in the inner circle of the revolutionary family. In spite of some complications, the working relationship between the bankers and the development-oriented Mexican officials was cultivated even during periods of deteriorating relations between the two governments. The Morrow appointment and the diplomatic fruits of his ambassadorship were directly connected to this relationship.

The attitudes and actions of Lamont and his colleagues provided an important basis for this working relationship. During the 1920s, Mexican officials had ample opportunity to compare these attitudes and actions with those of other foreign interests. The hard line put forward by the leading U.S. oil companies, combined with the numerous reports that these interests were involved in counterrevolutionary activities, made the investment bankers appear rather mild.

Lamont and Morrow were opposed to armed intervention and to policy tactics that relied on the threat of ultimate force. In January 1925, Pani informed Lamont that Mexico could not resume service on its exterior debt. When Lamont replied that the International Committee might have to declare the 1922 debt agreement (the Lamont–de la Huerta agreement) in "final default," Pani asked if this meant intervention by the governments involved. Lamont emphatically stated "that in his view it meant nothing of the kind and that he felt the time when a debt could be collected by force of arms was past."[35] On another occasion, when asked about government protection of foreign investments, Lamont referred to Morrow's article in the January 1927 issues of *Foreign Affairs* as "the latest and best answer." He concluded,

I hold with him [Morrow] that good faith on the part of a borrower is far sounder security for a lender than armed forces however great or powerful. The theory of collecting debt by gunboat is unrighteous, unworkable and obsolete. While I have, of course, no mandate to speak for my colleagues of the investment banking community, I think I may safely say that they share this view with Mr. Morrow and myself.[36]

In 1925, Morrow stated that businessmen who had differences with the Cuban government should seek remedies through the ordinary channels in Cuba: "They should not look to Washington."[37]

In his negotiations with the Mexican government, Lamont did not employ threats of retaliation by either the U.S. government or the bankers. Some of his associates on the International Committee considered him to be "soft on Mexico," but as Lamont noted in regard to one committee debate, "Millhauser [Speyer and Company] talks glibly about wielding the big stick or kicking them in the stomach. There is no big stick to wield and we have no boot that could possibly reach their remote and very tough stomach."[38]

Lamont and the Morgan bank stressed this type of low-pressure, quiet diplomacy in their dealings with the Mexican government. They were willing to negotiate on a give-and-take basis and emphasized specific issues rather than broad principles or legal technicalities. As Morrow wrote to Lamont in April 1927, "I hope you can see Teagle and Swain [Standard Oil of New Jersey] and get them to see that they can be helpful to themselves by thundering more about *oil* and less about *rights* to oil."[39]

Lamont and the bankers did not insist on winning every point and were even willing to accept defeat on some issues. An excellent example of this took place in 1925 when the Calles administration announced its plans for a central bank of issue and began to accumulate funds for a reserve. At first the International Committee, through Lamont, privately stated its opposition to various Mexican officials and then, on August 26, sent a formal protest through the U.S. State Department. After delivering the protest, H. F. Arthur Schoenfeld, charge d'affaires ad interim, reported that the New York bankers could wreck the new bank if they so desired.[40]

When the Mexican government proceeded to implement its plans, Lamont prepared an advisory memorandum for the International Committee. He stated frankly, "We have to face the facts: (I) Capital has been accumulated for Bank of Issue (legally and otherwise) which will open September 1st. (II) 49 percent of the capital local banks have subscribed. This shows their confidence. No use in effect bucking them."[41]

Lamont noted Pani's promise to renew full payments to the International Committee on January 1, 1926, and praised the "thoroughgoing financial reorganization" of the Mexican government. He advised,

I think they are getting out of the woods and we shall show ourselves unwise if we don't walk out with them. Now our gesture to prevent their opening the Bank of Issue has failed. This is a great disappointment and I don't quite see how we are going to save our face. Yet it is more important to save our bondholders than to save our face.[42]

The International Committee accepted these ideas, and Lamont informed the State Department that they did not desire any further action.

During the first half of 1927, Lamont, Morrow, and other officials of J. P. Morgan and Company met regularly with several influential Mexicans. Pani, Tellez, A. L. Negrete, David Montes de Oca (finance minister after February 1927), and Legorreta all took an active part in these informal meetings and dinners. In turn, they met with President Calles and presented the views of the bankers.

In late March 1927, Calles instructed Ambassador Tellez to deliver a personal message to Calvin Coolidge assuring him of a desire to adjust all differences and telling him that Calles would be pleased if Coolidge would send a personal representative to Mexico to discuss the situation privately, perhaps on his ranch. Secretary of State Frank B. Kellogg was present during the Tellez–Coolidge meeting, and as a result, the Mexican ambassador did not deliver the critical part of the message. Tellez then went to New York to see Lamont, and at a meeting at Lamont's house, the details were fully presented. Lamont advised the ambassador to explain in detail to Assistant Secretary Robert Olds the reasons for Sheffield's unpopularity and tell him of Calles's desire to get as far away as possible from the method of negotiating by notes. Tellez took this advice, and in all probability Coolidge received the information from either Olds or Morrow.[43]

Lamont himself also established contact with Calles through mutual friends, and the Mexican president informed one American visitor that he wished the U.S. government would let Lamont handle the situation in place of Sheffield and Kellogg, for he had complete confidence in the New York banker. As Lamont told Olds concerning a letter the former was sending to Ambassador Tellez, "You may think that I lay it on a bit thick about my friendship for Mexico, but that is in line with the repeated messages which I have received from President Calles."[44]

Morrow became ambassador in late 1927 and began to hammer out a compromise between the two countries. During these negotiations, Morrow's relationship with the Morgan bank aided him in his dealings with the oil men. Lamont, and other former colleagues of Morrow, worked to convince the oil executives not to rock the boat, either by harsh public statements or by an uncompromising stand on the legal issues. Morrow did not directly solicit this kind of behind-the-scenes assistance. But, as he wrote to Secretary Olds explaining why he had sent Lamont information on the oil issue, "Lamont's influence on the oil men in New York can be considerable if he desires to exert it."[45] The banker's efforts did not have to be solicited. He was interested not only in the success of a friend and former colleague but also in the practical settlement of the various issues complicating U.S.–Mexican relations. Vernon Munroe, a Morgan executive, wrote to Morrow explaining why the bankers had arranged a conference between Legorreta and Gen. Palmer Pierce of Standard: "There was perhaps the feeling that you would be very glad if the oil companies would approach the oil problem from the point of view of a practical settlement rather than of a purely legalistic settlement and undoubtedly Mr. Legorreta called on General Pierce because he and we felt that you would be glad to have him do so."[46]

Morrow believed that long-range Mexican stability would be achieved only by the complete financial reorganization of the country. The Sterrett-Davis report commissioned by the International Committee reinforced this conviction, since it convinced the ambassador that Mexico was in a condition of virtual bankruptcy (more liabilities than assets). He advised Lamont in November 1928,

I do not think any partial settlement [by Mexico] should be made with the International Committee, with the governments, with the specie banks or with any other group of creditors, because I think such partial settlements will most inevitably break down and delay the real financial reorganization of the country.[47]

Morrow probably wanted a Dawes Commission for Mexico. But even without such an instrument, he at least hoped to arrange a consolidation of the entire Mexican debt and a balanced budget that would allow Mexico to make payments to all claimants and at the same time provide funds for essential governmental functions, especially for the army and education. In short, Mexico should be handled as a bankrupt corporation.

Lamont did not entirely agree with the ambassador's views, but he cooperated with Morrow during late 1928 and early 1929 with the hope that Morrow would support some kind of revised agreement between the International Committee and the Mexican government. Other members of the committee, however, were pressuring Lamont to negotiate for additional funds for the bondholders. Mexico was negotiating en bloc settlements with several governments which were aimed at consolidating and funding the various claims of each country's citizens. The bondholders represented by the International Committee, rather than by governments, wanted a new agreement to ensure that they would not be left out, and Morrow believed that a series of uncoordinated settlements would completely wreck Mexican finances.

Over the opposition of Ambassador Morrow, Lamont negotiated a revised agreement with Mexico in July 1930. The Mexican Congress, however, faced with mounting economic problems caused by the depression, refused to ratify the Lamont–Montes de Oca Agreement. For the time being, the Mexican debt issue was placed on the back burner.

During the 1920s, Lamont also was concerned with issues in other parts of the world. The Nationalist revolution in China produced much instability and a call (from some quarters) for foreign intervention. Lamont used his influence in both Great Britain and the United States to oppose any forcible intervention and to support the commitments made to revise the treaty system (especially extraterritoriality). Lamont's views were sent back to President Coolidge, and in mid-1925, Secretary of State Kellogg informed the other signatories of the Washington Conference treaties that the United States was ready to attend a conference on the Chinese tariff issue and to send a commission to investigate the extraterritoriality question. By 1930, the Chinese government had recovered tariff autonomy and had made some revisions in the area of extraterritorial rights for foreigners.

Republican administrations also solicited Lamont's advice on questions concerning European financial stability. Several months after his inauguration, President Warren G. Harding asked Lamont to visit him at the White House. The banker found a dispirited president who wanted to be informed about intergovernmental debts. Thus, Lamont became involved in the negotiations that led to the Dawes Plan of 1924 and the Young Plan of 1929. Both involved bond issues designed to help Germany with reparations payments and to stabilize the European economy.[48]

During the 1920s, Lamont also played a key role in securing loans for Japan. In March 1927, J. P. Morgan and other banks purchased $20 million in Tokyo Municipal bonds. These were then sold to the public. Later that year, Lamont was a special guest of the Japanese government. He had an audience with the emperor, lunch with the premier, and numerous engagements with industrialists and government officials. During this visit, the government requested Lamont to obtain the support of the Morgan bank in issuing $30 million worth of South Manchuria Railway bonds. The State Department had opposed such U.S. involvement since it had surfaced in 1923 but had modified its views during 1927–28. When Japan sent five thousand troops to Shantung in April 1928, however, the department returned to its original opposition, and Lamont retreated in the face of official irritation over his efforts. In May 1930, a group of American bankers, headed by J. P. Morgan and Company, did underwrite a $50 million loan to the Japanese government.[49]

Lamont's efforts to promote cooperation and friendship between Japan and the United States sustained severe blows during the early 1930s. On September 18, 1931, Japanese troops began the military conquest of Manchuria. Then, in early 1932, the Japanese attacked Shanghai. Lamont's hopes for Japan were further shaken when his close friends, Junnosuke Inoue and Dan Takuma (both liberal political leaders), were assassinated by the army. As his friends were killed or muffled, Lamont's influence in Japan faded rapidly, but he did not support an economic boycott, even when full-scale war broke out between Japan and China in 1937. The Tripartite Pact (Germany, Italy, and Japan) of 1940 changed his position. In September 1940, after consultation with Secretary of State Cordell Hull and Stanley K. Hornbeck (head of the Division of Far Eastern Affairs), Lamont delivered a hard-hitting address to the annual dinner of the American Academy of Political Science. In it, he declared that the pact had made "Europe and the Far East a single, great struggle. The conflict becomes truly a world war." Lamont also called for a complete embargo on the sale of war materials to Japan. This speech was printed on the front page of the *New York Times*, and copies were sent to Chinese and Japanese officials; the latter were not too happy. In the process, he helped to move some elements in the business community away from an appeasement policy regarding Japan.[50]

During late 1940 and early 1941, Lamont worked with the White Committee (Committee to Defend America by Aiding the Allies) in its campaign for the Lend-Lease Act. In the process, he acted as a liaison between President Franklin D. Roosevelt and the committee and helped to moderate the committee's stand on several issues. He also acted to restrain the committee's criticism of the president's Far Eastern policy while encouraging the president to be more outspoken on China. When Roger Greene of the committee condemned the administration's "continued appeasement" of Japan, Lamont became quite angry, since this violated his policy to (in Warren Cohen's words) "work with the Department of State, work from within, never attack."[51] He then prepared a lengthy memorandum on the Far East for the State Department. While he wanted a sterner U.S. policy toward Japan, he still regarded Hitler as the main target and did not want to precipitate a conflict in the Far East that would harm the efforts to stop Germany. The Japanese and Germans solved these problems in December 1941.

In the mid-1930s, Lamont once more engaged in sporadic negotiations with Mexican officials over the debt issue. Draft agreements were worked out in 1936 and 1938, but the Mexicans did not accept these and periodic negotiations continued. Then in 1938, the foreign debt issue was complicated by Mexican nationalization of most of the oil industry. Negotiations over these issues began in 1940 between the two governments. This complicated Lamont's efforts, but Assistant Secretary Sumner Welles in March 1941 encouraged him to continue his separate talks and even told Lamont that the answer concerning concessions "is for you not to make *any concessions* beyond those embodied in the draft agreement that you reached two or three years ago. Make none, he repeated, they will do whatever you demand in reason!" Lamont considered this latter admonition to be "quite an order."[52]

By September, Lamont was convinced that the actions of U.S. negotiators in Mexico were encouraging Mexican officials to make more stringent demands on the bondholders. In a memorandum concerning a conversation with Secretary of State Hull, Lamont could not contain the frustration and cynicism engendered by over twenty years of negotiations with Mexican politicians. "He [Hull] was very cordial and helpful in his expressions, but whether he will be able to make an inch of headway against the Little Boys down there who dream dreams about the Good Neighbor policy, who want to buy up all Argentina's wheat, all Brazil's coffee, all of Mexico's silver for the purpose of having friendly banquets given to them when they go down there from a gang that has never stayed bought yet is more than I know."[53]

Lamont finally worked out a settlement in November 1942, and Mexico began to make payments on a small scale in 1943, thus ending some fifteen years of default. Although the settlement was set at 20 percent of the principal amount ($240 million out of a debt of $2,471 million, including back interest), Lamont argued that in reality the bondholders only received 10 percent of their total claims due to interest reduction under earlier agreements.[54] Thus ended a lengthy chapter in Lamont's career.

If such a thing as an "Establishment" exists in this country, then Lamont was certainly a member in good standing. He was consulted by every president from Wilson to Roosevelt and, in turn, assisted them in various ways. His career demolishes the Marxist-Leninist ruling class notion. Lamont disagreed with, and even worked against, other businessmen when he believed they were wrong. And he did not expect the government to bail out his interests either with the marines or economic pressure. He had some influence but did not always win his point.

Lamont believed that international cooperation was the key to nations living in peace, and to this end, he stressed negotiation. His negotiating strength was his sense of moderation and his emphasis on compromise. His efforts helped to produce compromise and moderate feelings, and his sense of humor facilitated negotiations.

Perhaps, more than many public figures of his period, Lamont had a respect for other cultures and races and could deal with Mexicans, Chinese, and Japanese in a spirit of dignity and friendship, without condescension. A nondogmatic view of international relations helped him to deal with foreign leaders with calmness and moderation.

Lamont knew the world was an imperfect place, and as a result, he stressed acceptance of political realities whether in dealing with the Mexican Revolution or recognition of the Soviet Union. He worked to try to produce good relations with Japan during the 1920s and early 1930s and with the Soviet Union during and after World War II. In the latter case, he stressed the need to coexist with the Soviets. He was unhappy over Stalin's policy in Poland and the Baltic states but did not want conflict over these issues. Lamont would also try to impress on Soviet leaders the need for a "humane" settlement of the Polish question.[55] But, as the old saying goes, "it takes two to tango," and in the case of both Japan and the Soviet Union, Lamont's tactics of compromise and moderation met the mailed fist. When this happened, Lamont's usefulness as a negotiator and moderator came to an end.

For over thirty years, Thomas W. Lamont brought to the arena of international relations a humane, moderate approach to the solution of problems. This did not always work, and Lamont probably underestimated the strength of some forces operating in the world. For a time, some U.S. historians were quite critical of Lamont's concept of international order and the liberal-capitalist system that he believed was an important part of that order. Yet, as the Berlin Wall has come tumbling down and Communist regimes have collapsed under the weight of their own failure, from Poland to Bulgaria, perhaps we can gain a new appreciation of Lamont's view of the world. It does not provide any easy answers, but as Lamont wrote in the conclusion to *Across World Frontiers*, "American foreign policy must be guided by accurate and adequate information regarding international conditions; and must be based upon a humane understanding of the world's needs. That is the only chance of salvation for mankind."[56]

NOTES

1. Remarks of Thomas W. Lamont before the Dutch Treat Club, Lincoln, Nebr., March 14, 1922; Thomas W. Lamont Papers, Baker Library, Harvard Graduate School of Business Administration (Cambridge).

2. Thomas W. Lamont, *My Boyhood in a Parsonage* (New York and London: Harper & Brothers, 1946): 176–177.

3. Thomas W. Lamont, *Across World Frontiers* (New York: Harcourt Brace & Co., 1951): 36.

4. Quoted in Warren I. Cohen, *The Chinese Connection: Roger S. Green, Thomas W. Lamont, George E. Sokolsky, and American–East Asian Relations* (New York: Columbia University Press, 1978): 36.

5. Memorandum of Interview between Mr. Lamont and Gen. Zambrano, January 11, 1917, Lamont Mss.

6. Egan to Lamont, May 31, 1917, Lamont Mss.

7. Lamont to Fletcher, July 27, 1917, Lamont Mss.

8. "Memorandum for President Wilson in reference to Mexico," by Thomas Lill and Henry Bruere, enclosed in Bruere to Frank Polk, August 15, 1918; Records of U.S. Department of State, Record Group 59, 812.51/542 (hereafter cited as SD and file number).

9. Lamont to Norman H. Davis, October 5, 1920, SD 812.51/600; Memorandum to Vernon Munroe from Lamont, November 19, 1929, Lamont Mss.

10. J. P. Morgan and Co. to Morgan, Grenfell & Co., October 10, 1918, SD 812.51/544.

11. Lamont to Fletcher, August 5, 1919, and Fletcher to Lamont, August 6, 1919, SD 812.51/554; William Phillips to Lamont, November 5, 1919, SD 812.51/557.

12. Lamont to Davis, October 25 and 28, 1920, Norman H. Davis Papers, Library of Congress (Washington, D.C.); Davis to President Wilson, November 2, 1920, SD 812.51/598a; Wilson to Davis, November 3, 1930, Woodrow Wilson Papers, Library of Congress.

13. Cohen, *Chinese Connection*, 51.

14. Ibid., 69.

15. Ibid., 70.

16. Lamont to Hughes, March 29, 1921, SD 812.51/724.

17. Lamont to Judge E. H. Gary (Chairman of the Board, U.S. Steel Corp.), February 15, 1922; Lamont Mss.

18. "Remarks before the Dutch Treat Club," March 14, 1922, Lamont Mss.

19. Lamont to Hughes, October 31, 1922, Lamont Mss.

20. Lamont to D. E. Pomeroy (vice president, Bankers Trust Company, New York), June 29, 1921, Lamont Mss.; Lamont to James F. McDonald (chairman, Foreign Policy Association), July 29, 1921, Lamont Mss.; Lamont to Hughes, June 9, 1921, Lamont Mss.

21. Lamont to Pomeroy, June 22, 1921, Lamont Mss.

22. Lamont to Egan, September 2, 1921.

23. Memo: Lamont to Martin Egan, September 2, 1921, Lamont Mss.

24. General J. A. Ryan (Texas Company) to Lamont, July 27, 1922, and October 4, 1922, Lamont Mss.

25. Memorandum of Thomas Lamont's Conference in Washington, D.C., January 30, 1924, Lamont Mss.; unless otherwise indicated, all material on this topic has been derived from this memorandum. The memorandum and the stenographer's notebooks were in a heavy brown envelope and secured with three wax seals.

26. Ibid.

27. Lamont to E. C. Grenfill (senior partner, Morgan, Grenfell & Company, London), June 10, 1921, Lamont Mss.

28. Ibid.

29. Lamont to Smith, June 23, 1921, Lamont Mss.

30. Memorandum of a conversation with Sir William Tyrrell, Permanent Undersecretary of Foreign Affairs, at the British Foreign Office, May 7, 1925.

31. Memo: October 7, 1925, by Vernon Munroe, Lamont Mss.

32. Reports sent to Lamont by Wilbur Bates at various times.

33. John W. F. Dulles, *Yesterday in Mexico: A Chronicle of the Revolution, 1919–1936* (Austin: University of Texas Press, 1961): 286.

34. Ibid., 324–325.

35. Memorandum of a conversation between Finance Minister Pani and Lamont, January 21, 1925, Lamont Mss.

36. Lamont to James E. Sabine, January 9, 1928, Lamont Mss.; the article was, "Who Buys Foreign Bonds," *Foreign Affairs* (Jan. 1927).

37. *New York Times,* April 23, 1925.

38. Lamont to Vivian Smith, November 20, 1928, Lamont Mss.

39. Morrow to Lamont, April 12, 1927, Lamont Mss.

40. Memorandum by Lamont of a conversation with Secretary Kellogg, September 16, 1925, SD 812.51/1201; Schoenfeld to Kellogg, August 28, 1925, SD 812.51/1201.

41. Memo for Subcommittee from Thomas Lamont, August 31, 1925, Lamont Mss.

42. Memorandum by Lamont, August 31, 1925, Lamont Mss.

43. Memorandum of a meeting at Mr. Lamont's house at 9:30 A.M., March 31, 1927, at which the Mexican ambassador, Mr. Lamont, Mr. Negrete, Mr. Prieto, and Vernon Munroe were present. Dwight W. Morrow Papers, Amherst College Library (Amherst, Mass.); Memorandum of conversation between Asst. Sec. Olds and Ambassador Tellez, April 1, 1927, SD 711.12/ 1084.

44. Lamont to Olds, May 16, 1927, Lamont Mss.

45. Morrow to Olds, January 3, 1928, Lamont Mss.

46. Munroe to Morrow, January 6, 1928, Lamont Mss.

47. Morrow to Lamont, November 29, 1928, Morrow Mss.

48. Lamont, *Across World Frontiers*, 218–219.

49. Cohen, *Chinese Connection*, 148–149.

50. Ibid., 232.

51. Ibid., 235.

52. Lamont to Munroe, March 5, 1941, Lamont Mss.

53. Memorandum by Lamont, September 11, 1941, Lamont Mss.

54. Lamont to Welles, October 21, 1942, Lamont Mss.

55. Cohen, *Chinese Connection*, 250–255.

56. Lamont, *Across World Frontiers*, 267–268.

CHAPTER 5

Walking the Tightrope
Adolf A. Berle and America's Journey from Social to Global Capitalism, 1933–1945

THOMAS J. McCORMICK

> There is order in the cosmos and if you can not apprehend it, then you make one up inside your head.
>
> Adolf A. Berle, Jr., 1961

Adolf A. Berle, Jr., was the quintessential servant of power during the New Deal and World War II eras. Brighter and more thoughtful than those he served, he nonetheless trimmed and transformed his own vision and views to conform to theirs. In the process, he tacitly abandoned a moral and intellectual model of social capitalism, one that sought to use government regulation to accommodate the economic rationality and efficiency of large corporations to the larger societal goal of equitable consumption. In its place, he increasingly accepted and advocated a deregulated world economy in which American corporate efficiency—unfettered by government controls—could produce for an unlimited market of global customers. Berle the intellectual, imaginatively confronting the pivotal issues of equity and efficiency, had metamorphosed into Berle the booster, energetically promoting economic internationalism as a way to evade and beg those issues.

Beatrice Bishop Berle said of her husband in 1934, "He has shown a surprising agility in business and in politics so that I expect he will be condemned to tightrope walking all his life. Even the most skilled tightrope walkers eventually fall off and break a neck or a leg, but do they become philosophers?"[1] With an academic base at Columbia

University's law school and a business base in corporate law and corporate directorships, Berle did indeed walk a tightrope during the period between the opening of the New Deal and the close of World War II. And a heady performance it was: a charter member of Franklin D. Roosevelt's brain trust; confidant and adviser to Fiorello H. La Guardia during his tenure as New York City mayor; assistant secretary of state, with imprecise but impressive responsibilities in economic matters, postwar planning, and Latin American affairs; and, climactically, chair of the Chicago Conference on Civil Aviation, that vital but neglected part of the triumvirate of postwar planning conferences that included Dumbarton Oaks and Bretton Woods.[2]

In the end, Berle did fall off the tightrope: he was relieved of his assistant secretary of state position and banished into purgatory as stopgap ambassador to Brazil. With Roosevelt's untimely death, Berle's exile from the center of power became permanent. During the last twenty-five years of his life, he remained a prominent national figure as sometime chair of New York's Liberal party and chair of the board of trustees of the Twentieth Century Fund, Berle's beloved center of social engineering in America. But never again did he enjoy the special status as idea man and troubleshooter for presidents and Free World leaders that he had experienced in the Roosevelt era. To be sure, John F. Kennedy returned him to Washington as head of an interdepartmental task force on Latin America, but the nebulous and short-lived nature of the appointment only confirmed that he had become more symbol and cheerleader than theoretician and counselor. Forever frustrated in his efforts to mount the high wire again, Berle tragically fulfilled his wife's fears that tightrope walkers do not become philosophers.

It might have been otherwise. Brilliant, learned, opinionated, and powerfully ambitious, Berle had all the intellectual tools to fulfill "his real ambition in life . . . to be the American Karl Marx—a social prophet." In 1932, he put that promise on prominent display when he and his co-author, economist-statistician Gardner C. Means, published *The Modern Corporation and Private Property*. Widely regarded as one of the most important books published in twentieth-century America, it offered a vision—inchoate but powerful—of social capitalism; that is, its potential for transforming itself from a narrow economic system of profit maximization to a broad social system that balanced and reconciled the general welfare of the national community with the individual perquisites of private property.[3]

Two connected ideas, as Thomas K. McCraw recently noted, formed the book's core: "Means's findings about economic concentration,

Berle's conjectures about the separation of ownership from control." Of the two ideas, it was Berle's concept of the separation of ownership and control that was the more innovative and constituted the heart of the book's conclusion and of Berle's own evolving vision of a future capitalist commonwealth. Over time, Berle argued, a managerial revolution had divorced "the control" from shareholder influence and invested it in autonomous centers of power, principally in the upper levels of management. Those corporate managers, largely unaccountable to economic shareholders and wholly unaccountable to the political electorate, constituted a new social class, a managerial class, and the modern corporation over which they presided constituted a new social institution. As Berle had told the American Economic Association three years earlier, "A Machiavelli writing today would have very little interest in princes, and every interest in the Standard Oil Company of Indiana. And he would be right; because the prince of today is the president or dominant interest in a great corporation." In *The Modern Corporation*, Berle foresaw a possible corporate oligarchy, "not only on an equal plane with the state, but possibly superseding it as the dominant form of social organization." Its economic choices had vast social consequences for society as a whole, but no mechanism existed to ensure that those choices were consistent with the general welfare.[4]

In that context, Berle thought it obvious that "the claims of the community" were not always consistent with "the rigid enforcement of the property right" and that "modification" of the latter might require it to "yield before the larger interest of society." Such was his stated belief in 1932 when his Columbia University colleague, Raymond Moley, enlisted Berle to be one of the social science experts advising Franklin Roosevelt on national issues in his bid for the presidency. Counseling FDR at the nadir of the Great Depression, Berle believed that economic concentration had been sharply accelerated by the economic contraction, as larger corporations drove out marginal competitors. He was also persuaded that there was "a slow parallel in the increasing intensity of depressions in the cycles, and increasing economic concentration," that the latter spread and deepened the downturn and produced "dislocation of the whole mechanism."[5]

Underconsumption (or overproduction) was the key to Berle's analysis of the depression and its relationship to corporate concentration. In the unequal contest between concentrated corporations and the mass of consumers and workers, the relative ability of the former to sustain price levels while deflating wages resulted in an aggregate decline in effective purchasing power. In the short run, Berle believed that this underconsumption could be remedied through bank deposit insurance, unemployment insurance, and social security programs that would "resume consumption and thereby reactivate manufacture and production." Otherwise, he feared, there was a "one chance in five" of "wholesale dislocation." "For the first time," he warned, "the United States has come within hailing distance of revolution along continental European lines." In the long run, Berle believed that more structural solutions were required to strike a balance between property's share of the national wealth (profits) and that of the general community (disposable income). If not, "some depression" in the future would produce "a revolution in fact, if not in name."[6]

Berle's proffered course of long-term structural responses rested on three premises. First, his given unit of economic analysis was the national rather than the global economy. He saw no opportunity in the foreseeable future to reverse the depression's wholesale contraction and devastation of world trade. Using the metaphor of *Alice in Wonderland*, he mildly ridiculed "the White Knight" and "his wondrous schemes of unlimited sales in foreign markets, though we had to lend the money to our customers to pay the shot." Second, each national economy would inevitably face recurring crises of underconsumption or overproduction. No national economy was sufficiently large or diverse to consume, at satisfactory rates of profit, the full product of its domestic manufacturers. Efficient national producers—taking full advantage of the economies of scale—would require large production runs beyond the limits of their national economy to consume. Inefficient producers, by contrast, might produce smaller production runs but at prices too high for mass consumption. Third, the only alternative responses to such long-term structural problems were either war and imperialism abroad or balanced management of the economy at home. "Heretofore," Berle noted, "depressions have been broken up by an economic miracle or windfall; a gold rush, the opening up of new territory, a war creating demand for goods, or some similar factor." Writing to Roosevelt in 1932, Berle argued that "such a windfall is not now on the horizon" and, moreover, that "it is not necessary."[7]

What was both possible and necessary was state intervention in the economy to ensure "that the modern corporation serve not alone the owners or the control but all society." "Ultimately," he hoped to see "a purely neutral technocracy, balancing a variety of claims by various groups in the community and assigning to each a portion of the income stream on the basis of public policy rather than private cupidity." Those impartial technocrats, for whom Berle was himself the prototype, would embrace the methods of "the social engineer who assembles and considers all the available information on a problem and then makes the best possible plan for action that time permits." They would provide the accountability necessary to transform American capitalism from a narrowly rational economic system to a broadly responsible social system.[8]

That vision of social capitalism informed Berle's role in FDR's brain trust, never more forcefully than in his ghostwriting of Roosevelt's famous Commonwealth Club speech in the 1932 presidential campaign. In a broad and brilliant survey of America's political economy from 1776 to 1932, FDR's speech replayed several key Berle themes. The end of the Western frontier had left the United States with "no safety valve . . . to which those thrown out of work by the Eastern economic machines can go for a new start." The imbalance between such decreased individual opportunity, on one hand, and corporate concentration and "economic oligarchy," on the other, was at the heart of the depression's overproduction/underconsumption crisis. "We know now," said Roosevelt, "that these economic units cannot exist unless prosperity is uniform—or, to put it differently—unless purchasing power is well distributed throughout every group in the community." Consequently, the economy would have to be rationalized and managed to ensure greater income equity and to eliminate the disequilibrium between supply and demand. "The day of the manager has come," proclaimed Berle.[9]

But who was to be the manager? Ever the tightrope walker, Berle self-consciously embraced a middle ground between free enterprise and state capitalism. The corporation, despite its past abuses, would do its own managing: "private initiative, inspired by high responsibility, with such assistance and balance as government can give." The private sector would plan cuts in production, while resisting the temptation to cut wage bills, thus restoring a balance between supply and demand. The government would legitimize this private planning and act in an oversight capacity to ensure some degree of accountability. Only as "a last resort," would it "enter and itself perform this function of economic regulation." That middle ground was safe ground, for it was the most-traveled road for practical-minded New Dealers; and traveling it with them protected Berle from being tagged a visionary, as was "rival ghostwriter," Rexford Tugwell.[10]

Berle believed that wise pricing was the key to successful private planning. Prices had to rise above "the crazily low prices of 1931 and 1932" if new investment was to be stimulated. However, prices had to rise more slowly than wages if mass purchasing power was to be revived. His views were consistent with those that produced the National Recovery Administration (NRA) in 1933, the New Deal's major venture in national industrial policy. In the absence of any direct state role in economic regulation, the NRA sought to achieve its goal by using organized labor "as a counterfoil" to guard against wages lagging behind prices. Section 7A of the NRA, indeed, sought to ensure the success of that countervailing strategy by sanctioning labor's right to organize and bargain collectively and by creating labor standards for "a minimum wage, short hours, decent conditions of work, and the like." In practice, it proved "impossible" to use organized labor as a general governmental counterfoil, and aggregate industrial prices outstripped "the desired increase in wage payrolls" and "purchasing power."[11]

To Berle's credit, he quickly understood why that middle ground failed. In a July 1934 study paper commissioned by Hugh Johnson of the NRA, Berle brilliantly transcended the conventional wisdom that the wage lag resulted simply from the lack of unionism in some industries and the dominance of corporate-controlled company unions in others. More fundamentally, he argued, even worker-controlled "organizations of labor" lacked any national industrial policy or perspective. "Organized labor as such in the United States has never undertaken to assume responsibility for a major national policy." Instead, "it conceives itself as a bargaining group, which means in substance that it aims to secure for itself such advantages as it can in a bargain and naturally to put itself in the strongest possible position in making such a bargain." Consequently, individual unions in individual industries made bargains that "advantage the particular group," but the consequences of their bargain disadvantaged unorganized workers and the consuming public as a whole. Rather than advancing "a unified policy" as "a champion of popular rights," organized labor—in exchange for higher wages for its union members—abstained from any effort to limit the rise in commodity prices. Indeed, they tacitly permitted industrial producers to invoke increased wages as the rationale for their unregulated price hikes. In short, organized labor bargained over income shares for their members but not over the inflationary consequences of that bargain for society as a whole. It was, in Berle's judgment, "exactly the same position held by an employing group."[12]

Without organized labor as a countervailing power, Berle had no recourse save to trust big business to make rational choices that transcended the impulse for short-term profit maximization and that opted for broader, long-range strategies that would be good for America and good for business. But organized capital proved as particularistic and short-sighted as organized labor in that respect. Largely unchecked, big business manipulated prices and wages in ways that benefited itself at the expense of either labor or small business competitors. Large corporations opted either for a low-wage, low-price strategy or for a high-wage, high-price strategy. The laboring class obviously lost in the first instance, though parts of organized labor gained in the second. Small business lost in both instances. In the first strategy, "the low price meant putting the small producer out of business" since it could not compete with "the cost of the most efficient" and "the largest producer." In the second strategy, high wages produced the same result because small producers were far less able than big ones to absorb the costs of higher wage bills. On balance, the consequent wage lag and small business bankruptcies impaired the revival of consumer spending and made the job of systemic reconstruction all the more difficult.[13]

The logic of Berle's own prior positions dictated an obvious solution to the failure of the NRA and the middle ground. Since the point of "last resort" had arguably been reached, a state-employed "neutral technocracy" was required to regulate price and wage movements in a fashion that would save capitalism from itself. Berle, however, balked at his own logic. His intellect prescribed one course of action, but his nerve—or more precisely, its failure—produced another. Contrary to Jordan Schwarz's assessment that Berle "liked catering to a market that wanted daring ideas," the New Deal brain truster made his ideas only as daring as the market allowed. Caught between his ambition to be "the American Karl Marx" and his self-defined occupation as "an intellectual jobber and contractor," Berle rarely ventured beyond the limits of the latter job description. He was a classic servant of power; and in the America of the late 1930s, those who held power—either in the public or private sectors—were not interested in hearing about state capitalism or technocratic management from those, like Berle, who served them. Such notions were beyond the pale—ideologically unacceptable and politically unfeasible; and Berle—ever the tightrope walker—was careful never to transgress those boundaries. Positions advanced in 1932 as a scholarly author could no longer be advanced in 1933 and beyond as a faithful (and ambitious) servant.[14]

Cramped by such limits, Berle's only solution to the contradictions of the middle ground was simply to do more of the same. Time and again, between 1934 and 1938, he argued that America's only alternatives to his middling course were state capitalism and "turning the clock backward" to an age of small-scale, competitive enterprise. He largely ignored the former, despite his earlier advocacy of it; but he heaped extensive scorn on the latter—gently when advocated by Louis Brandeis and bitterly when advocated by Felix Frankfurter, Berle's former law professor and lifelong adversary. Berle, however, did a more persuasive job of attacking the antitrusters than he did of defending his own de facto collaboration with big business. While acknowledging the possible correctness of Brandeis's attack on "the curse of bigness" ("Who shall say he is not right?"), his only rejoinder, "from the puzzled position of mid-career," was that he did not "see how the tide [could] be turned back."[15]

Not even the devastating downturn of the depression in 1937–38 could jar Berle from his intellectual torpor. Returning to the Roosevelt administration in the dual role of refurbished brain truster and assistant secretary of state, Berle's initial task was to help chart "a national policy" to deal "with the present depression in business." In a meeting with business leaders like Thomas Lamont and Owen Young and labor leaders like John L. Lewis and Philip Murray, Berle could only offer patchwork solutions. All of them were premised on the unlikely but conventional middle ground hope that the current "disunity" between and among business, labor, and government could be ended and "a harmonious agreement, so far as possible," could be reached. Angered by the antimonopoly campaigns of both old-line Progressives like Frankfurter and neo-Populists like Huey Long, Berle feared any "real retreat" from his moderate policy of informal collaboration between business, labor, and government. What he wanted, as he wrote in his diary four months later, "was an agreement to hold the line accompanied by a dramatic insistence on some kind of moral unity." In essence, he agreed with those who favored "making peace with business and letting matters run."[16]

Berle's 1938 positions were evidence of intellectual bankruptcy— both his own and the New Deal's. In a fascinating conversation with Eleanor Roosevelt in early 1939, he acknowledged as much in agreeing with her assessment "that the New Deal had bought time to think, but that the thinking had not been done." But he was also energized by her warning that "we have possibly a year or two, or until the next war, whichever comes first, and if we do not get something started by then, we are in for trouble." The result was one last, heroic effort by Berle to transcend the boundaries of servanthood and to act out his destiny as "social prophet," delineating for America the way to be both democratic and capitalist. It came on May 23, 1939, in virtuoso testimony before the TNEC, the Temporary National Economic Commission.[17]

Now heavily influenced by "the work of John Maynard Keynes," Berle retreated from his earlier emphasis on price-wage manipulation. Instead, he accepted the "Keynes multiplier" argument that "the amount spent on heavy capital construction" multiplies "the national income" by a factor of "about two and a half." Indeed, he argued that "there is evidence, based on the work of Schacht in Germany, that it stands up in practice" as well as in "theory." In the United States, however, lower levels of long-term capital spending had frustrated recovery from the Great Depression. The American banking system, geared largely to short- and medium-term commercial lending, could not meet the developmental needs of most corporations or of noncommercial institutions like hospitals. Because there was "no really modern system of long-term finance" in the United States, "the private capital markets have been in large measure closed since the year 1931."[18]

Drawing on his five-month stint in 1933 with the Reconstruction Finance Corporation (RFC), Berle argued that long-term government credit was preferable to increased government spending as the way to increase capital spending. The latter route would eventually lead to "the United States becom[ing] a Socialist country," since the "government will have to enter into the direct financing of activities now supposed to be private," and "over a period of years, the government would gradually come to own most of the productive plants of the United States." Socializing long-term credit, however, would achieve the same goal of increased capital spending without the ideologically unacceptable consequence of impairing free enterprise. Berle's proposed "capital credit banking system"—a kind of superpowered RFC—would have provided both "passive" credit for commercial institutions and "active" credit for "nonprofit" institutions. If funds from "investment banking houses" were insufficient, the capital credit bank would passively respond to private demand to ensure at "all times an adequate supply of cash for 'investment' purposes." In addition, Berle's bank would actively provide low-interest financing for nonprofit undertakings that the private sector generally eschewed, namely, infrastructural construction and health and human services that "fill[ed] certain needs of the community."[19]

At pains to make his proposal ideologically acceptable, Berle argued that it was not "radical" in any socialist sense. He did acknowledge, however, that his proposal would "shift . . . control" from private "investment banking" to "new centers" of capital credit—"centers which should be more responsible to the public and carried on by groups which, by their nature, assume greater responsibility for maintaining a continuous economic flow." In Berle's imaginative scheme, the free enterprise system would remain intact, but the capital credit bank would ensure that the social needs of the larger community were met and would encourage the private sector to stress long-term, productive investment rather than short-term profit-taking. Moreover, the new banking system and the nonprofit sector it partially served would provide socially useful outlets for the talents and energies of technocrats like Berle himself. "The drive which sets men to work is quite as much moral as financial," he affirmed. "Work like that of La Guardia in New York, of Nathan Strauss in the housing field, of Lilienthal and Morgan in the electric power field, efforts of hosts of men in less spectacular areas are quite as significant today, as the work of a Harriman, a Huntington or a Carnegie of yesterday." Yesterday's servants of power would become today's social capitalists.[20]

Nothing came of Berle's proposal. "Never worked out. The war came on," he wrote in a cryptic marginal note that summarized the fate of his economic policy. It was to be his last hurrah as New Deal brain truster. By America's entry into World War II, he had essentially given up the intellectual ghost, tacitly accepting the reality that domestic planning had given way to the economic "windfall" of war. "I am afraid," he said, "I do not see solution in any particular system. The corporate system has gone pretty thoroughly mad. A state political system could get even worse. Probably the two have to lever against each other to produce something like a balance." Berle's days as social prophet had ended in a sad acceptance of a latter-day "hidden hand." Only in the broader sphere of foreign affairs, where he was to implement inherited ideas rather than conceive new ones, would Berle's energies receive any outlet.[21]

In early 1938, Berle returned to Washington as assistant secretary of state, apparently at the instigation of Sumner Welles, the department's new undersecretary. He was to retain the position until early 1945. By Berle's own description, Welles and Roosevelt persuaded him that he was to be a "Brain Truster in immediate contact with the President," representing a department that had "too many careerists and too little free thinking." The description appealed to the vanity of a man more inclined to be the president's confidant and "Chancellor" than any mere bureaucrat. Berle's role, as the British ambassador ascertained it, was to "co-ordinate political and economic affairs in general without concerning himself with any question of routine." [22]

Berle brought to the job a modest amount of experience, an initial lack of enthusiasm, and a set of biases that made his conventional ideas look less so. His background in foreign affairs had been episodic: an instant expert on Russia at the Versailles conference in 1919, where his elegant resignation carried more weight than his prior recommendations; Sumner Welles's comrade-in-arms in Havana, carrying out Roosevelt's diplomatic intervention in the Cuban revolution of 1933; and his ad hoc participation in the American delegation to the Buenos Aires meeting of the Pan American Union in 1936.

The lack of enthusiasm was more persistent. From April 1937, when he was offered the position, to January 1938, when he accepted it, Berle steadily resisted pressure from Welles and Roosevelt to come on board. The domestic economy, paralyzed by the 1937–38 crisis, seemed a more appropriate outlet for his talents and ambition. "The economic situation is getting worse by the minute," said Berle, "and the President has no particular ideas as to what to do nor has any of his group." By contrast, the international scene seemed less promising, where no likely "prospect of a real peace move is going forward," but, by the same token, no real likelihood of war seemed yet imminent. Even Roosevelt's assurance that he could play a double role as domestic brain truster and assistant secretary of state failed to allay Berle's concern that "the State Department is the world's worst place to try it. You would be limited by a small job which carries with it no political protection because it is unimportant." Nonetheless, Berle eventually concluded, "Somebody has to do the work and I would rather do it myself than leave it to some second-rate intriguer picked from the political basket who will get us in a British alliance and a European Asiatic war." [23]

Six months later, a dissatisfied Berle submitted his resignation to Roosevelt. "State Department administrative work, which twenty men can do better than I," had proved frustrating, and Berle wished to do more substantive, long-term "thinking at least one lap ahead of the obvious financial and industrial crisis, which is plainly indicated within the next few years." The Czechoslovakian crisis, however, put the resignation on hold for six weeks. After the Munich conference—which Berle greeted with the relieved exclamation, "The 'break'! Thank God!"—he reactivated his resignation request, only to encounter resistance from both Roosevelt and Welles. Eventually, Berle settled for a leave of absence in early 1939, one that set in motion the capital credit bank proposal that he advanced before the TNEC in May.[24]

But even as Berle acted out his last scene as social prophet, the war's approach in Europe had already reengaged his energies and intellect. Persuaded that the German move on the rest of Czechoslovakia offered "at least an even chance of a world war" in the near future, he quickly turned his talents as "intellectual jobber" to the task of establishing the range of American options and the liabilities and advantages of each. Eighteen months later—after the momentous events of the German-Russian nonaggression pact, the invasion of Poland, the so-called Phony War, the German conquest of Western Europe, and the Battle of Britain air war—Berle concluded that "there is no more fascinating place in the world than the State Department, just now." For Berle, as for the whole administration, "Dr. Win-the-War" had already replaced "Dr. New Deal" as America's family physician.[25]

Having accepted his role on the global stage, Berle brought to the part a fairly coherent world view. Largely derivative and far less complex than his views of domestic society, his perspective did differ by degree from some of his colleagues, especially in his extreme distrust of the British and in his strident Russophobia. At the center of Berle's *Weltanschauung* was a vision of an ideal world order. Like the Wilsonianism that informed it, Berle's conceptualization projected his own image of America onto the planetary canvas. Having arrived at a nearly perfect order in the United States—both in its internal structure and in the framework of its relations with the Western Hemisphere—he could only hope that other great powers would abandon the course of empire and aspire to the American model.

The core of that perfect order was the American republic itself, and the secret of its historical success was its political-economic integration. Instead of being Balkanized into forty-eight small, contentious, barely viable nations, the American federation of states created a framework of cooperation in which broad sovereignty was conferred on the federal government, but certain residual rights were reserved to the states. Similarly, instead of fragmenting the economy into multiple, undersized, redundant markets, a continent-spanning common market had provided the demand stimulus that enabled America's great leap forward from Third World status to industrialized development in the nineteenth century.

Nearly as important in America's success was its more recent achievement in integrating Latin America. Its culmination had come with FDR's Good Neighbor Policy, institutionalized at the four major meetings of the Pan American Union held between 1933 and 1941. Repudiating earlier ventures in "gunboat" and "dollar" diplomacy, the Roosevelt administration sought and secured a more equitable and cooperative relationship with Latin American republics. It ended military interventionism and quasi-imperialist arrangements, promoted cultural understanding and mutual respect, and heightened economic integration through reciprocal trade treaties and Export-Import Bank loans. Berle candidly acknowledged that the arrangement was still fragile and that the Axis threat in Europe and Asia might yet force the United States to reimpose "a kind of *Pax Americana*." Moreover, he conceded that the Good Neighbor Policy still smacked of "empire"— a word he used with less embarrassment and far greater frequency than his colleagues. Indeed, answering in the negative his own query, "Is Empire Avoidable?" he affirmed that "neither great nor small powers have free choice in the matter." Nonetheless, the American mode of informal empire was far superior to the older European mode of formal empire—"with its translation of nineteenth-century conceptions of empire into cooperative arrangements in which a minimum of control and a maximum of cooperative effort are achieved for the inhabitants of the region." "Until world government arrives," he contended, "the need is to make the inevitable empires 'good.'" "We shall have to be either generous or imperialistic, and present history is showing that the generous policy is infinitely the more successful."[26]

In sharp contrast to the United States, Europe had failed to be wise in its intramural affairs. On the European continent itself, no significant degree of political and economic integration had taken place. The gaggle of small-to-middling European nations had been collectively victimized by an unstable balance of power and a string of dynastic, tribal, and imperial wars. Its fragmented, undersized, redundant markets—hemmed in by tariff walls and currency convertibility controls—had spawned economic inefficiency and more frequent, everdeepening depressions. In Berle's judgment, neither Europe nor the world would know enduring peace and prosperity until European divisiveness had given way to unity. Looking backward, he approved of the countervailing "European habit of seeking a center (a Pope, a Holy Roman Empire, or the like)." Looking forward, he thought that

the Austrian Empire, or something like it, must be invented; obviously a set of regional arrangements have to be made so that the countries are not strangled by their economics and their politics; obviously, all these have to work together. But how? One vague idea floating through my head has been the possibility of three or four great regions based on economics; with national units within the regions. . . . Thus, there might be an Anglo-French-Spanish region; a Danubian region; a German-Dutch-Scandinavian and Baltic region, or the like; an Italian-Balkan-Turkish region.[27]

If "a successful great Germany" would peacefully function as an important, even central component of an integrated Europe, then Berle was prepared to welcome its participation, content to leave to the German people "the internal question of the German Reich" and to let them "settle whether they like the Nazi regime for themselves." However, if Hitler's "real desire" was "the domination of continental Europe," then German hegemony would have to be opposed as an unacceptable road to European integration. Even more emphatically, German-Russian condominium or unilateral Russian hegemony were even more treacherous trails. That conviction lay at the core of Berle's extreme anti-Soviet feelings—a sentiment that had firmly emerged by 1939 and was only barely abated by the wartime alliance with Russia after 1941.[28]

The fundamental reason for Berle's attitude was fairly simple and straightforward—and not unlike the economic and strategic premise that undergirded the cold war less than a decade later. In Berle's view, there were four industrial complexes in a world where industrial power ultimately determined all other forms of power: North America, Western Europe, Russia, and Japan. German control over the Western European complex would be dangerous to American prosperity and security—but not necessarily fatal. The combining of both the Western European and Russian industrial cores would be an unthinkable nightmare, regardless of whether Germany, Russia, or a Russo-German alliance produced that combination. "There is a bloc running from the Pacific clear to the Rhine," was Berle's instant appraisal of the 1939 German-Russian nonaggression pact, adding that "this is a picture not unlike the picture of Europe after Napoleon had made his famous Russian treaty at Tilsit." Poland's fall only confirmed his judgment that "you will have two men able to rule from Manchuria to the Rhine, much as Genghis Khan once ruled; and nothing to stop the combined Russian-German force at any point; . . . and for the time being, Europe is gone." From that juncture forward, Berle's principal concern in Europe was the threat of a "Russo-German combination" becoming "dominant."[29]

Hitler's double-cross invasion of Russia in June 1941, which raised the possibility of German hegemony over both industrial cores, was crucial in transforming Berle into a prowar interventionist. Despite the Soviet-American collaboration that then ensued, Berle remained obsessed with the possibility that Russia would cut a separate peace with Germany and revive the threat of Russo-German condominium over Europe. In 1941, he cautioned Harry Hopkins, Roosevelt's closest confidant and sometime emissary to Russia, "The Russian denouement is unpredictable," and there could "be a violent change in party line. I mean this quite seriously. We nearly got killed by it in 1918 [the Peace of Brest-Litovsk]. The British were betrayed into an almost hopeless position by it in August of 1939." A day later, he recorded in his diary, "We are much better off if we treat the Russian situation for what it is, namely, a temporary confluence of interest." Once "the defeat of Germany" was accomplished, Russia would be left "as the only substantial military power on the continent" and would "exploit that position to the utmost"—like "the Tsar Alexander after the Napoleonic wars." When that occurred, Germany would have to be transformed from adversary to anti-Russian counterweight. As he told his colleagues in postwar planning in May 1942, "The thing you want is not a weakened Germany (it might not stay that way), so much as a re-educated Germany which will be a balancing and peaceable force in the world. After all, there will be Russia."[30]

If the lack of European integration had made a hash of affairs between its great powers, that same factor had fundamentally distorted Europe's relations with its overseas periphery in the Middle East, Africa, and Asia. Inhibited by their undersized national markets and the barriers to intra-European trade, European nations could only approach economies-of-scale production runs by creating closed colonial markets and resource bases abroad. Europe's predilection for formal empire—with its militarism, its administrative colonialism, and its economic monopoly—was in part a logical outgrowth of European economic inefficiency. It was, as well, an expression of the national chauvinism that so characterized Europe's political relations and that made the competition for empire not merely a logical economic choice but a lust for prestige and a will to power.

The "imperialistic" character of Europe's formal, colonial empires was, in Berle's judgment, manifestly less "successful" than the "generous" nature of America's informal empire, that is, the cooperative structure of Pan Americanism embodied in the Good Neighbor Policy. European empires and imperial preference systems artificially protected European producers from the discipline of market competition and thus fostered continued economic inefficiency. European imperialism inevitably produced indigenous responses that sparked anti-imperialist movements and revolutions and, in turn, produced imperial repressions that were morally repugnant and whose material costs significantly offset the profits of colonial control. And finally, European imperialism—in denying fundamental freedoms to its colonial subjects—made it quite difficult to enlist their voluntary aid in defending their respective metropoles during Europe's recurring, internecine conflicts.

Berle reserved particular anathema for the British empire. Part of this scorn derived from Berle's conviction that the British, more than other Europeans, ought to have known better because they had already created a constructive alternative to empire. "The British strength," he insisted, "had lain not in the Empire, but in the Commonwealth." The British "moral and intellectual ability to bring about common action among a great number of nations" made the British Commonwealth "a magnificent and civilized development" that was "analogous to the position held by the United States among the nations of the Western Hemisphere." In effect, the British had already discovered the superiority of informal empire over its formal counterpart; but British ethnocentricism and racism had limited the former's application to the white-dominated dominions of Canada, Australia, New Zealand, and South Africa. "Briefly," argued Berle, "we must look for common denominators, which must take in Chinese, and Burmese, and Indians, and Malayans, and Javanese, and so forth, as well as white sahibs and plantation owners."[31]

Berle's distaste for the formal British empire also had its base in more practical, short-term considerations. First, it hurt the British war effort. "Why should India defend a freedom she hasn't got?" was a query that he also directed to the rest of the empire as well. Second, the empire tilted the British toward economic autarky. Preferential treatment for British trade and investment in the empire constituted a monopoly position that the British were not inclined to abandon to the open competition of a free world market. Both in negotiations for Lend-Lease and in the Atlantic Charter, the British strongly balked at American efforts "at cracking the Ottawa agreements"—the imperial preference system. The obstruction led Berle to wonder if "the only economic effect of the war will be that we have moved a closed-economy center from Berlin to London"—a "British economic system as violently opposed to our own as the German system was." Finally, efforts to protect its semicolonies in the Middle East and the Suez Canal connection to its colony in India predisposed the British to cut separate deals with their Russian rival in the region. The natural trade-off, feared Berle, was British approval of Russian hegemony in Eastern Europe in return for British suzereignty in the eastern Mediterranean. That *quid pro quo* was later evident in 1943 when Britain recognized Russia's 1939 takeover of the Baltic republics and in 1944 when Churchill gave Stalin a free hand in much of Eastern Europe in return for British dominance in Greece and a half-share influence in Yugoslavia. Berle, however, believed that the British "had given a half-promise" to support Russian aims in Eastern Europe as early as 1941. Its consequences "would necessarily bring the Russian system considerably east of Vienna" and threaten to replace German hegemony with Russian hegemony.[32]

Berle's world view decisively colored his reaction to the outbreak of World War II. Unlike the globalism he later embraced, Berle placed overwhelming value on that "civilized island in the world composed of this hemisphere, possibly Great Britain and a considerable part of western Europe." The Far East, by contrast, was presently less important. The Pacific market economy was vastly inferior to the Atlantic as a contributor to world trade and enterprise; and there was far less likelihood of an Asian war threatening American security. "Even in the days of airplanes," said Berle, "the Pacific is a wide place; and behind that width you do have time to build up a very considerable striking power." However, Berle thought that the Pacific—especially China—had great potential value, and he opposed cutting any separate deals with Japan to free up America to deal with Germany. "The effect of sacrificing China would be to make permanent enemies of that whole population, which was there before the Japanese came and will be there after they go."[33]

Berle's ambivalence led him to oppose efforts "to force matters to that point" of Japanese-American conflict "during the entire year of 1940 and the summer of 1941." Like Welles, he sought to avoid a premature two-ocean conflict "which would at once cripple our aid to Britain in the Atlantic, and at the same time expose us to grave attacks in the Pacific." In effect, he sought to appease Japan and buy time, keeping open the option of more decisive action if the Atlantic situation came to warrant it and if American rearming made it feasible. That option became viable in the late fall of 1941. "German strength was sufficiently impaired" by its foolish choice in "attacking Russia," so that it could neither threaten "Suez and the Near Eastern life-line" nor "be of that degree of assistance to the Japanese which otherwise it would have been."[34]

The European theater engaged Berle's interest and his work far more intensely. Persuaded by March 1939 that war was inevitable,

Berle produced on April 2 his "Memoire: Foreign Policy of the United States" in which he posited five options for the nation. Clearly meant to influence superiors and colleagues, Berle advised active consideration of three of those options and clear rejection of the other two. His negative assessment of the latter flowed logically from his distrust of the British and his dislike of the Russians. Pledging unequivocal support "in advance" to "the Anglo-French combination" was wholly unacceptable because "we do not know, with any accuracy, the real designs of British policy." Indeed, Berle assumed that British policy would "take advantage of every chance to strengthen her own commercial and naval position at the expense of any ally," and he feared that the Anglo-French entente, if "victorious," would "promptly, as in 1919, again create a situation of short-sighted advantage to themselves, leaving our own country less happy, less prosperous." Equally unacceptable was any "attempt to reach an understanding with Russia as to a common attitude in the event of war or threatened war." Indeed, Berle's Russophobia was so uncompromising that he dismissed the option out of hand, concluding that "it is as far out of the question as would be an American-German alliance. There is no such community either of understanding or interest as would make the idea feasible or desirable." [35]

The other three alternatives did engage Berle's consideration. The first entailed an effort to prevent war by calling "a peace conference of some kind." Although he concluded that the "alternative is not to be ruled out" and he supported Welles's periodic initiatives in that direction, he regarded the efficacy of that route as so improbable that it defied any reasonable odds. The second "policy" of nominal "neutrality with plain indication of sympathy for the Anglo-French group" was "that actually being pursued." Such "biased neutrality" would likely be a reprise of the U.S. "entry into the World War," and it was "probable" that it would lead to the same "logical conclusion." Finally, the third option was "true neutrality," undertaken on the grounds that the European crisis was "no concern of ours" or that "we can do nothing effective about it." Later to be called the "Fortress America" policy by the public or the "quarter-sphere" policy by the State Department, it entertained a hemispheric "isolationism" that would immunize the Americas against Europe's contagious diseases. Building on the cooperation and solidarity of the Pan American Union, the policy would require considerable "defense work" against German as well as British efforts to establish "footholds in this hemisphere" and a substantial American effort to "assist the continent economically." [36]

Berle believed that choosing the correct option depended not only on the shifting international situation but on the results of "an intra-Administrative struggle for power" between three groups. Interestingly, the groups were essentially the same as those who had done battle over domestic economic policy in the depression. The first group, the "big business group," had always favored whatever course of action maximized the private prerogatives and profits of large corporations. This group had integrated itself into the War Department, and its leaders, like Edward Stettinius of U.S. Steel and Walter Gifford of AT&T, dominated the new War Resources Board that was "really in large measure the economic administration of the country"—a sort of proto-military-industrial complex. The second group consisted of "New York radicals" and "half-baked liberals" who adorned the "subscription list of the *New Republic*" and, as part of "the Frankfurter crowd," took their political cues from Supreme Court Justice Felix Frankfurter. Just as Berle had earlier viewed this group as irrational trust-busters and idealizers of a *petit bourgeois* past, now he damned them as dangerous supporters of both Britain and Russia, hell-bent on joining the war against facism—despite Berle's judgment that British and Russian war aims were largely incompatible with America's. (Frankfurter reciprocated the hostility, saying of Berle in his diary that "there is not one iota of doubt that Berle is almost pathologically anti-British and anti-Russian, and his anti-Semitism is thrown in, as it were, for good measure.") The third group was, of course, Berle's place of worship. Just as he had opted earlier for a domestic middle ground between big business and its trust-busting opponents, "steering a course between the big business group . . . and this group of highly inexperienced New York radicals" now became the "political task" for Berle and like-thinking souls in the State Department.[37]

From the outbreak of European war in September 1939 and American entry into World War II in December 1941, Berle steered the middle course—tacking through four stages as the international winds shifted. During the lull that followed the German-Polish war (the "Phony War"), Berle first focused on assisting Welles's mission to Europe and the peace feelers he took with him. When Hitler's invasion of Western Europe shattered those slim hopes, Berle energetically embraced the Fortress America option, proclaiming that "we have no need to seek a new international order. We have achieved an American order." His bravado belied his more desperate judgment "that the continent of Europe is now in German hands, and likely to stay so for some time; any other idea is wishful thinking." Concluding that "the Western world is beseiged on the two Americas," he believed that the rest of his life, or at least most of it, would be "spent in trying to defend various parts of this world from the economic, military and propaganda attempts to establish domination over it." On one hand, the United States had to deflect German "imperialist schemes in South and Central America." On the other hand, it wanted to do so without becoming "militarist" itself and being "forced into empire in order to preserve ourselves." In short, the United States had to insulate the Americas from the rest of a hostile world without transforming the hemisphere into a garrison state.[38]

Berle's search for "our substitute for imperialism" led him to play a prominent role in formulating "the South American plan," nicknamed the "cartel" and later renamed "the Economic Defense of Latin America." He viewed the central problem as "an unbalance of trade between the countries of the Inter-American group" which "is likely to continue for some time." South America historically ran a payments deficit with the United States and had financed that deficit from export earnings to Europe, its largest and most established customer. If the hemisphere was to be insulated from the German-dominated European market, how was South America to offset the loss of export revenue, necessary for its prosperity? And how was it to pay for continued and even expanding American imports, necessary for the prosperity of the United States? The problem could be resolved either by financing the deficit or by increasing America's imports from its southern neighbors. The latter seemed "simple enough." Private imports would be encouraged if the administration made the dollar into a "double-action currency" and one kind of dollar could only be spent on Latin American goods—"a blocked currency, good only inside the Hemisphere." In addition, the U.S. government could augment private imports out of its own pocket. "We shall have to buy surpluses, along the lines of the Surplus Commodities Corporation," said Berle, "so as to give the countries cut off from their markets something to go along with."[39]

Those measures alone could not eliminate the Latin American deficit. The residue would have to be financed. The Havana meeting of the Pan American Union, held in August 1940, provided a stopgap by increasing the lending power of the Export-Import Bank by $500 million. While potentially useful, it was Berle's belief that a more permanent solution required a governmental inter-American bank, one that would be a regional precursor of the World Bank and the International Monetary Fund. On one hand, it would provide long-term developmental loans for new Latin American industries, stressing product lines for which a ready market existed in the United States. On the other hand, it would also function as kind of a hemispheric central banking reserve system that could use its clearing house function to ease the problem of currency convertibility and might even engage in a limited amount of currency creation. Berle even hoped the hemispheric bank might serve as a laboratory, perfecting techniques that could later be used in postwar Europe. Congressional opposition to the regional bank frustrated that hope, but the scheme was resurrected in the late 1950s and became part of the Alliance for Progress in the early 1960s.

The Fortress America option was dead by early 1941. Acknowledging that it "has already been turned down by our people," Berle cast his reluctant lot with the "biased neutrality" approach. Both domestic and international developments prompted that tilt. At home, the formulation and passage of the Lend-Lease bill made it clear that Roosevelt himself had set aside the hemispheric strategy and emphatically opted to make America a nonfighting belligerent and de facto ally of Britain. Ever the faithful servant, Berle was not one to stray outside the range of possibilities deemed acceptable by the president. At the same time, the international balance of power had shifted slightly against German ambitions. Britain won the air war, thus thwarting a German cross-channel invasion; and Hitler made the risky and fateful decision to invade Russia, thus exposing Germany to the potential hazard of a two-front war. Both raised the possibility that eventual American involvement might indeed undo German hegemony in Europe.[40]

Even as Berle joined Roosevelt's crusade to make America "the arsenal of democracy" for Britain, he continued to articulate his distrust of British policies. Some remarks were pure pique—irritation at odd and sundry British traits that annoyed Berle. His diary during this period is filled with sarcastic asides: the British seemed not to understand that "Cecil Rhodes had been dead a long time"; "there is nothing more second-rate than a second-rate Englishman"; "British imperial officers treat [Canadians] as though they were Malayans and issue orders all over the lot"; "the conviction rose in me that these English have learned nothing and forgotten nothing"; "I trust the British as warriors but not as statesmen"; and so-and-so was "one of those fat, pudgy, ever so slow voiced Englishmen, with rapt expression and a soft tone and an air of injured innocence" who "began by pulling out the *vox humana* stop and saying Britain was fighting for her life, which he remembered all day and all night, and every night." By extension, he strongly opposed "extreme Anglophiles" in the administration who "take the English view: i.e., that there are only two civilized peoples in the world—English and Americans." As always,

Berle perceived the sinister hand of Felix Frankfurter at work. By October, he was convinced that "there is a lot of intrigue—largely because a good many of the new men coming in were brought in by Acheson, probably at Frankfurter's suggestion." In almost paranoid style, he complained that "Frankfurter is getting a little out of scale," repeating rumors "that Frankfurter proposed to direct the State Department through Acheson, making him Secretary when Cordell Hull should finally get through," and that Frankfurter allegedly had "remarked that when he had accomplished this he would be in substantial control of every Department of the Government."[41]

By fall 1941, the Russo-German stalemate abroad and the growth of prointerventionist sentiment at home persuaded Berle that he had erred in his 1940 judgment that "we are not going to [reconquer the Continent]." By late November, he was certain that American intervention was inevitable, though he was less certain than Welles that "there will be war very soon" and unsure how long it would last. About one thing he was unequivocal—"how the war will come out." American entry would guarantee an eventual Allied victory over Germany and Japan and make good his prophecy of a year earlier: "I have been saying to myself and other people that the only possible effect of this war would be that the United States would emerge with an imperial power greater than the world had ever seen." The United States would be "the inevitable economic center of the regime which will emerge," and its policy choices would largely determine the shape of the postwar world. "The British Empire was dead," and the United States "was supposed to inherit that empire"—though the American version would be a "system more nearly like that which we have in this hemisphere than anything which the British [would be] likely to produce with their experience."[42]

No lover of war, Berle nonetheless knew "an economic miracle or windfall" when he saw one. War provided an alternative to domestic regulation, and Berle found himself by November 1941 "trying quite definitely now to swing my own mind into the business of the post-defense economic and other settlements." In so doing, he built on "longer shot thoughts" that he had entertained since early 1940 about "what reconstruction of peace must look like" and how the United States could effect it. As he told a fellow New Dealer, "either we mean it, or we do not. If we do, the problem, in size and intensity, is staggering; no half measures will do; we shall have to go the whole way." Determined to do the job right, Berle set about in late 1941 "to try to create some financial sentiment for the only financial arrangements which will make possible something like open trade."[43]

Planning for the peace became Berle's overwhelming task for the next three years. In the State Department's extensive postwar planning operation, Berle was a principal player in the Economic Section, where intellectual consensus somehow survived the "poisonous atmosphere" generated by his "personal" animosity with Herbert Feis, who "probably has affected a working alliance with Acheson's office." Berle was to make an imprint on all facets of that economic planning, but he had special impact on finance and aviation, areas that had become his bailiwick in early 1941. The former engaged most of his interest in 1942; during this time, he worked to globalize his earlier notion of an Inter-American bank, anticipating the World Bank and International Monetary Fund that came into being two years later. Indeed, in an effort to concentrate more exclusively on international finance, Berle requested in September 1942 that he be relieved of international aviation as a responsibility and that it be turned over to one of the other assistant secretaries. He rationalized that the subject was so important that it deserved undivided attention. "I feel that aviation will have a greater influence on American foreign interests and American foreign policy than any other non-political consideration," he asserted. "It may well be determinative in certain territorial matters which have to do with American defense, as well as with transportation matters affecting American commerce, in a degree comparable to that which sea power has had on our interests and policy.[44]

Ironically, Berle's plea served to talk himself out of one job and into another. Finance ceased to be his special preserve, and aviation became his primary duty. In early January 1943, he received "authority to work up an interdepartmental group" on international aviation composed of peers from War, Navy, Commerce, Civil Aeronautics, and Budget. To be sure, Berle continued to have significant input into financial matters for another year. But the departmental reorganization that followed Welles's forced resignation ended that influence in early 1944. With archrival Acheson now in control of overall economic matters, Berle "*emerge[d] as in charge of all technical operations*," that is, "shipping and radio as well as aviation," chiefly the latter. Lamenting that he "had not fared too well" in the reorganization, Berle, ever the good servant, nonetheless swallowed his "slight disappointment" and continued his new task with characteristic vigor and self-importance.[45]

Security and commerce were the Janus-faced sides of international aviation. The latter ultimately occupied far more of Berle's time and labor, but the former engaged him first. Berle was an early convert to the importance of air power in modern warfare. He had "bad dreams of this whole air warfare business," fearful that any industrial power could be "master of the air" if it was "prepared to organize its industrial life and its productions for warlike ends." Reports that Germany had sunk a British "capital ship by air bombardment" in 1940, coupled with "the fact that the *Bismarck* was sunk (substantially) by air power" in 1941, persuaded him that "air can definitely overcome the sea defenses"—an assessment validated by the successful Japanese aerial attack on the American fleet at Pearl Harbor.[46]

On January 10, 1944, "Secretary Hull assigned" Berle "the job of getting up negotiations for the air bases required by the United States after the war." Acknowledging that "the collection of a string of bases" constituted "what might be called the 'American Empire,'" he hastened to add that it would be an informal empire quite different from its European predecessors. Selecting the base sites was largely the job of the Joint Chiefs of Staff, but initiating negotiations for base rights was Berle's responsibility. By late February, Berle had "tentative indication from Brazil that they will go along" and that "the Mexicans will join." He also assumed that "we have no worries about Central America" and that "we shall simply go out and take" the "bases in the Japanese mandated islands" of the South Pacific. By mid-year, he had gone "to work with Canada" and commenced talks with Britain over the "few British islands" not covered by the prewar Destroyers for Bases deal. "Tough" talks still lay ahead over possible bases east of the Mid-Atlantic Ridge, in the Iberian, Canary, Cape Verde, and Angolan basins; but Berle felt confident enough to relinquish those negotiations to others while he concentrated during the remainder of 1944 on the issues of civil aviation that would climax in the Chicago Aviation Conference in December. Evidently, progress on base negotiations had been sufficient that Berle could "feel that [the United States] had gotten out of this war reasonably safe."[47]

Berle's larger task of effecting an international agreement on postwar civil aviation operated within broad guidelines established by President Roosevelt himself. Articulated informally in late 1941, Roosevelt codified his thoughts in November 1943 in a lengthy meeting with Berle, Harry Hopkins, Welch Pogue, chair of the Civil Aeronautics Board, and Robert Lovett, assistant secretary of war for air. The president's points addressed U.S. policy toward its own companies as well as its general policies toward all international carriers. His domestic policies included the following. *First,* aviation should not become a tool of economic imperialism in Third World countries. While he hoped that other nations would employ American pilots and "would buy American equipment," he "did not wish Americans to own or control their internal aviation"; nor did he wish them to hire American or other foreign companies as managers of their internal aviation. *Second,* aviation should not be monopolized. "American overseas aviation should not be handled by a single line." Disagreeing with Pan American, which "wanted all the business," the president believed that "the scope of international aviation was too great to be trusted to any one company or pool." *Third,* opposition to monopoly did not rule out the possibility of "various companies having 'zones'"; that "there might be a company for the western side of South America, another company for the eastern side, one company having the North Atlantic, another, the Mediterranean, and so forth." *Fourth,* "there was no need for [government] ownership." Even in instances in which initial "traffic could not support" a private company, there ought to be a clear "understanding that if ever a private line was prepared to bid for the route, the Government would promptly retire from the business" and that such privatization might be further encouraged by selective government "subsidies" for such marginal routes.[48]

Roosevelt's policies toward all international carriers stressed four additional points. *First,* "as to air and landing rights, the President said that he wanted a very free interchange." Each country "would have a number" of terminals designated for international traffic, and all countries would have the right "of discharging traffic of foreign origin and accepting foreign bound traffic." International carriers in transit, however, would not have the right to compete with domestic carriers in the internal market of a given country. *Second,* all international flights ought to have "the right of free transit" across domestic airspace that was not set aside as military corridors; and all ought to have "the right of technical stop—that is, the right to land at any field and get fuel and service, without, however, taking on or discharging traffic." *Third,* any "general party or conference about aviation" ought to be postponed until the United Nations was ready to deal with the related problems of collective security and international finance (Dumbarton Oaks and Bretton Woods in late 1944). In the meantime, "talks with Britain and other countries could be handled quietly as a part of the preparatory discussion." *Fourth,* when the conference did meet, it ought to create an international organization "to handle such matters as safety standards, signals, communication, weather reporting, and the incidental services that went with airports; and also to handle the problem of competitive subsidies or rates."[49]

Berle's interdepartmental committee had already anticipated Roosevelt's guidelines in its April 1943 report. It agreed that free competition—"the widest generalization of air navigation rights"—would ensure "that the best interests of the United States are served." Both American airlines and aircraft manufacturers would be served, thought Berle, if "properly documented aircraft of any nation may reciprocally . . . use the airports of any other nation as freely as foreign vessels may enter seaports." The latter would clearly benefit from a competitive ethos that multiplied the number of companies and nations making "applications to buy planes and spare parts."[50]

That demand stimulus would favor an American aircraft industry that "during the war period" had come "to control the supply of aircraft." Indeed, Berle took note of a corporate "lobby . . . whose interest generally is to sell as many aircraft as they can, and who, in general, will oppose the monopoly idea of Pan-Air." Not only was that "aircraft manufacturing industry" an important one to the postwar prosperity but it was "a vital defense industry" as well. Similarly, American airlines would suffer from a closed door aviation policy while benefiting from an open one. If international aviation returned to the prewar status quo, American airlines would find themselves largely limited to the "western hemisphere" but with "no entries into Europe, or Asia, aside from" Pan American's "very limited rights" into the British Isles, Portugal, Singapore, and Hong Kong. However, "the technical and business proficiency of the United States," operating in a liberated and enlarged world market, would virtually ensure American "supremacy in the field of international air transport."[51]

The advantages of an open sky world, however, went far beyond corporate commercial interests. Indeed, Berle sometimes argued that "this is not primarily a commercial interest, though in the United States it is commonly so perceived." In the narrow military sense, "the lines of invasion and defense will lie along the same lines as those of air commerce." In particular, Berle pointed to "four huge areas of rapidly growing military importance": the North Atlantic run, the Great Circle route, the Caribbean–Brazil–West Africa triangle, and the United States/Panama line to Australia and New Zealand. If the United States was excluded from any of those areas, it might "lead to an influx of European technical advisers, etc.," who might act as an entering wedge for a hostile strategic presence. In the broader diplomatic sense, the omnipresent participation of America in international aviation might well provide "the only real lines through which we can maintain contact with and exert some influence over the underlying situation." Air policy would be a "leverage" by which the United States could help persuade others to accept its postwar hegemony and its rules of the game. "The commercial interests, though they are important in some respects, are incidental to the maintenance of the general moral and diplomatic position which we have, and which we will need." [52]

Two barriers—one domestic and the other international—obstructed Berle's efforts to secure an international agreement on terms that would serve those perceived national interests. The adversaries on the home front were "the extremists and narrow nationalists in the aviation industry," principally associated with Pan American Airlines. Having enjoyed a monopoly of overseas American flights prior to World War II, Pan Am wished to preserve its position against the expected efforts of domestic rivals to compete in old routes and to exploit America's postwar dominance to open up new routes. Berle, however, opposed that monopoly not only in principle but on the grounds that Pan Am had grossly abused its privileged position as the "chosen instrument" of American foreign policy, chiefly by putting corporate profits ahead of national security. He apparently believed and repeated rumors in early 1940 that "Pan Am had been helping to run a German line in Colombia and had been using it to train German pilots—presumably to bomb the Panama Canal when the time comes." [53]

Pan Am's alleged treachery reinforced Berle's vigorous opposition to that company's ongoing effort "to stamp out every kind of competition" from other airlines trying to enter the international sphere. Consequently, Berle strongly backed the efforts of the newly created American Export Line to establish "a competing line across the Atlantic, to Portugal," and to purchase several British-owned "freight air lines in Central America." Specifically, Berle appeared before the Senate Appropriations Committee to speak for an export airlines "subsidy," against the vigorous "lobbying" of Pan Am, still defending its position as "a single, monopolistic air line." ("As dirty a piece of business as I have seen," is how Berle characterized Pan Am's "fighting, tooth and nail" against the subsidy proposal.) Moreover, he encouraged the Civil Aeronautics Board to pursue its investigation of Pan Am's operation, even in the face of a Justice Department decision "to withdraw its anti-trust suit." [54]

Those prewar clashes formed the context in which Berle dueled over American air policy in 1943 and 1944 with Juan Trippe, Pan Am's chief executive. The airline's goal was to create an Anglo-American cartel that would divide global air routes and exclude both foreign and domestic competition. Berle opposed such monopolization, not simply because of Pan Am's past abuses but because he believed that competition made for more "rapid and healthy" industry development through an "increase" in "efficiency." He pointed to the superior service produced by "the more competitive air development inside the United States" as well as to Pan Am's own improved performance when it was forced during the war to confront "competition introduced when the army brought in other air companies as contractors, who promptly ran the routes in accordance with the higher domestic standards."[55]

Pan Am, in its efforts to overcome Berle's opposition, made common cause with the British airline industry and with key American congressmen. In early 1944, it made "a cartel agreement" with British Overseas Air Company (BOAC). According to British intelligence reports, the agreement called for Pan Am "to have the bulk of the North Atlantic traffic" between the United States and Great Britain, while BOAC "was to have substantially all of the European traffic." Pan Am retained an essential monopoly on its Latin American and Pacific basin routes but permitted BOAC to operate in South America "under Pan Am franchise" and to have a "Hawaiian stop, making possible a connection between Canada and Australia." British spheres in Africa, the Near East, and South Asia remained off-limits to Pan Am. Concurrently, Pan Am acted "industriously" on the domestic scene to build "up a very powerful lobby" that would recognize the Pan Am–BOAC cartel and support its "proposition that all American foreign civil aviation after the war should be allowed to associate." In particular, Pan Am used Senator Ralph O. Brewster, key member of the Commerce Committee's special subcommittee on international aviation, to prepare a Senate resolution "favoring the chosen instrument theory and conferring on Pan-Air the right to handle American air interests in foreign negotiations."[56]

Berle countered Pan Am's moves by turning to the British government to undermine its BOAC agreement and to Pan Am's domestic rivals to thwart its congressional lobbying. First, he confronted his British co-negotiator, the Lord Privy Seal, Lord Beaverbrook, with rumors of the cartel agreement. Beaverbrook not only confirmed the rumors but agreed that "these people had no right to make agreements of this kind," and he made "clear that no such arrangement could be binding." (In fact, the cartel pact was quite consistent with the British government's own air policy, but it was an embarrassment to that government to have news of that agreement surface while the two governments were negotiating.)[57]

On the home front, Berle tacitly cooperated with "an equally powerful lobby . . . being built by other airlines which have done an excellent job for the army: notably, Northwestern Airlines, Northeastern Airlines, American Export Airlines, American Airlines, and three or four others." They were joined by another "lobby being created by the manufacturers of aircraft," who feared that "the monopoly idea of Pan-Air" would inhibit their overseas sales. Those "independent airlines got busy and started a campaign throughout the country" to block the Brewster resolution. Berle supported those efforts by doing some personal lobbying with Democratic members of the Senate Commerce Committee, especially Bennett Champ Clark, chair of the aviation subcommittee. At the same time, he tried to discredit Pan Am by encouraging "the Truman Investigating Committee" in the Senate "to release publicly the data concerning the Pan Am airport contracts, particularly those in South America." He also urged "General Bissel, Chief of Military Intelligence," not to block the "disclosure" either, arguing his account of Pan Am's malpractices "might well tip the scale against the 'chosen instrument' theory."[58]

The other obstacle to Berle's diplomacy was international: "Two great empires, the British and the Russian, the former trying to save her territory and get guaranteed trade positions in various parts of the world; the latter out to capitalize to the last inch on her military victory." In the aviation sphere, the Russian imperial threat proved quite empty. While willing to cooperate in "technical processes of control, licensing, signaling, and so forth," the Russians were "very clear in their determination not to yield what they consider[ed] sovereign powers." In essence, "all operations of air routes in Soviet territory" were "to be carried on by Soviet planes and Soviet flyers." International carriers could only fly to "agreed points" close to but not in Soviet territory; and there, Soviet planes would transship passengers and cargo into or across the Soviet Union. As of late 1944, Moscow seemed uninterested in establishing any "northern contact" in the Baltic and regarded Cairo as its "Near Eastern terminus," meaning "that no commercial plane headed for Russia would come east of Egypt." As Berle aptly characterized Russian policy, it looked "toward a closed area, but with agreements permitting entry of persons and goods (but not planes) into it." In the end, the Russians proved more isolationist than expansionist, so uninterested in global aviation issues outside their own sphere that they made a last-minute decision not to attend the Chicago aviation conference in December 1944, much to the disappointment of Berle and to the detriment of the conference's prestige.[59]

Self-isolation was not an option for the British empire. Possessing colonies and dominions noncontiguous and far-flung and commercial interests worldwide and vital, Britain had to concern itself with the arteries of air and water that were the lifeblood of Britain's global system. Aware of its growing weakness vis-à-vis the United States, Britain was predictably appalled at the prospects of competing in an unregulated open sky. Defining "Air" as more important to Britain "than India or the Colonies or solvency," Prime Minister Churchill lamented that "we live in a world of wolves" (Americans), adding "Bears" (Russians) only as an afterthought. Moreover, *Canus lupus americanus* had "a vision of the future" that was "expansive and far surpasses the outlook of the most optimistic British advocate of civil aviation"—a judgment that led Lord Beaverbrook to fear that "civil aviation must pass to control of the U.S.A. on the manufacturing and operating basis."[60]

British leaders pursued two alternative courses designed to forestall that eventuality. Lord Beaverbrook and the Air Ministry favored an Anglo-American cartel agreement along the lines privately negotiated by BOAC and Pan Am; and despite his disclaimer to Berle, Beaverbrook supported that agreement and hoped to build on it. The Foreign Office, however, regarded cartel building as a futile enterprise, feeling that American ambitions were too expansive and avaricious to settle for a self-limiting division of postwar spoils in any sphere, including aviation. British diplomats, therefore developed a fallback strategy to employ when the cartel scheme inevitably floundered. In essence, it proposed creation of an international aviation commission that would have full powers to set rates and distribute routes. Dubbed "internationalization," in a clever theft of American ideological language, British leaders hoped their plan would avoid American dominance of that international body by a coalition of Britain, France, their respective colonies and/or dominions, and smaller countries hoping to establish their own national airlines as local and regional carriers. All would have a vested stake in opposing American air hegemony. The agency, through its rate-setting and route-distributing powers, could perform the same service envisioned for the cartel, that is, protect British aviation preeminence in the European continental market and in long-distance flights to much of Africa, the Near East, and South Asia.

Berle's counterstrategy for the United States was fairly simple. Firmly but politely, he would resist both the cartel and internationalization schemes, while pushing the British to accept the American position—informally in Anglo-American negotiations (sometimes brokered by the Canadians) and then formally at a multinational conference. If that approach failed, then he would aggressively raise the ante, so that any final compromise would still reflect the original American position. The firm-but-polite mode prevailed in the Anglo-American negotiations between Lord Beaverbrook and himself—at London in April 1944 and at Washington and New Brunswick, Canada, in July. The more expansive and belligerent mode characterized most of his negotiations with Lord Philip Swinton, Beaverbrook's successor, at the Chicago Aviation Conference in November.

Berle's negotiations with the British began in February 1944 shortly after the State Department reorganization had left him with aviation as the only sphere in which to make his mark. Ever driven and ambitious, he sought to make the most of it in an effort to recoup his losses and revive his own hopes for higher and more powerful office—perhaps undersecretary if Hull retired and Stettinius moved up. He expected "quite a battle when it comes," since he had already had wind of the BOAC–Pan Am negotiations as well as rumored British cartel negotiations "with the continental Europeans designed to exclude the United States from the whole European area." By early March, however, "various preliminaries" had suggested that "the British now have come fairly close to our projected method." In that moderate climate, Hull and Roosevelt dispatched Berle to London on March 29 for a week of formal talks.[61]

The London talks, and the more informal talks in July, gradually unmasked the incompatibility of the British and American positions. Berle dashed any lingering hopes that Beaverbrook might have entertained about an Anglo-American cartel agreement, even a quite limited one in which the two split the trans-Atlantic traffic "50/50." However, he did grant Britain the right of "Colonial cabotage," which permitted Britain to treat flights to and from its colonies as domestic rather than international flights and hence not necessarily subject to competition. In addition, Berle agreed to accept the notion of internationalization as the basis for future discussions. The concessions, however, gave the British a misleading picture of American flexibility. The cabotage concession grew largely from the American desire to claim the same right for its formal empire ("Hawaii, Alaska, Puerto Rico, and Guam"); and internationalization meant something quite different to the Americans than it did to the British. "The British favored an international authority with power to fix rates, frequencies, etc. The American felt that the international authority should deal only with technical matters related to air traffic."[62]

The subsequent Berle–Beaverbrook meetings in July made the distance between those positions abundantly clear to Beaverbrook. "We have come to the parting of the ways," he told the War Cabinet on his return. "We can either go forward with the Americans or we can stand on our previous policy of international collaboration excluding the United States. The issue involves the whole future of British Civil Aviation." Indeed, he urged that the Chicago conference be postponed indefinitely because the two sides were in "fundamental disagreement." None of this, however, was at all clear to Berle. Gullibility and perhaps wishful thinking led him to extrapolate from his July conversations "that at the appropriate time the British Government [would] recede from its position," following a face-saving "several days' battle at an international conference." So he steadfastly pushed ahead with conference plans, perhaps hopeful that the expected British capitulation to America's open sky position would be the crowning achievement of a career whose best days still lay ahead.[63]

The Chicago Aviation Conference was a no-lose situation for the American government and a must-win situation for Berle. Since the United States had both the commitment and the power to block either the cartel or the internationalization strategies of the British, only two possible outcomes remained; and both (or some variation in between) were acceptable to the Roosevelt administration. Ideally, the British might wholly acquiesce to the American position, making possible an orderly and rapid entry of American airlines into all the routes of the world. Less ideally, the British might stand by their guns and scuttle the conference; but without the protection of a cartel or an international authority, the British would quickly find themselves overwhelmed by a torrent of American-initiated bilateral agreements that would push American airlines, aircraft manufacturers, and technicians into areas historically dominated by the British. As Berle told a Canadian delegate, "If the British do not play ball with the United States on air transport, the U.S. could make deals with other countries and leave the British out completely." The competitive, bilateral approach would slow American entry into new routes, but in the end, the United States would achieve the goal articulated by Clare Boothe Luce: "We want to fly everywhere. Period."[64]

Unlike his government, Berle could not accept impasse with Britain as an outcome of the conference. He had wagered that the conference would produce British capitulation and a triumphant agreement in which the fifty-three delegations accepted America's new order in international aviation; and the size of his bet was no less than his future career. The Chicago conference was one last, grand opportunity to effect a reversal of fortunes as he looked back on a year that saw him deprived of Welles's patronage and, as well, of any role in international finance and as he looked forward to an uncertain future in a department increasingly dominated by adversaries like Stettinius, Acheson, and (*ex officio*) Harry Hopkins. As an astute Canadian friend put it, "If Berle had felt his position to be secure and particularly if he felt that there was a chance of his getting the Undersecretaryship of State he might even at the last moment have been able to save the conference." But insecure and desperate about his future, "he played his cards badly." [65]

Indeed, he did play them badly. Even before the conference began, the American air attaché in London aptly characterized British policy as "a holding and delaying attitude to the limit that can be done without seriously threatening the overall relations between it and the United States." In effect, the British had decided in advance (as Beaverbrook put it) that there was no way they could "drive" the United States "into accepting a regulatory Authority" and that they would have "to recognize the failure" of their internationalization strategy. Since the British, in turn, had no intention of accepting the American position (save perhaps in a token way), it meant that the British delegation went to Chicago not in search of substantive agreement but in search of a rhetorical formula that would mask the extent of Anglo-American disagreement. Beaverbrook, in fact, saw no reason to commit his energies and prestige to an already doomed enterprise and withdrew as head of the delegation. His place was taken by Lord Swinton, a colonial bureaucrat and faithful follower of orders who was ideally suited to conduct "a holding and delaying action." [66]

A more objective Berle, less self-absorbed, might have recognized the inherent limits of the Chicago negotiations and tried to make the best of them. Instead, six days into the conference, he had deluded himself that "the major issues have been met and cracked with a minimum of public debate, largely because the British receded from their position directly they got the feel of the situation." He predicted that a difficult "ten days" of "putting the solutions into form" would end the conference business. "If my analysis is correct," he concluded, "the climax has been reached and passed." His analysis, however, was quite incorrect; yet six days later, despite a stormy meeting with the British that saw Berle "in a raging temper" that Swinton matched, Berle still assured Stettinius that Anglo-American accord was imminent and that the conference would end successfully within ten days. [67]

That self-defined pressure pushed Berle to extraordinary and often ill-advised limits in his search for a diplomatic triumph. He lobbied like a stump politician to line up Third World countries against the British; he labored assiduously to use Canada as a lever to disrupt Commonwealth solidarity; he conducted public press conferences that not only violated protocol but publicly aired his differences with the British; he whiningly complained to Undersecretary Stettinius, who was Juan Trippe's brother-in-law, that Pan American Airways had "attempted to embarrass the Delegation" by engineering a hostile "press campaign" by the *Chicago Tribune* as well as "a Senate investigation" of an alleged "protest from the War Department to the State Department, in connection with our plans"; and he even importuned Roosevelt to intercede directly with Churchill, thus requiring the president to put his own relationship with the British prime minister on the line. The potential price must have been abundantly clear to FDR when his two personal messages to Churchill—including a thinly veiled threat—provoked a British threat to "adjourn" the meeting as well as an antihegemonic rebuke that the United States, whose "navy," "air force," "trade," and "gold" already dominated the world, "will not be given to vainglorious ambitions but rather will be guided by justice and fair play."[68]

Some of Berle's moves may have been useful, and none need have been fatal. What was fatal, however, was Berle's foolish gamble in introducing the so-called fifth freedom issue into the conference deliberations. This fifth freedom was an unannounced add-on to the American proposals, which Berle had packaged as the "four freedoms." Consensus on the first two had essentially been reached prior to the conference; so there was no need to negotiate further for the right of "transit" (to overfly another nation's nonmilitary airspace) and the right of "technical stop" (to refuel or to effect repairs but not to discharge or collect passengers and cargo). Three and four, however, were the sticking points with the British: the right to discharge passengers and cargo from the country of origin and the right to collect passengers and cargo bound for the country of origin. Britain had nominally "conceded" those rights; in reality, however, it tried to gut those rights by insisting that the frequencies of flights from one country to another be rigidly fixed by quotas. Predictably, the United States strongly opposed fixed frequencies and quotas, arguing that it violated the concept of open skies and inevitably mutated into "either cartels or national combinations to benefit themselves at the expense of other countries." Nonetheless, it did advance the notion of "escalation" as a compromise. It would accept quotas as a starting point, if additional flights could be added "when planes were running at 65% load factor, which in operating language means substantially full." Ultimately, then, competition rather than regulation would determine flight frequencies; and the American position would come to prevail.[69]

When the British dug in their heels against the escalator clauses, Berle tried to change the terms of the negotiation by introducing the so-called fifth freedom—"the right to pick up" and discharge "traffic at intermediate points." To use Berle's own example of an American flight between New York and Cairo, the third and fourth freedoms would have merely extended the right to discharge passengers and cargo from the point of national origin (New York) and pick up passengers and cargo bound for that point of national origin (again, New York). Under the fifth freedom, however, that New York-to-Cairo flight could conceivably discharge and pick up passengers and cargo at intermediate points along the way, for example, Lisbon, Madrid, Rome, or Athens. Berle argued that routes like the New York–Cairo run could not be made into "an economically self-supporting route" without access to intermediate traffic. The British (and the French), however, saw it as an American gambit to compete with them for intra-European and European–Near Eastern trade, making American long-distance carriers into competitors of European short-haul and medium-haul lines. As expected, the British rejected the fifth freedom unless the number and location of intermediate stops were fixed in advance by quotas, while the United States once more proposed an escalator clause compromise. The debate over the fifth freedom seemed a reprise of that over the third and fourth freedoms.

According to Schwarz, Berle's apparent intent was to use the fifth freedom as a negotiating chip that he would bargain away in exchange for British acceptance of the third and fourth freedoms. If so, it was a disastrous miscalculation (though not for the reasons his biographer suggests). In one blundering moment, Berle gave the British the opportunity to break the pro-American, anti-British climate that had prevailed at the conference. Heretofore, European continental countries and Third World countries had been united in their desire to break prewar British monopolies so that they might create their own local and regional carriers, presumably using cheaper and better American aircraft. Now, the introduction of the fifth freedom opened the possibility that their market shares might be usurped by long-distance American lines exercising the right of intermediate stop. That threat made it possible for Britain to present itself as defender of small national carriers against the aggrandizing American giant. It justified its insistence on fixed quotas for the fifth freedom as "protection for small nations"; and it curried favor with European continentals by "insisting on all European powers agreeing to the fifth freedom" before it could be implemented. Despite Berle's confidence that the British ploy would be "simply blown out of the water," he eventually conceded that "the debate was not the happiest since countries which had disagreed with Britain the day before were nevertheless not prepared to go all the way out, and the result was a session not very satisfactory from our point of view."[70]

The sorry denouement of Berle's gamble left him with no further room for maneuvering. By December 2, he was inclined to accept the British position that "the disputed sections of the air transport agreement" simply be deferred for further study. For more than a month, he had attempted to pound out an agreement on explicit American terms, and now the votes were simply not there. Moreover, the personal imperatives of career that had so driven him were now moot. On November 27, Hopkins had carried personal word to him that he was being relieved of his rank as assistant secretary of state and being reassigned as ambassador to Brazil. In part, he was the victim of a general departmental reorganization that followed Hull's resignation and Stettinius's promotion as his successor—and Roosevelt's blanket authorization to let the new secretary name his own subordinates. But he was undoubtedly the victim of his own ineptness as well. So many promises of success unkept; so many self-proclaimed deadlines passed; so much unnecessary furor generated—all with no more result than an Anglo-American "impasse" marked by an embarrassing admonition from the British prime minister that the American president not abandon "justice and fair play." Despite FDR's face-saving promise that he would bring Berle back from Brazil after VE Day, there was little doubt that the reassignment was a tacit rebuke to the president's longtime servant.[71]

Berle characteristically tried to put the best face on the Chicago conference. He was helped in this regard by a key member of his delegation—old friend and patron, Mayor La Guardia of New York. Cutting through Berle's malaise of December 2, La Guardia made "an eloquent plea for getting together with the British on something," rather than lamely referring matters for further study. He proposed that the conference draft two documents and that it leave to individual countries the option of signing one or both. The first document, "The Two Freedoms Agreement," committed signatories to accept the right of transit and the right of technical stop. The second document, the "Five Freedoms Agreement," carried an additional obligation to accept freedoms three through five, dealing with the right to load and unload passengers and freight—both in long-distance direct flights and (the fifth freedom) in intermediate traffic. Viritually all the delegations, including the British, indicated a willingness to sign and ratify the first document. The second faced a more divided and uncertain future. Berle, in a burst of forced bravado, called it "a notable victory for civilization" and "new in air history. It took two hundred years of squabbling and several major wars to get this result on the sea." While later acknowledging the "bitter struggle at Chicago," he claimed to "proudly bear" its "honorable scars."[72]

Despite the hyperbole, Berle's assessment was not wholly without substance. His friend and sometime critic, Escott Reid of the Canadian delegation, insisted that the "Chicago conference worked a minor miracle" and that "it failed by a hair's breadth to work a major miracle." Reid's assessment was clearly an overstatement—and perhaps a bit self-serving, since he was generally allied with Berle's efforts at the conference. But he was clearly right in his judgment that the Chicago conference was an important chapter in the history of aviation. It created the International Civil Aviation Organization (ICAO) that came to have advisory input on international rates and that established the "rules, routines, and practices" that are "essential to participation in the vast process of world communication by air." It secured nearly universal agreement—outside the Soviet bloc—on the right of transit and technical stop. It articulated principles and posed options in the Five Freedoms Agreement that later had impact on many bilateral and multilateral agreements.[73]

In the last analysis, however, the Chicago conference was only a small step on the road to American hegemony of the air. The giant steps came with the multitude of bilateral agreements, including one with Britain in 1946, that both preceded and followed the conference. Given its general economic wealth and military might and given its specific dominance of aircraft manufacturing, the United States encountered little difficulty in persuading individual nations to open the doors of their airports to American planes and to place themselves in agreement with American aviation principles. The Chicago conference, had it succeeded on Berle's terms, might have hastened that process considerably. Its far more limited success, however, meant that it hastened the process only marginally.

It did, of course, hasten Berle's fall from the tightrope. Berle had begun his public life with the high ambition of being "America's Karl Marx—a social prophet." Both his joint authorship of *The Modern Corporation and Private Property* and his campaign penmanship of classics like Roosevelt's Commonwealth Address had made clear that real promise lay beneath the pretension. But seven years of New Deal brain trusting, overlapping with seven more years as assistant secretary of state, had transformed him into a conventional thinker and servant of power. Only his appearance before the TNEC in early 1939 showed flashes of the old brilliance and originality, and it was quickly cast aside during the maelstrom of war. In the end, the role of prophetic intellectual was incompatible with his function of "intellectual jobber and contractor." Selling his intellectual services as servant of power meant that those he served would pose the questions he would answer and set the agenda he would follow. It meant that an implied condition of his servitude was that his ideas not go beyond the acceptable ideological boundaries of his employers. It meant that the validity of his ideas would be measured by the pragmatic standard of whether they worked. It meant that the workability of those ideas would in part be determined by his bureaucratic efforts to implement them: to think and then to act on those thoughts. And it meant, finally, that the success or failure of those efforts would determine his share of power and prestige as a servant of power, whether he continued to serve "upstairs" or was exiled "downstairs." In the context of those many meanings, Berle's fall from grace in late 1944 was the personal tragedy of a man unable to reconcile his dreams of intellectual originality with his taste for power and prestige. It was also, perhaps, the more general tragedy of many "action intellectuals" in Berle's day and since. Confronted with the never-ending national demands of both equity and efficiency, and burdened with the complex task of both thinking about and acting on those demands, it sometimes became easier to evade and export those burdens abroad than to shoulder them at home—especially when world wars and cold wars provided the "windfall" opportunity.

NOTES

1. Jordan Schwarz, *Liberal: Adolf A. Berle and the Vision of an American Era* (New York: Free Press, 1977): 335.

2. Ibid., 90.

3. Ibid., 62.

4. Thomas K. McCraw, "In Retrospect: Berle and Means," *Reviews in American History* 18 (December 1990): 582; Schwarz, *Liberal*, 56, 67.

5. Schwarz, *Liberal*, 66–67; Beatrice Bishop Berle and Travis Beal Jacobs, eds., *Navigating the Rapids, 1918–1971: From the Papers of Adolf A. Berle* (New York: Harcourt Brace Jovanovich, 1973): 45. (Hereafter abbreviated and listed in the notes simply as *NTR*.)

6. *NTR*, 45.
7. Ibid., 60; 43.
8. McCraw, "In Retrospect," 590; Schwarz, *Liberal*, 353.
9. *NTR*, 62–70.
10. Schwarz, *Liberal*, 83; *NTR*, 119, 69.
11. Ibid., 99–100.
12. Ibid., 99–100.
13. Ibid., 100–101.
14. Schwarz, *Liberal*, 83, 82.
15. Ibid., 83.
16. *NTR*, 154–157, 171, 176.
17. Ibid., 198.
18. Ibid., 218–219.
19. Ibid., 220–221.
20. Ibid., 221–223.
21. Ibid., 239; 240. Berle to Richard A. Atkinsen, April 28, 1942. Berle Papers, Box 28, Franklin Roosevelt Library. (Berle Papers will hereafter be abbreviated as BP, followed by a hyphen and a number that indicates the box number: *e.g.*, BP-28 above.)
22. *NTR*, 149, 179; Schwarz, *Liberal*, 143–144, 119.
23. *NTR*, 152, 126, 152, 148.
24. *NTR*, 182, 188.
25. Schwarz, *Liberal*, 125.
26. Ibid., 128, 374–375, 257.
27. *NTR*, 281, 183, 270.
28. Ibid., 183, 188–189.
29. Ibid., 241, 273.
30. Ibid., 374–375, 390, 442, 412.
31. Schwarz, *Liberal*, 183; *NTR*, 403.
32. *NTR*, 404; Patrick J. Hearden, *Roosevelt Confronts Hitler: America's Entry into World War II* (DeKalb: Northern Illinois University Press, 1987): 236; Schwarz, *Liberal*, 164, 167.
33. *NTR*, 138, 391, 233; Hearden, *Roosevelt Confronts Hitler*, 150.
34. *NTR*, 386.
35. Ibid., 206–210.
36. Ibid., 206–210.
37. Ibid., 238; Schwarz, *Liberal*, 182.
38. *NTR*, 305, 328, 254, 230.
39. Schwarz, *Liberal*, 127; *NTR*, 324–325.
40. Hearden, *Roosevelt Confronts Hitler*, 233.
41. Schwarz, *Liberal*, 177, 179; *NTR*, 366, 365, 377.
42. Schwarz, *Liberal*, 145–146; *NTR*, 378; Hearden, *Roosevelt Confronts Hitler*, 241.
43. *NTR*, 378, 290.
44. Ibid., 481–482.

45. Ibid., 450, 454.
46. Ibid., 296, 310, 370, 385.
47. Ibid., 484–485.
48. "Memorandum of Conversation," November 11, 1943, BP-215.
49. Ibid., BP-215. FDR also railed against any Axis nation being allowed to "fly anything larger than one of these toy planes that you wind up with an elastic."
50. "Memorandum," April 30, 1943, BP-54; *NTR*, 483; "Berle to Hull," March 11, 1943, BP-54.
51. Ibid., April 30, 1943; ibid., May 24, 1943; "Memorandum: International Aviation Conference," September 16, 1944, BP-216; Schwarz, *Liberal*, 219.
52. "Memorandum," May 24, 1943, BP-54; September 16, 1944, BP-216. *NTR*, 467.
53. "Memorandum," April 30, 1943, BP-216. *NTR*, 301.
54. *NTR*, 337–340, 357, 361–362, 364.
55. "Memorandum," April 30, 1943, BP-216.
56. "Diary," May 13, 1944, BP-216; "Diary," June 23, 1944, BP-216.
57. "Memorandum," April 30, 1943, BP-54; "Memorandum," June 23, 1944, BP-216.
58. "Diary Entry," July 4, 1944, BP-216.
59. "Diary Entry," April 1, 1945, BP-216. *NTR*, 488–489, 495–496.
60. Schwarz, *Liberal*, 224, 235.
61. "Diary Entry," February 22, 1944, BP-215; *NTR*, 486.
62. Schwarz, *Liberal*, 229; *NTR*, 486.
63. Schwarz, *Liberal*, 236; *NTR*, 491.
64. Schwarz, *Liberal*, 245, 230.
65. Ibid., 252.
66. Ibid., 236–237.
67. *NTR*, 501; Schwarz, *Liberal*, 245.
68. *NTR*, 502–503; Schwarz, *Liberal*, 247–248.
69. *NTR*, 503, 502.
70. Schwarz, *Liberal*, 246–247. Schwarz's analysis argues that the fifth freedom was an empty threat, since it would have opened internal American traffic, like the New York–Chicago run, to international competition—something opposed by domestic airlines and by Roosevelt himself. On the contrary, the fifth freedom as Berle formulated it, could only be applied to international traffic. Moreover, its position had been explicitly endorsed by FDR a year earlier. ("Memorandum of Conversation," November 11, 1943, BP-215.) *NTR*, 505–507.
71. Ibid., 506–507.
72. Ibid., 506–510, 512; Schwarz, *Liberal*, 252.
73. Ibid., 252; *NTR*, 512–513.

CHAPTER 6

Thomas C. Mann and the Devolution of Latin American Policy
From the Good Neighbor to Military Intervention

WALTER LaFEBER

In the quarter century between the outbreak of World War II and the mid-1960s, U.S. policy toward Latin America devolved from Franklin D. Roosevelt's Good Neighbor approach to Lyndon B. Johnson's intervention of 22,000 troops in the Dominican Republic. These years have turned out to be exceptions in the history of U.S.–Latin American relations. Before and after this era, these relations have been dominated more by Washington's use of its military power and its inability to work out an effective cooperative economic policy with its southern neighbors than by the noninterventionism and economic cooperation that characterized the Good Neighbor policy.

Not that FDR's approach proscribed interventionism. But U.S. officials intervened with a subtlety and effectiveness—through the use of military supplies, training of the Latin American military, and massive economic domination—that demonstrated U.S. control of the hemisphere and the growing dependence of Latin Americans on the northern giant instead of on their traditional European ties. The more indirect interventionism of the Good Neighbor transformed through a series of stages and climaxed with armed intervention in 1965. These stages included an attempt to retain U.S. leverage through economic sanctions in the early 1950s; the use of covert, especially Central Intelligence Agency (CIA), activity to overthrow unwanted governments; a massive aid program to create a friendly, middle-class

Latin America in the early 1960s; and, finally, the use, once again, of U.S. troops, a use that signaled the failure of the previous policies. In 1965, normality, at least as measured by long historical precedent, returned. As in the pre-Good Neighbor days, Washington again depended on overt military power, open economic pressure, and the unilateralism of the Monroe Doctrine rather than the multilateral cooperation of the Organization of American States (OAS) that had been created in 1948 at the tag end of the Good Neighbor era.

This quarter-century transformation can be understood by examining the career of Thomas C. Mann, who first entered government service in 1942 as a lowly assistant stationed in Uruguay and left in 1966 after holding—simultaneously, no less—the three most powerful offices that made Latin American policy. There is no biographical study of Mann's career, and he never rose higher than the number three State Department office, but his career is a case study of how the United States moved from Good Neighbor to the overt use of military power in the hemisphere. His service, moreover, spanned the era that began with the belief that the world had entered the American Century and ended with the morass in Vietnam. Mann was by no means primarily responsible for the devolution. His career is worth studying precisely because he understood the growing U.S. dilemmas in Latin America, confronted and analyzed them with a professionalism and cold-bloodedness that earned him respect in southern capitals as well as his own, and rather ruthlessly followed the logic of Washington's policies in the hemisphere to its conclusion. Since World War II, the top U.S. policymaking apparatus for Latin America has appeared to be less an office than a revolving door through which persons moved freely and frequently between enjoying public power in Washington and private profits in the marketplace. Mann, however, remained at his post, a constant when all around him changed. "I'm very bad on names," he told an interviewer after he left Washington, "because I was there [in government] so long and people changed so often."[1]

Mann was born in Laredo, Texas, in 1912. "I was born right on the Mexican border," he recalled, "and learned Spanish before English and I have known Mexico all my life. I spent vacations in my childhood in Monterrey [Mexico] and Saltillo just because it was cooler." His father, a lawyer, imparted a sternness, a love of law, and the morality of the Southern Baptist church ("We didn't even play cards") to his son. In high school, Mann stood out as a scholar and especially as a 138-pound quarterback who took Laredo to an undefeated season in 1927; he confused monolingual opponents by calling out signals in a mixture of Spanish and English. At Baylor University, he met Nancy Aynesworth. They married while he was in his final year of Baylor Law School. He practiced law (at $100 a month), with his father, and thereafter—especially as he later gained international renown—identified himself only as a "Texas country lawyer." Mann tried to join the navy after Pearl Harbor was attacked. He was rejected because he could not read even the largest letters on the eye chart. "I had a muscle-freeze in my eyes" from overly intensive study of law books, Mann remembered. So he volunteered for the State Department and in 1942 was assigned to Montevideo, Uruguay, to monitor Nazi shipping in the South Atlantic.[2]

His work was so good that in 1943 he was recalled to Washington to watch Axis business operations throughout Latin America. In this post, he became intimately familiar with Argentina, the one nation President Roosevelt had not convinced to break with Hitler's Germany. Long an outspoken opponent of U.S. dominance in the hemisphere and tied closely to Central Europe through trade, Argentina was also moving to what U.S. officials feared was a Fascist-type political system under military strongman Juan Perón. In 1945, Mann participated in the Mexico City conference that passed the Act of Chapultepec. That act was specifically a mutual hemispheric agreement to resist aggression. More generally, it sealed off the hemisphere from unwanted interference from the new United Nations. The Americas, not least in Mann's own mind, were to remain a community unto themselves. But Perón continued to relish living on the wrong side of the tracks in the otherwise Good Neighborhood. In 1946, Mann became chief of the Division of River Plate Affairs, which was responsible in part for overseeing policy toward Argentina.

The following year he decided to join the Foreign Service, although this career choice cost him a 40 percent pay cut from his $11,000 civilian-status job at the State Department. After serving as second secretary in the U.S. embassy in Caracas, Venezuela, in 1947–48, he returned to Washington to become special assistant, then in 1950, director of the Office of Middle American Affairs. At the relatively young age of thirty-eight, Mann had become one of the most respected and powerful U.S. officials making Latin American policy. The meteoric rise had not been without cost. In Caracas, his first son swallowed brightly colored fireworks thinking they were candy and died of phosphorus poisoning. Salaries were pitiful. "One never stays more than one jump ahead of the sheriff as long as he is in the Foreign Service," Mann wrote a fellow diplomat in 1953.[3]

Burying himself in work, by 1950, Mann had no illusions about either Washington or conditions in Latin America. Calling on fellow Texan Sam Rayburn, the powerful, salty, speaker of the House of Representatives told him, "Young fellow, you may wonder why the U.S. Government doesn't function better than it does. . . . After you have been around awhile, you'll wonder how it works as well as it does." As for Latin America, the cooperation that had shaped the Rio military pact of 1947 and the OAS the following year turned sour as southern economies deteriorated. Latin Americans felt betrayed because they had cooperated with Washington during the war, often by selling raw materials to the northern war machine at unduly cheap prices, but now found the United States to be undependable as a buyer, a buyer who spent $13 billion for the Marshall Plan to rebuild Western Europe yet virtually nothing to build an economically functioning Latin America—other than to invest heavily to extract oil and minerals and integrate the products into the U.S. industrial complex. When the Korean War erupted in June 1950, Mann grew frustrated in attempts to obtain help from Mexico and other former wartime allies. After rumors spread that Bolivian troops might be sent to Korea, riots broke out in the capital city of La Paz. A disgusted Mann told the Bolivian ambassador "that if the Bolivians were complaining about spilling their blood for Yankees, a lot of Yankees were also complaining about American blood already being spilled in Korea for Bolivia and other countries of the hemisphere." Much of Latin America remained unmoved by such arguments.[4]

It was, however, Argentina and the Peronist threat that preoccupied Mann, much as that threat haunted all U.S. policy toward Latin America in the first postwar decade. The lessons he drew from his firsthand dealings with the Argentines came on several levels. One was political. During the 1946 Argentine election campaign, he had helped Spruille Braden, the U.S. ambassador to Argentina (and a tutor who convinced Mann to join the Foreign Service in 1947), draw up the soon-to-be-infamous "Blue Book" that publicly detailed Perón's supposed pro-Nazi crimes against the hemisphere. Perón promptly told Argentine voters that the choice was between himself and the "pig" Braden. Washington suffered an unexpected, stunning defeat as Perón enjoyed an electoral triumph. Thereafter, Mann ordered U.S. diplomats to stay out of Latin American political campaigns, even in such a quasi-U.S. colony as Cuba. During the 1950 Guatemalan balloting, Mann told a press conference that "at election time it is just political suicide to try to defend the United States. . . . I think on the whole people in the other American Republics understand and support us, but it isn't good politics to say so at election time. We are a sort of punching bag during elections. Everybody likes to take a swing at us, and makes sure he does every time you say something." The same rule applied to private firms. When U.S. companies were being enticed to contribute to Venezuelan candidates, Mann warned that corporate "long-term interests" were "best served by . . . strict impartiality in local politics." Anticommunism was not even a reason for political involvement because "Communist strength [was] relatively small" in Venezuela.[5]

The second and quite different lesson came from the economic level. Mann concluded that direct and powerful U.S. interference was justified to prevent the highly nationalist, state-controlled economic system that Perón seemed to be creating. As close philosophically to being a free-marketeer as one could find in Washington during the autumn days of the New Deal, Mann assumed that the global capitalist system planned by his State Department and Treasury colleagues in 1944–1946 offered the best hope by far for Latin American development, as well as for United States economic and political interests. He sought more social justice in the south, but any success—he privately argued forcefully in 1951—was "often related" to destroying "economic and political nationalism" typified by Perón and by Lázaro Cárdenas's nationalization of U.S. oil properties in Mexico a decade earlier. The following year, Mann tried to educate a reporter about "the three principal movements . . . that together condition all phases of our foreign relations with the American states." Mann emphasized that "the first is the doctrine of 'ultra-nationalism' or 'colonialism.'" This doctrine, he believed, blamed all problems in the region on the U.S. domination of southern raw materials, services, and capital investments. Mann lamented that this idea "has gradually gained wide popular acceptance in Latin America," although it "often has little to do with either logic or economic reality."[6]

This "ultra-nationalism," in his eyes, existed apart from, and was more dangerous than, communism. The point is pivotal: Mann feared communism and later became obsessed with fighting it, but his approach to that danger—and indeed to his entire Latin American policy—emerged out of his fear of a series of closed Latin American nationalist blocs, exemplified by Peronism and spread like contagion by anti-Yankeeism, that could wreck the possibilities of market economies, U.S. investment, and Latin American development on North American terms. Communism, he instructed his State Department superior in 1951, was "separate though related" to "nationalism." Communism was apparently less dangerous because it rested less on mass support than on "Latin American intellectuals who lost faith in democracy and adopted socialism during the great depression" of the 1930s. Communism also found support from certain labor groups. The solution was not a Marshall Plan for Latin America, as many urged, but help targeted through the U.S. Export-Import Bank that helped finance private exports, loans from the World Bank that was controlled by the United States and largely dependent on private funds, and "United States private capital investments." To obtain such help, the Latin Americans had "to act in a responsible way toward us" and meet their "responsibility." An example was a current crisis in Chilean copper caused by low U.S. copper prices. The crisis, Mann suggested, could best be handled by the Chileans acting less nationalistic and less anti-Yankee and understanding that the "only way" to deal with it was "to decontrol copper and let the world market fix the price."[7] Latin American nationalism had to learn elementary economic truths.

Mann feared an economic domino effect, and he moved to reinforce the dominoes. The "confiscation" of U.S. property was dangerous, he recalled, because "this would lead to confiscatory measures and semi- or quasi-confiscatory measures in other countries in the world." He especially condemned the "Mexican oil monopoly which is confiscated from American and other foreign interests." It "was an indirect encouragement [to others for] the same thing." Mexico actually expropriated (i.e., paid a settlement for) the U.S. oil holdings and did not confiscate (or simply seize) them. By 1949, the Mexicans even were contracting with private U.S. firms for exploration and drilling. But when Mexico asked for a loan to develop its oil industry in 1950, Mann advised President Harry S. Truman to reject it on both political and economic grounds. Because "experience elsewhere (as in Venezuela and the Middle East) indicates that this is a job for private enterprise," Mann believed, Mexico should be forced to give concessions to private oil firms in return for the loan. Truman at first demurred, but after the Korean War began and U.S. funds were squeezed, he acquiesced. Mann also acted to prevent a first domino from falling. When Brazil applied for a $350 million Export-Import Bank loan in 1953, State Department pursewatchers recommended a token $100 million. Mann successfully urged the new secretary of state, John Foster Dulles, to give $300 million, not only because Brazil was "our traditional and principal ally in the inter-American system" but because a refusal created "a serious risk that Brazil will become more nationalistic."[8]

Bolivia provided the best example of how Mann and his colleagues caught and controlled one pivotal domino in midfall. With its economy totally dependent on three giant tin-producing mines and world tin prices, Bolivia sank toward chaos as tin prices dropped in 1951. As part of its Korean War economic policy, the U.S. government used its awesome purchasing power to drive down world tin prices and hence obtain cheaper metal for its war industries. Mann begged that the policy be reversed before the Latin Americans, who believed they were "exploited as 'economic colonies,'" sank into revolution or formed anti-Yankee cartels. It was too late. In April 1952, the MNR party (Movimiento Nacionalista Revolutionario) took power after two days of fighting in Bolivia. A conglomeration ranging from former and present Communists to pro-Fascist army officers, the MNR disbanded the army, began dismantling the feudal land system, and nationalized the tin mines. It appeared to be the most revolutionary Latin American movement since Mexico had erupted forty years earlier. After six months of careful watching, the United States recognized the new government, then stunned observers by actually giving economic aid, especially through tin purchases. Mann privately explained why aid could be sent to supposed revolutionaries: Bolivia had agreed to compensate the former tin owners, especially the relatively few American owners, through arbitration; such arbitration could be a most important precedent elsewhere in case of other nationalization; if Washington did not help, it would be charged with trying "to bring chaos and starvation to Bolivia"; and U.S. bargaining leverage over Bolivia was great because of its purchasing power in the tin markets. If, moreover, the MNR regime fell, "it would probably be replaced by a government of even more pronounced leftist leanings." Mann's reasoning was followed. U.S. economic aid flowed, the Bolivian revolution stagnated into failure, and in 1964, the MNR was overthrown. Bolivia moved sharply to the Right. This particular nationalist domino never fell.[9]

In late 1952, as the newly elected Eisenhower administration prepared to move into power, Mann sent the White House a forty-two-page analysis of "our situation in Latin America." The document perhaps was intended to do for that "situation" what George Kennan—Mr. "X"—had done six years earlier for U.S.–Soviet relations, that is, provide a fresh analysis and a set of solutions for complex and confusing problems. Mann began by acknowledging U.S. power: "The most conspicuous physical characteristic of the Western Hemisphere is its isolation from other major landmasses; its salient political feature is the predominance of the United States." Thus the problem was not, as in Asia or Central Europe, the threat of Communist invasion. The problem was instead to strengthen the U.S. hold for "security, political, and economic reasons," including access to "readily accessible essential strategic materials." Mann noted that 100 percent of vanadium imports and more than 80 percent of crude petroleum imports came from Latin America. Moreover, "in 1950 Latin America purchased about $2.7 billion of United States goods; by comparison, United States exports to Western Europe . . . were valued at $2.9 billion," and $2 billion of that was "financed out of Marshall Plan funds." U.S. direct investment in the area was about $6 billion (compared with $4.6 billion everywhere else except Canada), and most of the money was in oil and vital minerals.[10] North America and South America, in other words, were forming a natural economic unit on which U.S. prosperity and security largely rested.

The "basic problems," Mann continued, were both demagogic Latin American demands "for immediate reform" and "a great disparity in wealth and power" that kept "alive anti-Americanism and stimulates economic nationalism." Communism simply "exploits" such conditions. When he listed specific "problems," Mann started with "Argentine nationalism in its present form of Peronism" that was trying to destroy "the inter-American system" and form an "anti-American bloc." After Peronism, Mann listed "infiltration of Communists" and "a threatened increase in the tempo of nationalization of foreign-owned properties." Because the United States produced 90 percent of the hemisphere's wealth, it was a most inviting target. Washington had made life even more difficult for itself by correctly accepting "the principles of non-intervention and juridical equality." This acceptance had "the effect of giving to Latin Americans a new sense of power and security which greatly complicated our ability to use our superior military and economic strength and reduce[d] our bargaining power."[11]

Mann then faced squarely the possibility that, confronted with threatening nationalisms and communism, the United States might have to ditch the Good Neighbor policy and return to direct interventionism. He defined two special conditions under which such intervention would be justified: "if a clearly Communist regime should establish itself in the hemisphere" and if intervention was by "multilateral action by the inter-American system." The latter, he admitted, was improbable because Latin Americans, from bitter experience with the U.S. military, had learned to fear even "limited multilateral intervention." Such intervention, moreover, could be too easily controlled by the northern giant. As for the former condition, any appearance of communism was apparently to be assumed to be under external control and not indigenous. Mann was direct: Latins must understand the United States would react and that their "own self-interest is best served by cooperating with us. In doing so, our purpose should be to arrest the development of irresponsibility and extreme nationalism and their belief in their immunity from the exercise of United States power."[12]

Specifically, the United States had the right to protect its investments, including those in strategic materials, "against abuses and discrimination which are the product of extreme nationalism." He hoped this protection could be found through "pressures" exerted by the State Department and "cooperation of the business concerns discriminated against." Otherwise, a domino effect could occur. If, for example, Venezuela succeeded in nationalizing its oil, "the temptation for other countries to follow suit might be considerable." The solutions included top-level attention to Latin Americans; strengthening an inter-American system that institutionalized U.S. interests and power; an increase in the grant aid given the region; "primary reliance on private capital to finance Latin America's economic development"; and a battering down of nationalist barriers that discriminated against private capital. Of special importance, "extremists" in Brazil ("our traditional ally") and the "extreme nationalism" in Argentina had to receive priority attention.[13]

Mann's analysis anticipated and elaborated key points of NSC 144/1 of March 18, 1953, which stated in top secret form the Eisenhower administration's initial Latin American policy. He realized, no doubt more than the incoming officials, that the Good Neighbor had outlived its usefulness. The stakes, especially economic access and strategic routes, were simply too high in a long cold war where the future of the U.S. system depended on an orderly, cooperative home hemisphere and on the raw materials needed to wage the struggle and maintain that system's prosperity. Given such stakes, ultra-nationalism and the less-threatening communism (which Mann's analysis mentioned as specifically causing problems in Guatemala) could not be tolerated. Contrary to the Good Neighbor policy, direct U.S. intervention had not only become thinkable but Mann had moved ahead to define the conditions for such intervention. After all, as he wrote to a colleague in September 1954, "It is literally true that economic stability and progress, on the one hand, and political stability, on the other, are indivisible."[14] Political stability in Mann's mind meant an absence of ultra-nationalism in any form.

He now thought of himself as a nonpartisan professional, "sort of like the Army and Navy," who had no intention of leaving government just because Republicans replaced Democrats in power. He later observed that in 1953, State Department officials were termed "Truman Democrats," and in 1961, the same people were "accused of being 'Eisenhower appointee[s].' . . . It's really absurd." Mann thought himself above such bickering, but he also saw firsthand the State Department casualties of the McCarthyite witchhunts of 1950–1954. Remembering later that he got "fed up with all the McCarthy stuff," Mann asked for an overseas post and became counselor of the U.S. embassy in Athens, Greece. He oversaw the pumping in of dollars to maintain a conservative regime that had been saved from Communist-supported rebels between 1947 and 1949. Greece, indeed, had become the first success of Truman's containment policy. It turned out to be appropriate training for his next Latin American assignment. In September 1954, Secretary of State Dulles ordered Mann to Guatemala. Just three months before, a CIA-directed group of rather bedraggled Guatemalan exiles had managed to overthrow the elected government of Jacobo Arbenz, who, Eisenhower and Dulles had concluded, was tolerating a Communist takeover of Guatemala.[15]

Mann knew the situation intimately. Indeed, between 1950 and 1953, his reaction to Arbenz is a case study of the stages through which U.S. policy passed on its way to direct, if supposedly covert, intervention. The 1944 revolt that overthrew a Guatemalan dictatorship and instituted perhaps the most liberal system in the region had been welcomed in Washington. By 1950, however, the State Department so feared the growing "influence of Communists and extremists" that Mann, the director of Middle America Affairs, set out to isolate the Communists by warning "moderate groups," including the army, of the possible harm to U.S.–Guatemalan relations. This policy of divide and conquer seemed to be working until the newly elected Arbenz took office in 1951. After attending the inaugural ceremony, Mann concluded that the new president was a Marxist. Moreover, top officials of the United Fruit Company (UFCO), long the dominant economic force in Guatemala and now feeling the heat of Arbenz's reforms, worked on Mann. Thomas ("The Cork") Corcoran, a powerful Washington power broker since the early New Deal and now a UFCO lobbyist, warned Mann in 1951 that the U.S. companies intended "to bring the moderate elements to power in Guatemala." Mann had to tolerate the well-connected Corcoran, but he had less use for other UFCO officials, who seemed arrogant and crude. When one official complained that Arbenz refused to give guarantees that Guatemala would pass no law for three years which increased UFCO's costs, Mann drily observed that such a demand possibly conflicted "with the government's sovereign rights." The UFCO execu-

tive replied that he failed to see the conflict. Mann then urged UFCO
to publish its financial figures and even consider following the decision of U.S. oil companies in Venezuela to divide net profits fifty-fifty
with the government. Such actions could undercut "demagogues"
and "make the company's and the Government's interests mutual."
The apparently stunned executives made no response to Mann's attempt to educate them.[16]

He cared less about UFCO's problems than he did about how Guatemala's growing Communist strength could set a dangerous example. After all, "Latin America is in the throes of a social revolution," the deputy assistant secretary of state for Inter-American
Affairs told twenty-one top U.S. officials in June 1951. With the failure
of the divide-and-conquer approach, it was necessary to move to the
next level—economic pressures. "Mr. Mann felt the economic pressures would be effective since 85 percent of Guatemala's exports are
sold in this country and 85 percent of their imports come from the
United States," recorded the minutes of the meeting. There was,
however, a slight problem: "He [Mann] emphasized that we should
proceed quietly since this proposed policy is, in effect, a violation of
the Non-intervention Agreement [of 1947] to which we are a party.
He pointed out that this policy has a risk involved, because the Non-
intervention Agreement is a corner-stone of our Latin American
policy." Any revelation of this violation "would strengthen the hands
of the nationalists and communists in that country. He pointed out
that these proposed actions would be the first of its kind since the
establishment of the Good Neighbor policy." Mann had a sense about
history as well as about "nationalists."[17]

The stakes in Guatemala were rising. By late 1951, they seemed to
be nothing less than how U.S. corporations were to be treated
throughout the Southern Hemisphere. "[I]f the experiment [sic] in
Guatemala should be successful," he told a U.S. owner of Guatemalan power plants, "it should have a salutary effect on the way in
which all countries in Latin America, not only Guatemala, treated
United States business interests." Arbenz was to be a lesson for other
overly enthusiastic nationalists. But the economic sanctions failed to
work. U.S. assistance stopped, but no way could be found to shut off
Guatemala's profitable coffee exports. Mann and other officials, moreover, did not want to move too fast. When they learned that Nicaraguan dictator Anastasio Somoza was ready to attack Arbenz militarily
and wanted only a green light from Washington, Mann told Nicaragua to back away: "non-intervention was one of the very keystones
of the Inter-American system," and, after all, American troops were
dying in Korea "for the non-aggression principle."[18]

Mann and U.S. policy toward Guatemala seemed boxed in. As he repeatedly pointed out, direct intervention could wreck the inter-American system. But weapons short of that failed to work. Arbenz, moreover, was not the usual Latin American *caudillo* but a constitutionally elected president of an increasingly liberal nation—a problem that reportedly led Mann to conclude privately that Washington should not "support all constitutional governments under all circumstances." On February 26, 1953, Arbenz greeted the new Eisenhower team by expropriating 234,000 acres, largely vacant, of UFCO land for redistribution. Eisenhower ordered the CIA operation to be prepared. It was executed under cover of an OAS resolution, passed at Caracas in March 1954, declaring that a Communist-controlled or Communist-dominated government posed a threat to the American states. (Mexico and Argentina abstained on the vote; Guatemala opposed.) Mann was now stationed in Athens. He returned after Arbenz, deserted by the Guatemalan army, fled into exile in June 1954. Determined to make Guatemala a shining example of the good things that came to those who cooperated with him in rejecting radicalism, Secretary of State Dulles called Norman Armour, one of the most respected U.S. diplomats, out of retirement to lead the U.S. embassy in Guatemala City. But Dulles knew the real work would be done by Mann, the new second in command.[19]

Mann found a confused, corrupt Guatemala presided over by the CIA's handpicked leader, Colonel Carlos Castillo Armas. The key to success was a quick economic upturn, for, as Mann wrote a State Department friend, "economic stability and progress, on the one hand, and political stability, on the other, are indivisible." Coffee prices were good, and Castillo Armas was nothing if not cooperative. When one of his advisers wrote a new oil law, the United States objected because it "would logically obstruct the entry of responsible oil companies into the local field." Castillo Armas saw the light: "Mr. Mann had criticized it," and so the colonel "was rejecting it." There would be "no final decision without consulting with Mr. Mann," the Guatemalan president promised. The question of Castillo Armas's "handling the army," Mann told the State Department, "was the only one in which the Embassy had not become involved." But then the embassy did not have to be involved; Guatemala's army was totally dependent on U.S. training and aid. The best of intentions and the greatest of leverage, however, were not enough. By April 1955, Mann described Guatemalan politics as an "incredible maze of intrigue, fathered by ignorance, inexperience, and native suspicion." That same month, Mann reported that the country's internal indebtedness, already boosted to $50 million by Arbenz's reforms, was rising as business slumped. The country's international reserves dropped to a crisis level. U.S. grant aid tripled in 1956 to $14 million as Dulles warned Castillo Armas that Guatemala must be "an example . . . to the free world of the success of a people in recovering after a period of Communist rule." But to no avail. The colonel was so inept, the CIA reported in 1956, that the Communist party "seem[ed] to be well on its way toward recovery." Mann had been promoted to ambassador to El Salvador in 1955, but he kept close watch on neighboring Guatemala. In 1957, he reported that opposition movements had "been put down with bloodshed. Leaders of opposition are in exile." In July 1957, Castillo Armas was shot by a member of his own guard. Subsequently, the country sank into more than thirty-five years of military rule and internal brutalities that marked it with the worst human rights record in the hemisphere.[20]

That same year, 1957, Mann returned home to become assistant secretary of state for economic affairs. He arrived to find that Central America's overwhelming economic problems, and the ultra-nationalisms they produced, had become the hemisphere's problems. An economic downturn, triggered by a U.S. recession in 1957–58, squeezed Latin America as if in a vise. The Southern Hemisphere's raw materials plummeted in value at the same time foreign investment capital dried up (and, in large amounts, moved instead into the new, rich, and stable Western European Common Market). Until the late 1950s, Washington thought it ensured stability by working closely with military dictators in the region. During the 1957–1960 years, several of the most important were replaced by democratic, nationalist regimes. The new leaders found their nations' urban slums filling with the world's fastest population growth, their extractive industries in decline, and the gap between their rich and poor greater than in any other Third World region. U.S. economic leverage remained impressive (its private companies alone accounted for 10% of Latin America's gross national product and 30% of its exports), but Yankee capitalism, its Latin American associates, and the remnants of the Good Neighbor policy were not doing the job. The region's demands and its nationalism rose as economies declined. All this occurred, moreover, as the Soviet Union's growth rate (and its attention to Third World demands) rose faster than did the rate of the U.S. gross national product. Dulles told the cabinet in January 1958 that Soviet leader Nikita Khrushchev had declared "economic war." The crisis became vivid later that year when Vice President Richard Nixon visited key Latin American nations, was met by mobs and spit, and nearly had to be rescued from Venezuelan protestors by U.S. paratroops.[21]

Mann, however, confronted a greater long-term danger on his return to Washington. If remedies were not quickly found, Latin Americans would turn inward, seek state-directed solutions, and begin import-substitution measures that cut off U.S. exports. In other words, their neighbors would attempt to create more self-sufficient national blocs. With antennae tuned to precisely this problem since the early 1940s, Mann publicly defined the crisis in speeches during early 1958. Outlining the U.S. economic downturn, then explaining Latin American dependence on northern capital and trade, he concluded that Washington's economic policy had to have three objectives: to promote U.S. economic power, to promote the "economic strength of the rest of the free world," and to "build and maintain cohesion in the free world. These parts of our policy," he added, "are inseparable." "Cohesion" clearly meant cooperation, openness, and the opposite of nationalism. He followed up by devising and/or implementing policies designed to destroy Latin American plans for autarchy. He began by pushing for a renewal of that traditional New Deal approach, multilateral reciprocal trade agreements.[22]

The Good Neighbor's tactics, however, were no longer enough. Mann worked hard to pass the Development Loan Fund (DLF) in Congress during 1957. The DLF provided long-term, low-interest loans repayable in either local currencies or dollars. It was a breakthrough in U.S. aid policy. More pointedly, it was an admission that private capital could not handle the growing crisis. Mann, no doubt swallowing hard, then successfully pushed for commodity agreements that stabilized slumping coffee prices. He hated to tamper so with the marketplace, but he later rationalized the deal as "bad principle but a good thing to do as a temporary tactic." *Time* magazine later claimed that Mann brought the crucial U.S. involvement into the coffee agreement "almost singlehandedly" over the free-marketeer objections of Eisenhower's other advisers. Finally, he helped create the Inter-American Development Bank (IADB) in 1958–59, a lending institution the southern neighbors had long demanded. As the largest contributor, the United States controlled the $1 billion fund of the IADB, but its great virtue, as Mann understood, was that it could intervene in, and demand certain obligations from, Latin American economies under a multilateral guise. No longer would lone U.S. efforts to make southern borrowers behave properly have to take all the heat generated by nationalists.[23]

These new policies, it must be emphasized, had begun to be developed by Mann and his colleagues before Nixon's disastrous trip. They also began before Fidel Castro materialized in Cuba on January 1,

1959, like Marley's ghost, to haunt U.S. officials with Washington's policies past. Castro represented a different kind of nationalism. Mann and other U.S. officials initially responded not to Castro's early, vague Marxism but to a larger failure of U.S. policies that threatened an entire system resting on access to markets and political cooperation among nations that accepted Washington's economic principles— a system, as Mann phrased it, that assumed "cohesion," not autarchic nationalism.[24]

By 1959, the central question was whether the United States would have to save the system by taking the ultimate step, which he called "a Marshall Plan for Latin America." The year before, Brazilian President Juscelino Kubitschek had publicly asked Eisenhower for an "Operation Pan America" that would provide $600 million in economic aid annually so Latin American living standards could rise from $300 to $500 per person within the next two decades. In a cabinet meeting of February 27, 1959, Mann outlined how the Eisenhower administration should respond. He began with a history lesson. The Good Neighbor policy had greatly improved hemispheric relations, but as early as "the middle 1940s the honeymoon was showing signs of strain" over economic problems. "Whatever the cause," he emphasized, "the fact remains that currently, for the first time, a, if not the, primary Latin American objective is economic." The southern neighbors, he continued, demand "a Marshall Plan" and stable raw material prices. "As an alternative," Mann urged greater use of the multilateral banks and the development of a regional common market. If Latin American capitalisms could not work properly within their present small spheres, he seemed to be suggesting, perhaps they could work in a larger arena modeled after the European Common Market or the United States itself. (The regional market idea became a favorite, and also a frustration, of Mann's. Both a Latin American and a Central American common market were created in 1960, but nationalisms tore both apart within a decade.)[25]

Mann then introduced his main theme. Latin Americans first had to help themselves. They especially had to create hospitable conditions for private investment. Obstacles did exist. "The old established order" was unfortunately giving way to "the power of governments and labor unions"; "men of stature and conviction" were "too few" compared with the "vociferous minorities"; grass roots demands overloaded the system; and "Latin American intellectuals" made their living by unfairly blaming their own nation's sins on U.S. and European capital "exploitation." "We know," Mann told the cabinet (once described by a journalist as being made up of 9 millionaires and a plumber), "that Wall Street is seldom popular on Main Street." This did not mean that Main Street was correct. To the contrary, the Latin American "rationalizations are, in the main, false." The future had to rest on the private capital of Wall Street. The alternative, Mann stressed, was a massive government-to-government aid program that the U.S. Congress—burdened with possible deficits, military spending, and domestic demands—could never sustain, "or, equally important," the program would fail because Latin "governments would not find it politically possible to ask commensurate sacrifices of their people." Latin Americans, he warned, "would later feel themselves deceived."[26]

Mann had outlined the decline and fall of the Good Neighbor, relentlessly followed out the logic of his own post-1940s views, and warned, accurately, that a program resembling the later Alliance for Progress would not only fail but perhaps be a disaster for hemisphere relations. Yet more had to be done, quickly. In May 1959, he flew to an OAS meeting in Buenos Aires and barely stopped a Castro-sponsored proposal that the United States, for its past misdeeds, should create a $30 billion hemispheric aid program. "We are thinking," Mann responded with some consistency, "in terms of interdependence rather than the dependence on any one state or another." A year later at Bogotá, Colombia, Mann's boss, Undersecretary of State Douglas Dillon, went part of the way. He proposed a plan for social development that required tax, land, and especially health and education reforms in Latin America. Dillon offered $500 million in soft loans to fund the reforms. Back home, President Eisenhower carefully explained that perhaps "additional sums" would be necessary, but he was not thinking of "anything . . . remotely resembling the Marshall Plan." In the "long run," he added, the useful funds had to be "private investment." "Normally" the new "public loans" were only made "to encourage and make better opportunities for the private investments that follow." Perhaps to cover his new bet, Eisenhower tightened U.S. ties with Latin American armies by raising military aid from $38 million in 1951 to $67 million in 1959 and by asking Congress for $96.5 million in the 1960 fiscal year.[27]

To make this point clearer about the importance of private funds, Eisenhower named Mann assistant secretary of state for inter-American affairs. In an unusual move, the White House called a press conference to announce Mann's elevation. When a reporter asked whether Mann's expertise in economics was a major reason for the appointment, Press Secretary James Hagerty responded, "That would be correct." The Texan thus occupied a pivotal post when John F.

Kennedy's New Frontiersmen moved into power during early 1961. Mann thought he would be posted overseas, or perhaps leave Washington to make money in the private sector, but Kennedy sent Vice President Lyndon Johnson—a fellow Texan but not a personal friend of the assistant secretary's—to convince Mann that if he remained a while, he could later become ambassador to Mexico.[28]

Big plans were forming. In March 1961, Kennedy announced a ten-year Alliance for Progress to which the United States would contribute as much as $10 billion each year to raise growth rates dramatically and create a large, democratic middle class in Latin America. In return, the southern neighbors would be expected to undertake massive tax and land reforms to make their societies more equitable and to contribute about 80 percent of the needed funds themselves. Accompanied by the early New Frontier's usual blare of trumpets and overoptimism, the Alliance seemed to be exactly what Mann had warned the Eisenhower cabinet against in early 1959. He later saw little difference between Kennedy's actual performance in the Alliance and Eisenhower's Bogotá program of 1960. But "the rhetoric was entirely different," even "to an unrealistic extent." To think, as some New Frontiersmen did, that Latin American problems "would be solved in ten years" was "patently absurd." U.S. officials, Mann recalled, too easily fell into the habit of calling their policies revolutionary: "We here in this country refer to nearly everything as a revolution, from the Industrial Revolution down." Kennedy had even said that under the Alliance, "every American Republic will be the master of its own revolution." But Mann feared that Latin Americans had a quite different view, for to them, "I'm convinced . . . , revolution means blood in the streets and shooting." "I never believed we should compete with revolutionaries," Mann recalled. Quite clearly, his emphasis on private investments, common markets, and soft rhetoric was unrevolutionary. He especially opposed holding out promises of vast land reform. It was not only that the U.S. Congress would never spend public funds for massive land redistribution (and it never would). It was not only that the Alliance's rhetoric held out unrealizable hopes that could only frustrate and even radicalize landless peasants. It was also, in Mann's view, that "confiscation" of land was wrong and that redistributing it to small farmers who lacked credit, training, and skills ensured a lethal failure for a nation's productivity and political stability.[29]

He also harbored doubts about a second, more secret Kennedy project—armed intervention to overthrow Castro's regime in Cuba. By mid-1960, U.S.–Cuban relations had reached a breaking point because of intense Washington opposition to Castro's growing ties with the Soviet Union, seizing of private property, and squeezing out more pro-U.S. advisers. Mann and his colleagues finally resorted in 1960 to cutting off all exports to Cuba except food and medicine. They also virtually stopped Cuba's vital sugar exports to the United States. These actions, as the earlier sanctions against Arbenz's Guatemala, could be interpreted to violate the OAS charter's provision that "no state may use or encourage the use of coercive measures of an economic or political character in order to force the sovereign will of another state." Mann's office responded disingenuously that it really was not trying to "coerce" Castro, then pointed to the 1954 Caracas declaration that the United States had the right to protect its neighbors "against the intervention of international communism."[30]

Truth be told, Mann seemed to be in continuing agony over the question of intervention. At least since the early 1950s, he had made public and private statements that tried to sort out the question. He especially tried to reconcile the promise of the Good Neighbor, and the solemn U.S. pledges in the OAS charter about nonintervention, with the need to save Latin Americans from "dictators," especially of the Communist variety, when the Latin Americans seemed incapable of saving themselves. In a November 1960 speech that resembled a cry from the heart as well as a rationalization for conservative approaches, Mann demanded to know, how "can anyone correctly claim that the United States is responsible for dictators in other countries when Latin American states regard the nonintervention principle as essential to good relations with the United States . . . and when this obligation is held by Latin America to override other obligations concerning democracy?"[31] Communism in Cuba was different, however. The 1954 Caracas resolution could be used to demonstrate that difference. The 1954 Guatemalan operation, moreover, could be repeated to solve the problem and cut through the frustrations imposed during that earlier and different era of the Good Neighbor.

Eisenhower and the CIA originated a small invasion plan using 300 men in March 1960. Mann later declared he knew nothing of it until the autumn, a strange situation for the top, highly trusted Eisenhower policymaker on Latin America. The plan changed several times until it involved 800 to 1,500 Cuban exiles, trained and directed by the CIA, who would land on the island and either wait for the Cuban people to rally around and overthrow Castro or, with U.S. help, destroy Castro's forces directly. Eisenhower never fully endorsed the operation. At least by early 1961 when Kennedy inherited the plan,

Mann had questioned both CIA assumptions. Indeed, as Kennedy was told, Mann and the top CIA planner, Richard Bissell, were the "real antagonists" in the debate. A popular uprising, Mann believed, was "unlikely." (Or as he phrased it later, the CIA plan foolishly assumed "an uprising of the Cuban people, sort of 1776 style, where everybody grabbed a musket and went out.") Any direct U.S. military intervention could wreck the inter-American system. In top secret meetings, Mann led the attack that destroyed the CIA's plan to seize a landing strip that would allow large, highly visible, U.S. Air Force assistance to the invasion force.[32]

The logic of Mann's position seemed to dictate opposition to the entire operation. He did not believe the Cuban people would rise up against Castro. He was convinced that only direct U.S. power could assure victory, but he opposed the use of such power. Mann nevertheless reluctantly went along with Kennedy's final decision to land 1,500 exiles at Cuba's Bay of Pigs without direct U.S. support. He did so because of his intense frustration with Castro and the Good Neighbor–OAS restraints. He also went along because the 1954 operation had succeeded in overthrowing Arbenz; it seemed the same team of operatives, including Mann, was running the Cuban plan. At the climactic decision-making meeting on April 4, 1961, only Senator J. William Fulbright (D.-Ark.) fervently opposed the landing. As part of a solid proinvasion State Department group, Mann half-heartedly agreed to the operation because, he claimed, the plan was so far advanced and, moreover, this could be the last chance to destroy Castro. The invasion of April 17, 1961, turned out to be "the perfect failure," as it was soon labeled. There was no uprising. Castro's forces quickly killed or captured 1,300 of the 1,500-man exile force. Mann's reasoning up to his illogical conclusion had been admirable, but he later drew another questionable conclusion: "In retrospect I would never again vote for any large clandestine operation because . . . you can't keep anything secret in our society." Secrecy was certainly not the main problem. Four years later, however, Mann did follow a quite different path of intervention into the Dominican Republic, and his hopes for the inter-American system were destroyed.[33]

Between the two invasions, Mann served as ambassador to Mexico. He resigned his top State Department post in early April 1961 so he would not arrive in Mexico City visibly tarred by the residue of the Bay of Pigs. He nevertheless had continued to participate in the planning. It was therefore ironic that the Senate internal security subcommittee, in one of its periodic witchhunts, charged him both with being "duped" by Castro and losing Latin America to communism.

Mann found that such charges did not necessarily hurt him in his new post. Mexico, despite qualms about the growing Soviet–Cuban links, acted as Castro's strongest Latin American advocate. With their constantly refreshed memories of 1846–1848 and 1914–1917 when U.S. troops invaded their country, Mexicans, in Mann's words, were "the foremost champions of the non-intervention policy. . . . In fact, that's the cardinal point in their foreign policy." His growing differences with that "cardinal point" never appeared publicly because, as a practical, professional diplomat, he kept the differences behind the closed doors when he talked with Mexican officials. Having little liking for most journalists, neither did he have much affection for pro-Alliance liberals such as White House official Richard Goodwin, who flew to Mexico City and apparently asked Mann to invite some leftists to the embassy. Mann refused: "Not in my house. There were a lot of restaurants. . . . They could meet somewhere else." When the president's youngest brother, Edward Kennedy (then running for the U.S. Senate), arrived in Mexico to debate leftists at the embassy, Mann apparently handled the request the same way with the same results. He had no intention of giving such Mexican figures any "respectability," and if any visitor thought he was "accomplishing anything" by talking with such people, he was "whistling Dixie." Mann preferred the leaders of Mexico's one-party state, where the single party kept "balance between the left and the right. And I have always thought this was a pretty sensible thing to do," the ambassador recalled, "instead of polarizing and letting the two extremes go at each other." Such understanding paid off. Mann successfully ended a decades-long border dispute between the two nations by negotiating the Chamizal Treaty that ceded a section of El Paso, Texas, to Mexico.[34]

U.S.–Mexican relations were never better than in late 1963 when Lyndon B. Johnson replaced the slain John Kennedy. But the president realized that the Alliance for Progress was failing. Unable to reach planned 1963–64 growth targets, torn in Latin America by military takeovers and civil wars, divided in Washington by bureaucratic warfare and congressional skepticism, the Alliance, in the words of one LBJ adviser, "was a thoroughgoing mess." The inter-American system bitterly divided over how to handle Castro. Mann had warned of all this years before. Johnson, whose memory was legendary, no doubt recalled those warnings. The ambassador's quiet diplomacy had scored successes in Mexico, the one Latin American nation the president believed he knew intimately. Mann, moreover, "not only didn't have charisma," a Washington journalist observed, "he didn't believe in it." He knew his place as a professional diplomat. Johnson liked that humility in his State Department officials. The president also liked to show his independence of the Kennedys and their failing policies whenever politically possible. In Vietnam, where Kennedy had committed 16,000 troops, it was not possible. In Latin America, however, it was, and it was possible to do so in a way that sent warnings across the Washington bureaucracy that Johnson was going to run a tight ship whose captain was clearly recognizable.[35]

On December 14, 1963, the president named Mann assistant secretary of state for inter-American affairs. Four days later, he named him special assistant to the president. "We expect to speak with one voice in all matters affecting the hemisphere," LBJ announced. Nine days later, Mann became head of the Agency for International Development (AID), which ran the Alliance for Progress. The Kennedys and their supporters were stunned and bitter. Key liberals such as Senator Hubert Humphrey (D.-Minn.) tried to prevent the appointments. LBJ paid no attention. U.S. corporations operating in Latin America were delighted. "The news of Tom Mann's appointment created more favorable reaction in Latin America than the launching of President Roosevelt's Good Neighbor policy," cabled the vice president for Brown and Root Overseas, Inc., a powerful Texas firm with close ties to Johnson. "I know him well and consider him the greatest." Some liberals, including Senator Ernest Gruening (D.-Alaska) applauded the appointments in the hope that Mann could finally make Latin American policy work.[36]

Mann intended to accomplish that by doing away with much of the original Alliance. He had analyzed the problems in several speeches during 1963. In a Mexico City address, he set the priorities, priorities with which many New Frontiersmen disagreed. The economic ranked above the political:

One cannot imagine that any people will benefit from an equitable distribution of property. It is necessary to think, first, of economic development—of the ways to produce wealth—before theories about the distribution of that wealth become meaningful. Or, as we say at home, it is necessary to make a mighty big pie before one can distribute large pieces to every member of a large family.[37]

That statement could be read as meaning the United States should be willing to work with any government, democratic or not, as long as it promised to make a larger "pie." In the same speech, Mann gave instructions about the pie's ingredients. "Mercantilism has failed," now as it had in the eighteenth century. Statist controls were as ineffective now as they were then and had to give way to "economic freedom." Mann was not merely giving a history lesson. Four months after he took over the nation's Latin American policies, a CIA analysis warned that "statism (state capital) is probably growing in the area" and that, consequently, except for Venezuela and Mexico, "the climate for private investment, domestic and foreign," was deteriorating. Castro's example was dangerous: Latin America was watching Cuba's "almost total state socialism," and if it were at all successful, it could "have an extensive impact on the statist trend elsewhere in the area." Quite clearly, Castro's threat went beyond the Soviet strategic threat.[38]

It was precisely the danger Mann had been warning of since the 1940s, long before communism had posed any threat to the inter-American system. He had barely returned to Washington when he declared that two kinds of Latin American nationalism existed. One was good and meant "knowing who you are and what your country stands for." One, however, was bad: "xenophobic nationalism" that "can impede the achievement of the *Alianza* goals" by rejecting the idea "that their country's interests lie on a parallel course with another—like ours." All these ideas came together in Mann's off-the-record speech of March 18, 1964, to U.S. officials serving in Latin America. Its main points were leaked and reported by Tad Szulc in the next day's *New York Times*. Mann never mentioned the Alliance. The story's headlines outlined his argument: "U.S. May Abandon Efforts to Deter Dictators. Mann Is Said to be Against Trying to Separate 'Good Guys and Bad Guys.'" Tellingly, Mann went back to the 1930s to point out that even FDR had failed to prevent or unseat dictatorships such as Perón's and Somoza's. Instead, he continued, U.S. policies must have four objectives: "economic growth . . . , the protection of $9 billion in United States investments there, non-intervention in the internal political affairs of the hemisphere's republics, and opposition to Communism." That the second and fourth objective could contradict the third did not have to be emphasized. Szulc added that the speech was seen in Washington as a "radical modification" of Kennedy's emphasis on democracy moving hand in hand with economic and social development. Mann was even quoted as saying that he saw no difference between the elected president of Mexico and the military dictator of Paraguay.[39]

This "Mann Doctrine," as it became known, and the policies that followed became significant in the history of U.S.–Latin American relations for a number of reasons. First and of special importance, Mann had cut through the problem that bedeviled U.S. officials since at least the time of Woodrow Wilson's emphasis on democracy and

Wilson's determination to teach Latin Americans "to elect good men." The problem was, how could North Americans ever implant their idea of democracy in Latin America without being blatant, and too often armed, imperialists? For sixty years, Mexico and Argentina had led their neighbors against this Wilsonianism. U.S.–Latin American ties had suffered, but democracy advanced little, if at all, it seemed. Mann was now proposing a policy many Latin governments, including the most progressive, had long desired: the halt of U.S. interventionism on behalf of supposed democratic processes that had too often helped destroy, not advance, those processes. Mann, of course, was questioning Kennedy as well as Wilson. It was even reported that he called Kennedy's beloved Peace Corps "a cliché."[40]

But second, Mann carefully indicated that under one condition, a Communist threat, the United States would intervene. He had pondered the question of intervention for years and now came out with half a Good Neighbor policy: noninterference against military dictatorships that promised stability, U.S. access to economic resources, and strategic cooperation but interference against Communist regimes that offered only the first virtue. This formulation seemed to leave in limbo what Mann had called "ultra-nationalists," such as Perón. But not in reality. Mann's emphasis on the protection of U.S. investments, and his stress in other recent speeches that "statism" threatened such interests, left room for dealing with future Peróns as well as Castros.

Third, Mann had given fair warning that he was going to take a personally uncharacteristically public hard line against governments that opposed the hemispheric system as he had long conceived it—open, controlled by private capital, and free of "mercantilist" apparatus. His reputation mushroomed to the extent that McGeorge Bundy, Johnson's national security adviser, warned the president that Mann's speeches had to be carefully monitored because his "hard line," even if "sound," too often emerged. It provided opportunities for those "too willing to paint him unjustifiably as a reactionary," Bundy added. One opportunity arose in June 1964 when Mann gave the commencement address at Notre Dame. Emphasizing U.S. intentions to discourage the overthrow of "constitutionally elected governments," he then detailed (quoting a favorite reference, Arthur Whitaker's *The Western Hemisphere Idea*) how Washington's attempts since Theodore Roosevelt and Woodrow Wilson to instill order had only turned Latin Americans against the United States. Mann even twisted history with an insouciance that had to be admired by arguing that in 1954 "the Guatemalan people" had acclaimed Castillo Armas's overthrow of the elected Arbenz government; therefore Washington had no business trying "to restore a Marxist-Leninist [Arbenz] to power against the will of the Guatemalan people." The CIA's role was not mentioned. In a September 1964 speech in Houston, Mann said much about Latin Americans having to "reorganize their own societies and economies . . . in ways which open the door to growth" but very little about how that "growth" might be distributed. If Kennedy's unrealistic idealism marked the first three years of the Alliance, Mann's overrealistic hard line shaped the next three until the original Alliance existed only in form (the commitment to growth), not in spirit (the commitment to reform and equity). In late 1965, Johnson gave the Alliance a surprising boost by pledging U.S. support after 1971, but it was a promise that never had to be fulfilled.[41]

Fourth, Mann meant what he implied in his March 18 remarks when he juxtaposed an emphasis on economic growth with an emphasis on private capital. Working closely with David Rockefeller (chair of Chase Manhattan Bank) and business leaders of thirty-eight other companies belonging to Rockefeller's Business Group for Latin America, Johnson, at Mann's suggestion, told them, "In no other sector of foreign policy is understanding and cooperation so important between business communities and the U.S. government." In 1965, the democratic presidents of Chile and Peru pleaded with Mann to create a reserve fund to guarantee Latin American agrarian reform bonds. Mann and Johnson rejected the plea and instead hoped that private capital would somehow do the job. Felipe Herrara, president of the Inter-American Development Bank, later testified how Washington's policy changed after 1964 to restrict drastically both U.S. contributions and Latin American access to the IADB. The switch, Herrara thought, was partly due to the worsening U.S. balance of payments. But Mann meanwhile encouraged private capital to move south. And he could be more direct, even brutal, when U.S. capital was threatened. In Peru, Fernando Belaunde, elected to replace a discredited military regime, was committed to agrarian and other reforms. Belaunde clashed with International Petroleum Company (IPC), a Standard Oil of New Jersey subsidiary. When IPC wanted new oil field rights, Belaunde asked for subsoil rights and back taxes. After Belaunde refused to give ground, Mann cut off all foreign aid to Peru. (In 1968, when the chastened Belaunde surrendered to some IPC demands, he was overthrown and replaced by military rulers who nationalized the oil industry.) Promoted once again by LBJ to undersecretary of state for economic affairs in 1965, Mann gave up his assistant secretary position, but he was in an even more powerful office to supervise proper development policy in Latin America.[42]

Fifth, Mann's dedication to creating stable conditions for private

investment helped lead him to violate his first principle of nonintervention, even in areas where the Communist threat was small, if not
nonexistent. During the 1964 Chilean elections, Mann paid little attention either to that principle or to his lesson, learned during the
Argentine election of 1946, that U. S. interference in foreign political
campaigns usually backfired. Eduardo Frei, a moderate reformer, ran
against Salvador Allende, suspected of Marxist leanings and, as
Mann phrased it, "extremist supporters." The U.S. economic stake
was huge, especially in industry and in copper mines that Washington feared Allende might nationalize if he won. Mann ordered complete support of Frei, threatened economic retaliation if Allende triumphed, and wanted "no doubt in Chile as to where the United
States stands." Frei won, but the Allende problem was only delayed
for six years.[43]

Even more important was Mann's involvement in the 1964 military
overthrow of the civilian government in Brazil, which, as Mann often
observed, had long been the most important U.S. ally in South
America. Brazil was in a bind by 1964, however. A massive development program begun in the late 1950s had angered the rich, unduly
raised expectations of the poor, created rampant inflation, and built a
large foreign debt. Kennedy had tried to help with money and understanding when President João Goulart moved to buy the U.S.-
controlled American and Foreign Power Company. Mann's sympathy
was considerably more restrained. His AID office viewed Goulart as
"an inept president, easily influenced by extreme leftist advisers and
cronies." When Goulart learned of Mann's concerns, he tried to build
support at home by promising reforms, including extensive nationalization, to millions of poor rural Brazilians. That was bad enough,
from Mann's point of view. Equally alarming was Goulart's attempt to
put his own officers in charge of the army. The Brazilian military had
been a special U.S. ally. Washington sent it more assistance in the
early 1960s than it gave to any other Latin American force. When the
threatened military officers decided to overthrow Goulart on March 31,
1964, they received support from disenchanted middle-class Brazilians and also from Mann and U.S. Ambassador Lincoln Gordon. It
was the opportunity to implement the Mann Doctrine announced
just two weeks before: destroy restraints on economic growth
through private help by recognizing the new military regime. And in
this case, it meant ensuring that the military won by encouraging it.
The United States sent a heavy attack aircraft carrier and support
ships to stand off the Brazilian coast, while supplying arms, ammunition, and petroleum to the plotters. The arrangements were made

through Gordon and Gen. Vernon Walters, who knew the Brazilian generals well and later became deputy director of the CIA and U.S. ambassador to the United Nations and to West Germany.[44]

Mann, Gordon, and others later claimed that the military saved Brazil from communism. That can now never be proven one way or another, but no evidence exists that either Goulart or the country was endangered by a Communist takeover. The night before the overthrow, the U.S. House Foreign Affairs Committee released a report that criticized Goulart's tolerance for Communists but concluded "there is little prospect for [a] communist takeover there in the foreseeable future." Secretary of State Dean Rusk, probably after a briefing from Mann, immediately tried to counter the report by telling reporters that Brazil was "increasingly subject to communist influence." That remark helped short-circuit criticism when President Johnson quickly congratulated the victorious generals. But it did not address the more important aspects of U.S. policy. Goulart had challenged not Mann's anticommunism but his belief in the need for more private capital and less statism. In his few months in office, moreover, Mann had systematically undercut Goulart by channeling aid to Brazil's states, not the central government, and had worked closely with, although not instigating, the planned military coup.[45]

The aftershocks were many. Gordon had confidently predicted that the military would soon restore a more sensible civilian rule. Instead, in what they called "Operation Cleanup," the generals arrested thousands of politicians, labor leaders, and intellectuals who were non-Communist. As human rights violations multiplied, Gordon suggested that the State Department explain that a "purge was clearly in order" because Communists had planned to seize power. Mann, however, was preoccupied with larger concerns. As the generals urged private investment and promised effective agrarian reform, he turned back on the aid spigot that poured $1.5 billion in U.S. help over the next four years. The generals' success and the Mann Doctrine's handsome response were also played out in Bolivia and Argentina. In Bolivia, Mann (and key U.S. congressional leaders) became critical of, and began distancing the United States from, Paz Estenssaro's formerly revolutionary MNR party. When the military seized power in 1964, opened the door to foreign investment, promised agrarian reforms, and smashed urban labor demands, Mann responded with aid. At Notre Dame, three months after the Brazilian coup, Mann had declared, "It has long been, and continues to be, our firm policy to discourage any who conspire to overthrow constitutionally elected governments."[46]

During these early months that Mann turned Washington's policy toward the Alliance, Brazil, and Bolivia, he and President Johnson took a historic step to transform sixty years of U.S.–Panama relations. Since 1903, when Theodore Roosevelt's navy helped Panama gain independence from Colombia in return for the right to build an isthmian canal, the United States had unilaterally operated the ten-mile-wide Zone and the waterway that divided the country. In the 1950s, Eisenhower bent to Panamanian demands and agreed to fly both the American and Panamanian flags over public buildings in the Zone. In January 1964, U.S. students ran up only their own flag. Bloody anti-Yankee riots erupted. The riots were fueled by chronic economic problems as well as Panamanian and U.S. patriotism. Mann and Johnson attempted to stop the riots, only to find that President Roberto Chiari demanded a new treaty to replace the 1903 agreement. Johnson, facing an election campaign, refused to agree as long as he believed Chiari was using the riots as a gun to his head. As the death toll reached 20 and casualties climbed to 400, Mann flew to meet with Chiari but could find no agreement. Talks continued while Mann applied pressure by reducing U.S. aid. He had no "wish to even give the appearance of rewarding irresponsibility."[47]

Otherwise, Mann urged Johnson to begin negotiations that would rule out no topic. Such an approach could lead to an entirely new treaty. At one point in March 1964, Mann thought acceptable wording had been found, but at a late Sunday night meeting, Johnson said, "I'm sorry, Tom, but I'm going to have to pull the rug out from under you." Johnson was not going to let "a country the size of St. Louis" (as he once described Panama), complicate his election campaign. Once he won a landslide victory in November 1964, however, Johnson agreed, on December 18, to seek a new treaty that would terminate the 1903 pact and "recognize the sovereignty of Panama" in the Zone while maintaining U.S. rights to use and protect the canal. The two countries thus entered the path to the 1977–78 treaties. Acting usually with restraint, showing patience with both Johnson and Chiari, Mann had succeeded, although he, rather than Johnson, became the lightning rod for critics of U.S. policy toward Panama throughout 1964. But then issues of nationalization, investment, and communism were not involved. Indeed, Mann understood that a new treaty would cost the United States little, while it would effectively neutralize more radical Panamanians.[48]

Such restraint did not mark Mann's policies toward the Dominican Republic. The results were an invasion by 22,000 U.S. troops, the long-term paralysis, if not the near-destruction, of the OAS, the splintering of crucial congressional support for the Johnson administration, and the beginning of the end for Mann's own career. Justified at the time by Mann, Johnson, and other officials as a necessary invasion to prevent another Communist-controlled country in the Caribbean, it had more complex origins. These origins were especially significant because of Mann's desire for order and his growing suspicion of Left-leaning, reform-minded groups, even if they were not Communist controlled. Walt Whitman Rostow, who replaced Bundy as Johnson's national security adviser, later described the Dominican crisis as, "in substance and in timing, a kind of dress rehearsal for the debate on Vietnam." But the crisis also looked back, for the landing of the U.S. troops ended with a crash any pretense that remained of the Good Neighbor policy. A historical era, as well as a career, finally ended when the troops began to land on April 28, 1965.[49]

Throughout the previous year, Mann's growing fear of Castroism had shaped much of his policy. At a National Security Council meeting on February 19, 1964, he attempted to find support so he could tell "the Russians and Cubans that we regard subversion as 'armed aggression'" and that we therefore would have "a juridical umbrella for any future forceful retaliation we have to take." The idea was promptly shot down by Attorney-General Robert Kennedy, who asked,

First, how do you define subversion? *Second*, subversion is hard to prove even when, on rare occasion, we have the evidence. . . . *Third*, retaliation by force is no simple matter; our decision-making experience of October 1962 made this clear. Finally, time-lag is a problem; the arms cache occurs [strong evidence indicated that a three-ton arms cache discovered in Venezuela had been sent by Castro to rebel groups] and three months later, after the research is completed we retaliate—this is somewhat unrealistic.[50]

Mann, however, refused to give up. In March, he proposed having the hemisphere's nations consider a new resolution that defined subversion as aggression. No longer would simply an "armed attack" trigger U.S. and Latin American responses under the OAS and Rio pacts. Although he could not line up the necessary Latin American votes for writing such a blank check, he was delighted in July 1964 when the hemisphere foreign ministers specifically defined Castro's attempt to subvert the Venezuelan government as "aggression" within the 1947 Rio treaty. They voted to sever diplomatic and trade relations with Cuba. During a September speech in Dallas, Mann warned that a neighbor's "fires have a way of spreading" and that Washington "stood ready" to stop "Communist subversion. As President Johnson said clearly last April, 'Our first task must be, as it has

been, to . . . frustrate [Cuba's] efforts to destroy free governments.'"
The Alliance for Progress clearly was not any longer the "first task,"
if, indeed, it had ever been.[51]

The Dominican Republic became a classic case study for Mann's
spreading-fires theory. In 1961, the nation, half the size of the state of
Virginia, had finally overthrown the brutal dictatorship of Rafael Trujillo. The United States played at least an indirect, if not direct, role in
assassinating the increasingly unpredictable dictator and ensuring
that his friends would not assume power. But Washington was not
pleased when Juan Bosch won the 1962 elections. Supported by peasant, labor, and student groups, Bosch was viewed by U.S. officials
as a soft-minded intellectual with knee-jerk favoritism of left-wing
causes. Nevertheless, when business and large landholders supported the army's overthrow of Bosch in September 1963, the Kennedy administration refused to recognize the new military regime.
Johnson and Mann did so, however, in mid-December with one of
their first Latin American policy decisions. Despite substantial U.S.
aid, the regime, led by Gen. Donald Reid Cabral, could not improve
the corruption-plagued economy. When it tried to raise its credit rat-
ing for international lenders by increasing the price of staple goods,
discontent spread. On April 24, 1965, middle-rank army officers, led
by Col. Francisco Caamaño Deño, moved to overthrow Reid Cabral's
isolated regime. The plotters were joined by liberals and leftists of
various stripes, including small pro-Castro groups. The rebels arrested Reid, then pushed to restore the elected president, Bosch, to
power. Bosch represented by far the best hope for a fairer, reformist,
not to mention democratic and constitutional, government.

Mann, however, believed himself to be squeezed between the de-
bris of Kennedy's ill-formulated Alliance and Castro's militant revolutionary expansionism. He wanted to waste no time on Bosch,
whom he called (in probably the most contemptible terms he could
think of) a "poet-professor type" and "do-gooder" who like "many
Latin American politicians would make an allowance with the devil
himself if he thought it would get him into office." As fighting increased on April 27–28, the chaos led to uncertainty about whether
the conservative military could maintain the upper hand. As Mann
defined it on April 27, the problem was order, not communism. The
U.S. objective, he told the embassy in Santo Domingo, was "to restore law and order and to see the establishment of a provisional government with general elections as soon as possible, in order to avoid
bloodshed and the political risk." The United States did not want
to intervene, he continued, but "the point was approaching when

there would be a lot of unnecessary bloodshed and risk." If "American lives" were threatened, "the United States would probably do something about it." On April 28, the U.S. embassy urgently reported that the approximately 4,500 Americans in the country could not be protected. The request from the provisional government, actually written mostly by the U.S. embassy, warned that without the troops, Communists would take power. But Mann was not ready for such an argument. He ordered that the request be rewritten and based on the need to protect U.S. citizens. The corrected cable immediately appeared. Johnson landed 500 marines to protect the Americans.[52]

To this point, both international law and opinion supported the president's response. The next morning, Mann noted the troops had given a "shot in the arm" to the anti-Bosch military junta, but Washington was "trying to give a picture of impartiality." He then ordered the embassy to urge the anti-Bosch junta, "with quiet assistance of a few United States officers," to aim "for the deliberate and systematic reduction of insurgent-held parts of [the] city." Mann and LBJ had been powerfully predisposed to restore order and an anti-Bosch regime, goals they doubtless saw as two sides of the same policy. The *New York Times* correspondent in Santo Domingo noted on May 1 that the United States, by landing troops, had "become identified with political support for the ersatz military junta that passes for this country's government. Thus the danger arises," the report continued, "that the United States may oversimplify the immensely confused and complex situation . . . by accepting the junta's interpretation of the rebellion here as—purely and simply—a Castro-Communist conspiracy." The correspondent contended that such an interpretation was inaccurate. By May 1, Johnson and Mann had indeed fallen into such a dilemma. With the embassy and the junta warning Washington almost hourly about the dangers of a Communist takeover, Johnson ordered in 22,300 more troops over the next week and kept another 10,500 offshore. On May 2, the president announced, in what became known as the Johnson Doctrine, that no more Cubas would be tolerated in the hemisphere even if military force were needed to prevent them. Led, not surprisingly, by Brazil's new military regime, other Latin American nations joined at Johnson's request, and under the OAS banner, to contribute troops to the operation.[53]

At the time, critics claimed that the Communist threat was grossly inflated and that Johnson had overreacted. Scholars later analyzed the evidence and concluded the critics were correct. The Communists were few (probably fewer than 50) in number, were not in a position to take over the rebellion, and were highly insignificant when compared with the junior military officers who had triggered the revolt. The U.S. embassy and the junta members whom Mann favored over-dramatized the threat; Mann and Johnson were captives of that information and predisposed to believe it. Motives probably differed. The embassy officials were frightened and misinformed and perhaps understood that advancement in U.S. politics or the bureaucracy had for some time depended on overstating, rather than understating, the Communist threat. The Dominican military simply wanted to save its own skin. But Mann, although doubtless understanding these motives, proved to be fully receptive to the warnings. He held Bosch in contempt, seemed to see little difference between pro-Bosch and pro-Communist factions, hated disorder, favored the military junta, and—as he had since the 1940s—wanted a government that would suppress nationalism for the sake of hemispheric cooperation. Constitutionally, Bosch deserved to be president. Mann and Johnson, however, were more concerned about order and cooperation. The rebels were defeated. On May 15, Mann headed a team that included McGeorge Bundy and Deputy Secretary of Defense Cyrus Vance to set up a provisional government. The mission failed, partly due to differences between Bundy and Mann, partly due to the refusal of candidates the United States deemed acceptable to cooperate. In September, a government was finally established under U.S. sponsorship. Elections held under U.S. supervision did not return Bosch to power. But brutal warfare continued until by 1971, one person was being murdered for political reasons on the average of every forty-eight hours. U.S. officials and the public paid little attention. A friendly government was firmly in power, and the victims were mostly young, militant leftists.[54]

In the debate that quickly erupted, Mann vigorously defended U.S. policy. Unfortunately, he raised the specter of the Communist threat until he lapsed into referring to the rebels as tools of the "Sino-Soviet bloc." Nearly all informed observers understood that the Soviets and Chinese now hated and feared each other so much that their "bloc" was history. Such obvious exaggeration, combined with the growing realization that the Communist threat had been wildly overstated, led the cooperative Latin American nations to feel they had been misled into an operation that—under the vague, U.S.-defined Johnson Doctrine—could lead to a new era of Yankee military intervention. "It was unquestionably a shattering experience for some of them," Sol Linowitz, the U.S. ambassador to the OAS, recalled. When Latins were asked to guarantee human rights in a particular country, he added, they would say, "'No, we don't want this because this would bring in a Dominican Republic situation and some other intervention in other areas.'" Mann had long grappled with the problem of how to intervene, had concluded that collective or multilateral intervention was the key to making it acceptable, and now discovered that the Dominican operation made such cooperative intervention virtually impossible. Cooperation in the Alliance for Progress had stumbled long before. Disillusioned Latin Americans observed that *para* (for) is also the third person present of the verb *parar* (to stop) and concluded the accurate translation was, "The Alliance Stops Progress."[55]

The Johnson administration, as well as the Good Neighbor policy, also became a victim of the intervention. As it became clear how the president and Mann had misled them about the Communist threat, congressional critics, led by Senator Fulbright, turned against the president. By turning against his once-close friend over the Dominican question, Fulbright also set the terms for the developing debate over Vietnam. Within a year after the intervention, nearly every key presidential adviser who had played a role in the decision to send in troops had either retired or moved on to another post. Lincoln Gordon became assistant secretary of state for inter-American affairs in early 1966, an appointment that in reality ended Mann's control of Latin American policy. At Gordon's confirmation hearings, Senator Fred Harris (D.-Okla.) told him he must make "a right-angle turn from the hard Thomas Mann line." Fulbright contented himself with noting wryly that those holding the job had a short life expectancy. Five men had held it in just five years.[56]

In May 1966, Mann resigned at age fifty-three after twenty-four years in the State Department. He planned to write a book. "If it resembles his career the book should be hard-hitting, controversial, and influential," *Time* observed. The *New York Times* called him "a complicated man of private charm and public abrasiveness" who had worked closely with Latin America in the 1950s when few others paid attention to the region. In commenting on his resignation, correspondent Max Frankel of the *New York Times*, who had known Mann well, concluded,

It is perhaps only possible to conclude that irrational elements are needed to give any reality to the quite irrational idea of the Alliance: that a measure of partnership rather than domination is possible between a powerful rich nation and its poor and neurotic neighbors. This possibility was notably lost on Mr. Mann.[57]

Perhaps. But Mann understood from the start, as he explained to Eisenhower's cabinet, that an Alliance as the Kennedy administration would later conceive it could do little but raise false expectations and worsen an already critical economic and political situation. The problem was, as historian Robert Freeman Smith wrote in 1965, that "the vocabulary was that of social revolution, but the concepts were a mixture of U.S.-oriented capitalism and New Deal economics."[58] Mann also understood this was a combustible mixture, which was why he moved so rapidly to dilute it in the 1964–1966 years. He could find no medicine to put in its place, however. He had begun with a Good Neighbor policy that was slowly undermined after 1945 by growing Latin American nationalism, poverty, inequality, and bitterness over U.S. aid policies. Believing in a Wilsonian world of openness and cooperation, Mann was too knowledgeable and realistic to believe in the 1950s that such a world could any longer be achieved through the Good Neighbor approach or Wilson's naive admonition to teach the Latin Americans to elect good men. Allegedly, Mann once remarked, "I know my Latinos. They understand only a dollar in the pocket and a kick in the ass." That quotation, even if accurately reported, also misled. Deeply experienced in, and respectful of, Latin cultures, Mann, at least until the Dominican intervention, was probably more highly respected by Latin Americans than any other U.S. official who specialized in the region.

The never-ending problem that Mann confronted throughout his career was how to reconcile Latin American nationalism with United States interests, especially the interests requiring a stable, open, cooperative region. These interests predated Mann's obsession with communism. Indeed, the anti-Communist obsession was only one more step rather than a new path in Washington's post-1945 policymaking. Attempting to reconcile southern nationalism and northern interests led Mann through economic sanctions, covert military operations, new economic institutions, and, finally, armed intervention by U.S. troops. FDR's Good Neighbor policy was finally in the past. Thomas Mann's policies were the future of U.S. policies in Latin America.

NOTES

1. Thomas Mann Oral History Interview, Dwight D. Eisenhower Presidential Library, Abilene, Kans., 66.

2. Thomas Mann Oral History Interview, John F. Kennedy Presidential Library, Boston, Mass., 31–32; *Time*, January 31, 1964, 14–17.

3. *Time*, January 31, 1964, 14, 17; Mann to Ambassador Fletcher Warren, January 16, 1953, Records of Deputy Assistant Secretaries of State for Inter-

American Affairs, 1945–1956, Box 7, "Venezuela 1953–1954" file, Lot File 57D 598, National Archives, Record Group 59, Washington, D.C. (hereafter cited as NA RG 59). I am indebted to David Langbart of the National Archives for drawing my attention to these and other Lot Files.

4. Mann Oral History, Kennedy Library, 54; U.S. Department of State, *Foreign Relations of the United States 1951*, II (Washington, D.C.: U.S. Government Printing Office, 1979): 1476–1477 (hereafter cited as *FRUS*, followed by year and volume number); ibid., 1145–1146.

5. *FRUS 1950*, II (Washington, D.C., 1976): 879; Harold F. Peterson, *Argentina and the United States, 1810–1960* (New York: University Publishers, 1964): 452–453; Mann to Ambassador Fletcher Warren, February 6, 1952, Records of Deputy Assistant Secretaries of State for Inter-American Affairs, 1945–1956, Box 7, "Venezuela, 1952" file, Lot File 57D 598, NA RG 59.

6. To Mr. Miller from Mr. Mann, Nov. 14, 1951, Records of Deputy Assistant Secretaries of State for Inter-American Affairs, 1945–1956, Box 6, "Policy Statements" file, NA RG 59.

7. Mann to Rogers Kelly, August 20, 1952, ibid., Box 4, "K" file, NA RG 59; Mann to Robert M. Hallett, June 6, 1952, ibid., Box 1, "C" file, NA RG 59; to Mr. Miller from Mr. Mann, November 14, 1951, ibid., Box 6, "Policy Statements" file, NA RG 59.

8. *FRUS 1950*, II: 950–954; J. Richard Powell, *The Mexican Petroleum Industry, 1938–1950* (New York: Russell & Russell, 1972): 48–49, 170–171; Mann Oral History, Eisenhower Library, 40–41; *FRUS 1952–1954*, IV (Washington, D.C., 1983): 607–608.

9. *FRUS 1952–1954*, IV: 513–516; Bernard M. Wood, *Foreign Aid and Revolutionary Development: The Case of Bolivia, 1952–1965* (Ottawa: Carleton University School of International Affairs, 1970): 1–8; *FRUS 1951*, II: 1152–1155; Mann to Messersmith, Records of Deputy Assistant Secretaries of State for Inter-American Affairs, 1945–1956, Box 4, "Messersmith, George" file, NA RG 59.

10. Bryce Wood, *The Dismantling of the Good Neighbor Policy* (Austin: University of Texas Press, 1985): 143, 146 n. 29; Memorandum to Charles S. Murphy, December 11, 1952, President's Secretary File, Latin America Folder, Harry S. Truman Library, Independence, Mo., 1–3. I am indebted to Professor Henry Berger of Washington University for a copy of this paper. Mann drew heavily from Norman Pearson's memorandum of April 2, 1952, in writing the paper. Gabriel Kolko, *Confronting the Third World: United States Foreign Policy 1945–1950* (New York: Pantheon Books, 1988): 97, is important.

11. Memorandum to Murphy, December 11, 1952, 4–16.

12. Ibid., 16–24.

13. Ibid., 24–42.

14. Mann to Raymond G. Leddy, September 17, 1954, Henry Holland Papers, Lot File 57D 295, Box 3, "Guatemala" file, NA RG 59.

15. Mann Oral History, Eisenhower Library, 10–12; *Time*, January 31, 1964, 17; Mann Oral History, Kennedy Library, 28–29.

16. *FRUS 1951*, II: 1447, has the conversation with UFCO officials; Richard Immerman, *The CIA in Guatemala* (Austin: University of Texas Press,

1982): 118–120. Mann to Miller, July 31, 1951, Records of Deputy Assistant Secretaries of State for Inter-American Affairs, 1945–1956, Box 3, "IADB" file, NA RG 59.

17. *FRUS 1951*, II: 1440–1442; Immerman, *CIA in Guatemala*, 82.

18. *FRUS 1952–1954*, IV: 1041–1043; *FRUS 1951*, II: 1448–1449; Wood, *Dismantling of the Good Neighbor Policy*, 140.

19. Blanche Wiesen Cook, *The Declassified Eisenhower: A Divided Legacy* (Garden City, N.Y.: Doubleday, 1981): 222; "Editorial Note," *FRUS 1952–1954*, IV: 1056–1057; Donald M. Dozer, *Are We Good Neighbors? Three Decades of Inter-American Relations, 1930–1960* (Gainesville: University of Florida Press, 1959): 340–342; Immerman, *CIA in Guatemala*, 178.

20. Mann to Leddy, September 17, 1954, Holland Lot File, Box 3, "Guatemala, 1954" file, NA RG 59. I am indebted to Jim Siekmeier for this document. Memorandum of Conversation, Col. Castillo Armas and Henry F. Holland, February 14, 1955, ibid.; Memorandum of Meeting, April 28–29, 1955, ibid., "Guatemala, 1955–1956" file; Memorandum of Conversation, July 22, 1956, Lot File, Office of Central American and Panamanian Affairs, Box 1, "Guat.-Castillo Armas" file, NA RG 59; Mann to Rubottom, July 10, 1957, 611.20/7/1057, NA RG 59; *FRUS 1955–1957*, VII: 87, 119; Graham H. Stuart and James L. Tigner, *Latin America and the United States* (New York: Prentice-Hall, 1975): 523.

21. Virgil Salera, "Beneficent Investment: The Department of Commerce Survey," *Inter-American Economic Affairs* 10 (Spring 1957): 71–72; Stephen G. Rabe, "Eisenhower and Latin America: Arms and Dictators," *Peace and Change* 11 (Spring 1985): 49–61; "Minutes of Cabinet Meeting," January 10, 1958, Cabinet Meetings of President Eisenhower (microfilm), Eisenhower Library, 1–2; Kolko, *Confronting the Third World*, 144–145.

22. Thomas C. Mann, "The Trade Agreements Program and American Prosperity," *Department of State Bulletin* 38 (April 28, 1958): 692–694; Thomas C. Mann, "American Trade Policy and the Lessons of the 1930's," *Department of State Bulletin* 37 (June 2, 1958): 895–899; Thomas McCormick, *America's Half-Century* (Baltimore: Johns Hopkins University Press, 1989): 141–142.

23. *FRUS 1955–1957*, VII: 995–996; Mann Oral History, Eisenhower Library, 40–41; *Time*, December 27, 1963, 14–15; Kolko, *Confronting the Third World*, 108; Burton Kaufman, *Trade and Aid: Eisenhower's Foreign Economic Policy, 1953–1961* (Baltimore: Johns Hopkins University Press, 1982): 152–182.

24. *New York Times*, May 17, 1959, IV, 4, has a useful overview of the pre-Nixon-visit roots of the policy, written by Tad Szulc.

25. "Comments on Inter-American Economic Problems," February 27, 1959, Cabinet Meetings of President Eisenhower.

26. Ibid.

27. *New York Times*, May 1, 1959, 11; ibid., July 12, 1960, 6; Edwin Lieuwen, "The Latin American Military," in U.S. Congress, Senate Committee on Foreign Relations, 91st Cong., 1st sess., *Survey of the Alliance for Progress* (Washington, D.C., 1969): 114–115.

28. *New York Times*, July 30, 1960, 1, 5; Philip L. Geyelin, *Lyndon B. Johnson and the World* (New York: F. A. Praeger, 1966): 96.

29. Mann Oral History, Eisenhower Library, 1–2, 7–8, 24–25; Mann Oral History, Kennedy Library, 9.

30. *New York Times*, October 13, 1960, 1.

31. Thomas C. Mann, "The Democratic Ideal in the Latin American Policy of the United States," *Department of State Bulletin* 43 (November 28, 1960): 811–814.

32. Barton J. Bernstein, "Kennedy and the Bay of Pigs Revisited— Twenty-Four Years Later," *Foreign Service Journal* (March 1985): 28–30; Mann Oral History, Kennedy Library, 16–20; Trumbull Higgins, *The Perfect Failure: Kennedy, Eisenhower, and the CIA at the Bay of Pigs* (New York: W. W. Norton, 1987): 50, 93–94.

33. Higgins, *The Perfect Failure*, 72, 111; Immerman, *CIA in Guatemala*, 194; Mann Oral History, Kennedy Library, 22; Theodore C. Sorensen, *Kennedy* (New York: Harper and Row, 1965, 1988): 307.

34. Mann Oral History, Kennedy Library, 27, 31, 33, 37–39; "Mann" in *Current Biography, 1964* (New York: 1964): 275; *Time*, January 31, 1964, 16; Rowland Evans, Jr., and Robert Novak, *Lyndon B. Johnson: The Exercise of Power* (New York: New American Library, 1966): 397.

35. Eric F. Goldman, *The Tragedy of Lyndon Johnson* (New York: A. A. Knopf, 1969): 89; Samuel Baily, *The United States and the Development of South America, 1945–1975* (New York: New Viewpoints, 1976): 105–106; Robert M. Sayre to Bundy, November 3, 1964, NSC Agency File, Alliance for Progress, Vol. II, Lyndon B. Johnson Library, Austin, Texas. I am deeply indebted to David Humphrey of the Johnson Library for his assistance. Ray S. Cline to McGeorge Bundy, April 17, 1964, with CIA's "Survey of Latin America," April 1, 1964, attached, NSC Country File: Latin America, Johnson Library; Geyelin, *Johnson and the World*, 97.

36. Evans and Novak, *Johnson*, 395–396, 397; Geyelin, *Johnson and the World*, 95, 98–99; Bill J. Clark to Johnson, December 17, 1963, White House Central File—Name File: Mann, Thomas C., Johnson Library.

37. Thomas C. Mann, "The Experience of the United States in Economic Development," *Department of State Bulletin* 47 (November 19, 1963): 772–773.

38. Ibid.; Cline to Bundy, April 17, 1964.

39. *Time*, January 31, 1964, 18; *New York Times*, March 19, 1964, 1; Robert Packenham, *Liberal America and the Third World* (Princeton: Princeton University Press, 1973): 95–96.

40. *Current Biography, 1964*, 275.

41. Draft Memorandum for the President from Bundy, May 4, 1964, NSF Agency File, Boxes 3–4, Johnson Library; Moyers to Bundy, June 5, 1964, NSC Files, Country File, Latin America, Box 1, Johnson Library. The Notre Dame speech may be found in Martin C. Needler, *The United States and the Latin American Revolution*, rev. ed. (Los Angeles: University of California, Los Angeles, Latin American Center, 1977): 145–153. Thomas C. Mann, "The Alliance for Progress: A Challenge and Opportunity," *Department of State Bulletin* 11 (October 26, 1964): 595–596; Geyelin, *Johnson and the World*, 274–275.

42. Mann to Johnson, March 15, 1965, CO 1-8, Executive File, White House Central Files, Johnson Library; Walter LaFeber, "The Alliance in Retrospect," in Andrew Maguire and Janet Welsh Brown, eds., *Bordering on Trouble: Resources and Politics in Latin America* (Bethesda: Adler and Adler, 1986): 353–354, 374–377; Felipe Herrera Oral History, Johnson Library.

43. "Latin American Policy Committee: Action Minutes, Meeting #90," July 9, 1964, NSF-Country File: Latin America, Vol. II, Box 2, Johnson Library; Memorandum for Mr. Bundy from Gordon Chase, Mar. 19, 1964, NSC Country File: Latin America, Vol. I, Johnson Library.

44. Phyllis R. Parker, *Brazil and the Quiet Intervention, 1964* (Austin: University of Texas Press, 1979): 58–59, 73–76, 92–93; Kolko, *Confronting the Third World*, 156, 158.

45. Thomas C. Mann, "The Western Hemisphere's Fight for Freedom," *Department of State Bulletin* 51 (October 19, 1964): 551; Parker, *Brazil*, 73, 92–93.

46. Lester D. Langley, *America and the Americas: The United States in the Western Hemisphere* (Athens: University of Georgia Press, 1989): 206–207; Kolko, *Confronting the Third World*, 158; Parker, *Brazil*, 81–82; Needler, *U.S. and Latin America*, 146; Robert M. Sayre to McGeorge Bundy, August 18, 1964, NSF-Country File: Latin America, Vol. II, Box 2, Johnson Library.

47. Geyelin, *Johnson and the World*, 100–101; Jules Dubois, *Danger Over Panama* (Indianapolis: Bobbs-Merrill, 1964), 286–290, 357; Bundy to the President, January 10, 1964, Memorandum of Meetings with the President, vol. 1, NSF, Files of McGeorge Bundy, Johnson Library; Memorandum for the Secretary of State from Mann, February 1, 1964, NSC Histories, Panama Crisis, Box 1, Johnson Library; Memorandum by Mann, January 24, 1964, NSC Histories, Panama Crisis, Box 1, Johnson Library; Mann to Martin, January 25, 1964, NSC Histories, Panama Crisis, Box 1, Johnson Library.

48. Geyelin, *Johnson and the World*, 109; Evans and Novak, *Johnson*, 400, 403; Walter LaFeber, *The Panama Canal*, updated ed. (New York: Oxford University Press, 1989): 109–114.

49. Walt Whitman Rostow, *The Diffusion of Power* (New York: Macmillan, 1972): 412.

50. Gordon Chase, "Memorandum for the Record," February 19, 1964, NSF File, Country File-Cuba, vol. 2, Memos, Box 25, Johnson Library.

51. Gordon Chase to McGeorge Bundy, March 17, 1964, NSF File, Country File-Cuba, vol. 2, Memos, Box 25, Johnson Library; Mann, "The Western Hemisphere's Fight for Freedom," 552.

52. Mann's view of Bosch is reported in *New York Times*, November 14, 1965, 1; Historical Studies Division, Department of State, "The Response of the Department of State to the Dominican Crisis of April–May 1965," NSC History File, National Security File, Johnson Library, 11–12, 19–20; Langley, *America and Americas*, 210–211.

53. Historical Studies Division, "The Response of the Department of State to the Dominican Crisis of April–May 1965," 23–24; *New York Times*, May 2, 1965, E1.

54.   Daniel Papermaster, "A Case Study of the Effect of International Law on Foreign Policy Decisionmaking: The United States Intervention in the Dominican Republic in 1965," *Texas International Law Journal* 24 (Summer 1989): 486; Thomas C. Mann, "The Dominican Crisis: Correcting Some Misconceptions," *Department of State Bulletin* 53 (November 8, 1965): 736–737, esp. for Mann's view of "reform"; Cole Blasier, *The Hovering Giant* (Pittsburgh: University of Pittsburgh Press, 1976): 247; Piero Gleijeses, *The Dominican Crisis: The 1965 Constitutionalist Revolt and American Intervention*, trans. Lawrence Lipson (Baltimore: Johns Hopkins University Press, 1978), has the best detailed analysis of the Dominican Republic's left wing; Evans and Novak, *Johnson*, 526; *Washington Post*, July 15, 1971, F7.

55.   Sol Linowitz Oral History, Johnson Library, 17–18; *New York Times*, April 6, 1966, 38; ibid., October 14, 1965, 6; LaFeber, "The Alliance in Retrospect," 354, 357.

56.   *New York Times*, April 24, 1966, 27; ibid., January 24, 1966, 12; ibid., February 8, 1966, 10.

57.   *New York Times*, May 1, 1966, IV, 1, has the Frankel evaluation; *Time*, May 6, 1966, 21–22.

58.   Robert Freeman Smith, "Whatever Happened to Baby *Alianza?*" *New Politics* 4 (Winter 1965): 90–95.

CHAPTER 7

Harry Hopkins with Hand Grenades?
McGeorge Bundy in the Kennedy and Johnson Years

LLOYD GARDNER

Early in the Kennedy administration, an anonymous insider quipped that National Security Adviser McGeorge Bundy was "another Harry Hopkins with hand grenades."[1] In some ways, it was an apt comparison. Like Franklin Roosevelt's famous confidant during World War II, dubbed "Lord Root-of-the-Matter" by no less an authority than Winston Churchill, Bundy played a role in elucidating key parts of the Kennedy and Johnson administrations' foreign policies. And the hand grenades reference, while too facile and hyperbolic, hit on a central theme of those years. As Bundy himself put it, policymakers believed that near the "very heart of all foreign affairs" was the relationship between "policy and military power."[2]

But the comparison is also misleading. Hopkins was FDR's messenger—and his eyes and ears abroad. Bundy was an organizer—and an agenda setter. He turned the office of National Security Adviser into a White House think tank. Control of the flow of information gave Bundy powers that Hopkins never had. Hopkins was a facilitator and intermediary; Bundy was an activist intellectual with a mission. He took it as a given that the world's salvation depended on his generation of Americans.

Born into a family with deep roots in the Boston aristocracy, Bundy grew up in a special tradition of service to the presidency even before he was sent off to the Reverend Endicott Peabody's care at Groton School. His father, Harvey H. Bundy, had served as Henry L. Stimson's aide both in the Hoover years, when Stimson headed the State Department, and in the Roosevelt years, when Stimson responded to the president's call to active duty as secretary of war. At Groton, where young men of his class began their preparation for leadership roles, the Reverend Peabody instilled a lifelong sense of duty and noblesse oblige.

Groton's motto, "To Serve Is to Rule," echoed the British public school tradition. On the famous playing fields of Eton and Harrow, generations of diplomats and colonial administrators practiced for the time when they would "play the great game of empire" and take up the "white man's burden." Americans had no formal empire (or not much of one anyway) to manage, but Groton's famous sons did not lack for work to do. Dean Acheson, for example, was especially busy at the outset of the cold war with the Marshall Plan and NATO.

Acheson was another powerful influence on Mac Bundy. "What he had learned from Dean Acheson," Bundy commented, was "that, in the final analysis, the United States was the locomotive at the head of mankind, and the rest of the world the caboose."[3] "McGeorge Bundy," wrote David Halberstam, "was the finest example of a special elite, a certain breed of men whose continuity is among themselves. They are linked to one another rather than to the country; in their minds they become responsible for the country but not responsive to it."[4]

But we must be careful in talking about elite control of American foreign policy, especially to avoid the risk of sounding like Vice President Spiro Agnew, who imagined (or professed to believe in) a liberal-dominated media conspiracy out to destroy the American Way and Richard Nixon. The crusade to make the world safe for democracy in World War I, when America achieved world power, was not the intellectual property of Groton School or any one class. Woodrow Wilson had instructed American schoolteachers in 1918 to explain to their pupils the profound differences between America and Imperial Germany. "Under your instruction," Wilson told the teachers,

children should come to see that it was the high logic of events and the providence of God that the United States and Germany, the one the most consistent practitioner of the new creed of mankind and the other the most consistent practitioner of the old, should thus meet in battle to determine whether the new democracy or the old autocracy shall govern the world, and under your instruction the children should be made to understand the stern duty and the supreme privilege which belong to the United States of being chief interpreter to the world of those democratic principles which we believe to constitute the only force which can rid the world of injustice and bring peace and happiness to mankind.[5]

A short time before, he had told Mexican newspaper editors what the outcome of the war would mean to their country. Once the war ended, and fair dealing and justice became the rule throughout the world, Mexico would prosper as never before, "because so soon as you can admit your own capital and the capital of the world to the free use of the resources of Mexico, it will be one of the most wonderfully rich and prosperous countries in the world."[6]

He could guarantee this happy outcome because, he told them, the Great War meant that the influence of the United States had become pervasive in the affairs of the world. America was thus compelled, by obligations to its very raison d'être and to the world at large, to wage such a war. This American ethos, with or without its subjective Wilsonian intensity, was commonly shared in the Progressive Era. It lay quiescent in the interwar period, sprang to life again in the aftermath of World War II as Americans responded to the problems of European reconstruction, and emerged full force in the 1960s in a variety of new forms, including modernization theory. Thus Secretary of Defense Robert McNamara updated Wilson's promise to Mexico by expanding it to the world in a 1965 interview with the *New York Times:*

If the U.S. withdrew from SVN, there would be a complete shift in the world balance of power. Asia goes Red, our prestige and integrity damaged, allies everywhere shaken (even those who publicly ask us to quit bombing, etc.). At home, he foresees as a result of these calamities, a bad effect on economy and a disastrous political fight that could further freeze American political debate and even affect political freedom. . . . On the other hand: If the U.S. achieved in SVN the objectives stated by LBJ in Baltimore, there would then be substantial political and economic and security gains. Way then open to combine birth control and economic expansion techniques in gigantic arc from SVN to Iran and Middle East, bringing unimaginable developments to this region, proving worth of moderate, democratic way of growth for societies.[7]

Vietnam was a long way off when Bundy was in prep school. But a schoolboy friend at Groton remarked, "He seemed to have been born older than we were."[8] As Europe trembled before Hitler and Mussolini, Yale University welcomed Bundy to the class of 1940. He had attained some of the highest marks on entrance exams ever recorded. In one case, he had even challenged a question as "silly." "If I were giving the test, this is the question I would ask, and this is my answer."[9]

Academic honors and Phi Beta Kappa came naturally. While pursuing majors in mathematics and classics, Bundy commented regularly in the student newspaper. As elsewhere in those days, the isolationist-internationalist debate had engulfed the university. "Let me put my whole proposition in one sentence," Bundy told his classmates. "I believe in the dignity of the individual, in government by law, in respect for truth and in a good God; these beliefs are worth my life, and more; they are not shared by Adolf Hitler."[10]

Using a friendly sergeant as an accomplice, Bundy passed the eye exam despite his glasses and served in the European theater. After the war, he worked for a time in Washington ironing out the details of the Marshall Plan, then assisted Stimson in the writing of his memoirs, *On Active Duty in Peace and War.* During the 1948 campaign, Bundy was a speechwriter and idea man for Republican nominee Thomas Dewey. When Dewey lost to Truman, Bundy found an academic niche for himself at Harvard University in the Government Department—even though he had never received his Ph.D. His course on American foreign policy became famous for a lecture on the folly of appeasement at Munich. Students crowded in to hear Bundy expose the failures of Europe's interwar generation in dramatic fashion. He never let them down.

When he became dean of Harvard College at the age of thirty-four, Bundy legends began to grow. Already, moreover, he had become a figure not only of awe but of fear. His tart self-assuredness put off and even frightened many colleagues, not only at Harvard but in the White House. "McGeorge Bundy is the iron priest of an iron faith in the definitiveness of his yes or no," one Kennedy insider confided to a reporter doing a profile of the national security adviser, "and he has such a marvelous storehouse of language to make everything he says sound plausible that he scares the hell out of me."[11]

"Ask not what your country can do for you," said John F. Kennedy at his inaugural, "ask what you can do for your country." Kennedy wanted Bundy to be his national security adviser. Bundy was a Republican, but he knew how he must respond. Bipartisan loyalty to the presidency was a hallmark of the Bundy character. When he was accused of party treachery by Republican conservatives for collaborating on a collection of Dean Acheson's speeches, published under the inevitable title, *The Pattern of Responsibility.* Bundy's reply was, "I was brought up in a school where the American Secretary of State is not the subject of partisan debate."[12]

Kennedy and Bundy had come to one another's attention in the late 1950s, as the Massachusetts senator began his drive for the White House. Bundy was precisely the sort of action-oriented intellectual Kennedy was looking for, a torchbearer for the generation that Kennedy described in his inaugural address as "tempered by the war, disciplined by a hard and bitter peace, proud of our ancient heritage."

He might have been named secretary of state, except for his youth

(Kennedy was leery of appointing too many young men to an administration headed by a very young president) and his Republican party background. Ironically, it was Walter Lippmann, later to be a determined critic of the Vietnam War, who pushed the idea that Bundy belonged at State.[13] Maybe it was Kennedy's way of keeping his obviously very talented and extremely energetic appointee in check that he described him to friends as the *second* brightest man he knew, next to his close friend, the British diplomat, David Ormsby Gore.[14]

Kennedy wanted a complete overhaul of the national security adviser's operation in the White House, so as to cut through the State Department's inertia, and he gave the assignment to the Harvard dean. When Bundy accepted Kennedy's invitation to become national security adviser in 1961, the position was little known to the public. Eisenhower had formalized the role of the national security adviser, but those who had served had carried out their assignments in the same obscurity as staff officers to a commanding general in the army. That was the way Eisenhower expected things to work. Eisenhower also used the full National Security Council (NSC) to develop ideas and for genuine debate of policy issues, a practice largely eschewed by both Kennedy and Johnson, who preferred working with smaller groups.

The upshot was that Bundy's control of the information flow to the president placed him in a far more powerful position than his predecessors. All this was, however, at Kennedy's explicit directions. When he announced Bundy's appointment on January 1, 1961, the president-elect said that he hoped to combine the NSC secretariat with "the continuing functions of a number of special projects within the White House."[15] When asked how Bundy was doing, Kennedy grinned and replied, "Mac has taken over in a great big way. I only hope he leaves a few residual functions to me."[16]

Whether the changes JFK wrought in the NSC organization and in the elevation of the national security adviser's role made for better policy decisions or, as Eisenhower scholars now argue, dangerously narrowed perspectives, the impact was felt almost immediately.[17] Roger Hilsman, an assistant secretary of state, quickly learned that Bundy was a key member of the "inner club" of the administration.

What did the president mean, Hilsman once asked after hearing JFK refer to the "inner club"? He meant, replied Bundy, that "now we had together the people who had known all along what we would do about the problem, and who had been pulling and hauling, debating and discussing for no other purpose than to keep the government together, to get all the others to come around."[18] Bundy's academic background, it turned out, prepared him well for integrating men and ideas on the New Frontier. The interpenetration of government and academy had begun, Bundy said in a 1964 speech, which turned out to be almost a personal review of his own career, with the Office of Strategic Services (OSS) in World War II, the precursor of the Central Intelligence Agency. "A remarkable institution," Bundy concluded, it was "half cops and robbers, half faculty meeting."[19]

The OSS had carried out the first area studies programs. Later, universities picked up the theme, he went on, and now government and the academy had a joint interest. One proposed answer to the Communist threat that engaged both the academy and government planners was regionalism, or, a basic, if somehow unrecognized, refinement of Dulles's "pactomania." Area programs, modernization theory, the applicability of social science techniques to foreign policy problems— all these intrigued and engaged the New Frontiersmen as they went about replacing the supposed Eisenhower/Dulles cold war simplicities with their own sophisticated problem-solving methodology.

"It was the golden age of development theorists," George Ball would recall. "A story current at the time told of the professor who boasted that he occupied 'The Pan American Chair of Development Economics.' By that he meant a first-class seat on Pan American Airways to any destination in the world."[20] But did the academic researchers and policymakers always share an identical interest? In the Kennedy years, it seemed easy to say so. When disillusionment sank in on both sides during the Vietnam War, it was not easy for either side to disengage. "But," writes Henry Fairlie, "'half cops and robbers, half faculty meeting' was a part of the spirit of the New Frontier: physical bravado joined to intellectual bravura."[21]

It began with the responsibilities assigned to the National Security Council experts. At the top, Bundy set up shop with another academic, Walt W. Rostow, as his principal assistant. Bundy assigned him responsibility for everything that happened east of Suez, while he attended to all the rest. As Rostow put it, he and Bundy "had divided the world."[22]

Bundy's expertise coming into the job was Europe, but the first two years of the Kennedy administration were dominated by Cuba; with Johnson, it would be Vietnam. Castro had become an obsession. The 1960 campaign had been run by the Democrats on the theme, "Who lost Cuba?" Over and over Kennedy attacked the Republicans for letting the Russians come within ninety miles of Florida. Their candidate, Richard Nixon, he gibed, boasted that he had stood up to Khrushchev in the Moscow "kitchen debate," but what had his party done about Castro when it really mattered? It was simple justice in cold war politics—and delicious revenge—for the party that had been pilloried by Republicans for "losing" China in 1949 to hurl back the charge. But Kennedy meant it—every word.

The trouble was that Cuba was no longer part of the regional grouping of the "Free World" in the Western Hemisphere. No members of the Peace Corps would be welcome there, and no economic specialists from the Alliance for Progress were likely to be invited to study Cuba's infrastructure.[23] Cuba had become a Russian satellite; Castro, a puppet tied to Kremlin strings.

As it turned out, Kennedy had trapped himself with all this rhetoric. Planning for an invasion by Cuban exiles had begun in the Eisenhower administration, overriding advice from the American embassy in Havana that the Cuban people, "whose nationalist batteries had been charged to the full by Fidel Castro," would never accept an external solution.[24] In televised debates with Nixon, the Democratic candidate had called for aid to Cuban exiles. So when CIA Director Allen Dulles presented Kennedy with the Bay of Pigs plan, it was put up or shut up time.

The New Frontiersmen were anxious to get going. "At this point," Bundy quipped to a friend before the Bay of Pigs, "we are like the Harlem Globetrotters, passing forward, behind, sidewise, and underneath. But nobody has made a basket yet."[25] The Bay of Pigs "team" did not make a basket for Kennedy, either. They did not resemble the Harlem Globetrotters at all. Instead, they looked like the patsies the Globetrotters always took along for straight men—or worse.

April is the cruelest month, began T. S. Eliot's famous long poem, "The Wasteland," and so it was for Kennedy. The Bay of Pigs invasion failed on every level from conception to execution. "Are you gentlemen telling us today," Republican Senator Homer Capehart asked of CIA and Pentagon officials in the aftermath, "that . . . our high military people who fought in World War I and World War II . . . approved this, what would appear to me to be a Boy Scout Operation?"[26]

Kennedy and his advisers became convinced that neither the Republicans nor Nikita Khrushchev would ever think of him otherwise unless somehow he redeemed the Bay of Pigs fiasco. Worse still, Kennedy himself seemed to read into the failure a generalized foreboding of defeat for his administration's policies. He feared most being labeled the president who somehow "lost" the cold war at the Bay of Pigs or in the jungles of Southeast Asia. Soon after the failure, Kennedy was ordering stepped up covert actions against Castro. Reading accounts of Operation Mongoose and other covert operations Kennedy authorized against Castro recalls to mind King Henry's obsession with that troublesome priest, Becket.[27] Both military contingency plans and covert schemes were set in motion.

Under the direction of Edward Lansdale, a veteran CIA operative from counterinsurgency campaigns in the Philippines and Vietnam, a series of bizarre assassination plots against Castro were designed. With each successive failure, Kennedy's frustration mounted. On August 23, 1962, Kennedy approved a directive that moved Operation Mongoose to a new phase, with contingency plans for provoking a full-scale revolt that might require U.S. intervention to succeed. His brother Robert, the attorney general, personally urged Operation Mongoose planners on October 4, 1962, to approve "massive activity" against Castro, including a priority for sabotage operations.[28]

Military plans were also speeded up by the Joint Chiefs of Staff, with a target date for October 20, 1962. Although the issue of Russian weaponry in Cuba added a new element to planners' concerns, these decisions were the result of a cumulative process that had been under way since the Bay of Pigs. All of the planning, moreover, preceded by months and weeks any intelligence of Russian missiles being placed on the island.

Only two days before the discovery of the missile sites, Bundy told a national television audience, "There is no present evidence, and I think there is no present likelihood, that the Cubans and the Cuban government and the Soviet government would in combination attempt to install a major offensive capability."[29] Such a statement does not refute, of course, Bundy's recollection (and that of others in the administration) that there was no intent to invade Cuba before the missile crisis.

Perhaps it is a matter of inertia and momentum. Forces had been set in operation to relieve the frustration that, as Bundy admits, was the dominant feeling in Washington during the summer of 1962. The covert program, he insists, was not "a prelude to stronger action but a substitute for it."[30] There were no plans to redo the Bay of Pigs and get it right the second time. "Nothing of that sort was in our heads." Indeed, asserts Bundy, administration thinking by the summer of 1962 was "180 degrees" away from an enlarged Bay of Pigs. "We were not going to repeat that exercise by adding a zero and throwing in the American army."[31]

But new elements Bundy now discounts were being added almost daily to the building pressures. It was not unlike 1898 when the sinking of the *Maine* precipitated war. Had that American warship gone down in a less fevered moment, the likelihood that the sinking would have caused a war diminishes considerably. From this reading, it could be argued that the missiles forestalled a *Maine* crisis, that they prevented a single dramatic event—like the assassination of Castro— from causing war.

However that may be, Kennedy, like William McKinley, faced a domestic political uproar about Russian weapons in Cuba. And, like McKinley, his chances of pushing the Cuban crisis off into some quiet corner grew slimmer each day. "The Congressional head of steam on this [issue]," Bundy warned the president on September 13, 1962, "is the most serious that we have had." Unless he provided "a very clear and aggressive explanation" of U.S. policy, said the national security adviser, Kennedy risked appearing "weak and indecisive."[32]

The president told a news conference that day that he would do "whatever must be done" to prevent Cuba from being converted into an offensive military base. The history of the Cuban missile crisis and its outcome have been explored by many students of the affair and, more recently, at conferences with Soviet participants. Khrushchev's reasons for putting the missiles in Cuba which were discovered by American U-2 overflights on October 14, 1962, were essentially those surmised by Americans: protection of the Cuban revolution and a quest for strategic parity. Which one came first is disputed by the Russians themselves.[33]

On the American side, there was no question about their staying there. "He can't do that to me!" snapped Kennedy when he saw the pictures on October 16, 1962.[34] The president then created a special committee, the ExCom, to advise him how to get the missiles out. Throughout the meetings of the ExCom, Bundy stressed the impact of whatever the United States did on Washington's relations with Europe. This is perhaps the most consistent thread in his thoughts as the debate ranged over such matters as whether to trade the missiles in Cuba for American missiles recently placed in Greece and Turkey, impose a blockade, or launch air strikes.

Bundy opposed the trade option as wrecking NATO faith in American commitments, a concern he now finds exaggerated. Yet it was also Bundy who asked the key question of Secretary of Defense McNamara about the difference the missiles made in the actual strategic balance. McNamara's response helped to cool off pressures for air strikes. "Mac, I asked the Chiefs. . . . And they said, substantially. My own personal view is, not at all."[35]

Bundy's own views about the best way to get rid of the missiles are not so easy to fathom—at least not at every stage of the crisis. He urged diplomacy but like others in the ExCom, feared that Khrushchev might use a private diplomatic demarche as an opening to take the issue to the United Nations, thereby forcing Kennedy's hand. When talk of the air strike option went around the table, Bundy pressed for the Acheson version—a limited attack on the sites themselves, not an all out against Castro's airfields and other military installations, as the Joint Chiefs wanted.

The political advantages are, *very* strong, it seems to me, of the small strike. . . . The punishment fits the crime in political terms, that we are doing only what we *warned* repeatedly and publicly we would *have* to do. Uh, we are *not* generalizing the attack.[36]

In the end, of course, Kennedy opted for the blockade, and, although dangerous straits lay ahead, a diplomatic resolution of the crisis proved possible. Khrushchev took the missiles out, and Kennedy gave a pledge not to invade Cuba. Bundy's retrospective comments twenty-five years later are nuanced, yet in some respects, too emphatic about the lessons learned from the crisis. Speaking of the matter of whether the Russian missiles in Cuba would have changed the political balance, Bundy quotes Kennedy's comment that the missiles would have "appeared to, and appearances contribute to reality." Bundy agrees but adds in a carefully worded sentence, "Indeed if it is right to conclude that the missiles in Cuba would have had this effect, it becomes clear that any change in the balance of power here would have been a change determined more by our own perceptions than by those of Khrushchev."[39]

In other words, at stake in Cuba were American self-perceptions. Here is a powerful key for unlocking the secrets of American cold war policies in the 1960s. It is really not very surprising that Bundy should say these things, however, because the memoirs of Kennedy aides are replete with evidence of the administration's great fear of appearing weak or not answering the Communist challenge. Soon after the Bay of Pigs debacle, notes Rostow, JFK told him,

The British could have a nervous breakdown in the wake of Suez, the French over Algeria. They each represent six to seven percent of the free world's power—and we could cover for them. But we can't afford a nervous breakdown. We're forty percent, and there's no one to cover for us. We'd better get on with the job.[38]

And, according to Rostow, that's what they did. The job after Cuba was Vietnam. Again in retrospect, Bundy writes that the lesson of the Cuban missile crisis "was not how to 'manage' a grave crisis, but how important it is not to have one."[39] At the time of Kennedy's death, and for at least two years after that, the Vietnam problem was dealt with largely as a crisis management issue.

Arguments about whether Kennedy would have plunged into the quagmire had he lived can never be finally settled. But it is clear that the two most powerful advisers who emerge at the outset of the Vietnam troop buildup are McGeorge Bundy and Robert McNamara. Bundy's recommendations for a graduated increase of pressure on North Vietnam are basically those Lyndon Johnson adopted.

Bundy's relationship with Johnson would not be the same—on a personal level—as it had been with Kennedy. LBJ did not get on with Bundy as well as Kennedy had; yet, as it turned out, Bundy's role was greater in those years, especially with regard to Vietnam. One story has it that the national security adviser went on vacation soon after Johnson succeeded Kennedy. During his absence, Johnson was frustrated that things simply did not move so well as when Bundy was on duty.[40] It helped also that Bundy chided Kennedy holdovers for their lack of enthusiasm for the new regime. He also wrote an article, "The Presidency and the Peace," for the elite journal, Foreign Affairs, that amounted to an absolute declaration of loyalty to the office. Presidential advisers, he wrote, had to separate what was essential from what was merely complementary. JFK's youth and grace and wit were wonderful, "but they were not the center." Loyalty to Kennedy and Johnson was not "merely naturally compatible, but logically necessary as a part of a larger loyalty to their common purpose."[41]

Bundy's criticism of the "Irish Mafia" for not having a proper sense of responsibility to the national interest presaged a more problematic discomfort, bordering on intolerance, however, for individuals outside government (especially former colleagues at Harvard) who disagreed with policy in the Vietnam years. In part, this discomfort was a general ailment among the New Frontiersmen. It was generally agreed at the outset of the Kennedy administration—by its members—that henceforth the universities would play a much larger role in government, and, perhaps with less awareness of the implications, that the reverse would also be true. As Bundy put it in his 1964 speech in regard to one aspect of the new situation, "I hope it will always be true that there is a big measure of interpenetration between universities with area programs and the information-gathering agencies of the United States."[42]

In Southeast Asia, Bundy said in a memo to Kennedy in late 1961, the United States was already committed. Victory there would "produce great effects all over the world." Laos was not important, however, because the world did not see Laos as "ours." "Laos was never really ours after 1954. South Vietnam is and wants to be. Laotians have fought very little. South Vietnam troops are not U.S. Marines, but they are usable."[43]

Hence Bundy joined Gen. Maxwell Taylor and Rostow in recommending a commitment of troops in the 5,000 to 25,000 range and the sending of a large number of advisers, helicopters, tactical bombers, and other weapons. The effect would be to deter the North and galvanize the South into an active pursuit of the guerrillas.[44] Recently, Maj. Andrew Krepinevich, in *The Army and Vietnam*, has dissected the military assumptions of the U.S. Army before and during the war, bringing them down to what he calls the "concept." His argument is that the military planned to fight a midintensity war in Vietnam, stubbornly refused to change in the face of evidence that the war had to be fought at the village level, and, to explain its failures, turned always to the dubious issue of external support for the antigovernment forces.

"The characteristics of the Army Concept are two: a focus on midintensity, or conventional, war and a reliance on high volumes of firepower to minimize casualties—in effect, the substitution of material costs at every available opportunity to avoid payment in blood."[45] Clearly, it was not only the military that adhered to the concept, however, because political advisers had other reasons for their faith in a *Pax Americana Technocratica*. As one former aide to Bundy wrote about the prevailing outlook of the National Security Council after resigning his position in despair, what endowed policymakers with such confidence was

first, our unsurpassed military might; second, our clear technological supremacy; and third, our allegedly invincible benevolence (our "altruism," our affluence, our lack of territorial aspirations). Together, it is argued, this threefold endowment provides us with the opportunity and the obligation to ease the nations of the earth toward modernization and stability: toward a full-fledged *Pax Americana Technocratica*. In reaching toward this goal, Vietnam is viewed as the last and crucial test. Once we have succeeded there, the road ahead is clear.[46]

By the summer of 1963, the greatest obstacle to clearing the road appeared to be not North Vietnam or the Vietcong but the man Americans had once called the George Washington of his country, Ngo Dinh Diem. Diem's inability to satisfy Buddhist complaints, his family's role in South Vietnamese politics, and the general corrosion evident throughout his regime, had led Ambassador Henry Cabot

Lodge to conclude that the war could not be won with him. "We are launched on a course from which there is no respectable turning back: the overthrow of the Diem government," he cabled Washington on August 29, 1963.[47] Lodge's meetings with a military cabal alarmed even the severest critics of Diem. Was he absolutely sure that was the only way, Bundy cabled back, and was he sure the generals could bring it off? Unless it was certain that the generals could achieve a "quick success," "we should discourage them from proceeding since a miscalculation could result in jeopardizing [the] U.S. position in Southeast Asia."[48]

Not only was Lodge sure of the generals but he raised a point (or threat) similar to one Allen Dulles had argued before the Bay of Pigs. What would be the result if the United States did not go along with the coup plan? Credibility with the generals would be destroyed, they themselves would be put at risk, and there could be little doubt that Washington's ability to influence the Diem regime toward reform, already negligible, would disappear altogether.[49] Bundy's qualms were never completely assuaged, but the general tenor of American policy in the summer of 1963, like the months before the Cuban missile crisis, had set in train forces that could not be reversed. Kennedy's threatened withholding of aid to the Diem regime was really the crucial matter, because the South Vietnamese military was faced with the prospect of being denied any chance for a victory. A coup was really their only alternative.

Bundy's final response to Lodge made the best of the situation: "Once a coup under responsible leadership has begun . . . it is in the interest of the U.S. Government that it should succeed."[50] The coup succeeded, but while Lodge cabled Washington his assurances that the chances of ultimate victory were now greater than ever before, once the celebrations ended in Saigon, the reality was that South Vietnam had no leader to replace Diem. By early summer 1964, Vietnamese trends were all downward. With Bundy leading the way, the concept came into full force.

It was also an election year. Johnson always worried about the thunder on his right, but there was another twist to the political situation. Aide Michael Forrestal advised Bundy that the military believed that the "strong forthright actions called for" might not be taken because "some advisors" were telling him his decisions should be determined by their impact on the election, "rather than what is required in terms of the 'national interest.'"[51]

In two late May memos to Johnson, the national security adviser reported on what plans were being made, at the president's direction,

to save the situation. One object was to provide Diem's latest successor, General Khanh, with what he had repeatedly asked for—"the
tall American at every point of stress and strain." Beyond this idea of
"marrying Americans to Vietnamese at every level," it was recommended in the second memo that the president "use selected and
carefully graduated military force against North Vietnam" until Hanoi realized that it had no hope of winning. Bundy placed great emphasis on public displays of American will and determination, to impress not only the North Vietnamese but also those, like France's
Charles de Gaulle, who were calling for the "neutralization" of Vietnam. These demonstrations should begin, he proposed, with an ap-
peal to the United Nations, which would no doubt encounter a Soviet
veto, to be followed by well-publicized meetings with the SEATO allies. Next would come a congressional resolution, followed by deployment of American military forces, and ultimately, if all these were
not sufficient, a "deterrent" attack on North Vietnam itself.[52]

The memo had a confident tone to it, born out of the ExCom experience in the Cuban missile crisis. Whether or not the crisis management approach really suited a war that had been going on, in one
form or another, for nearly twenty years, Johnson now faced a quan-
dary. The whole purpose of gradual escalation, accompanied, as
Bundy suggested, by a symbolic blare of trumpets and drum roll, was
to convince the "enemy" that he could not achieve his objectives, yet
not arouse American emotions to a war pitch.

Seizing on events in the Gulf of Tonkin in early August 1964, when
North Vietnamese PT boats launched a night attack or attacks on
American destroyers, Johnson asked Congress for authority to use
military force in Southeast Asia. Though they did not admit it in public, Johnson's closest advisers were aware from the outset that the
North Vietnamese attacks were retaliatory in nature for various South
Vietnamese and American operations against their territory. "What is
[the] 34-A role in all this?" a member of the inner circle asked immediately, naming one secret operation, at a White House lunch on August 4. "*Must* be [the] *cause;* no other is rational," was the answer
given, although perhaps not a sufficient cause. At a National Security
Council meeting, Johnson asked CIA Director John McCone if it was
his opinion that the North Vietnamese wanted a war. No, McCone
replied, they were reacting defensively. "They are responding out of
pride and on the basis of defense considerations." But it was a signal
they had the will to continue the present war.[53]

These tactics may have served crisis management purposes on the
Hill, by sending a supposedly not-too-subtle message to Hanoi that

LBJ's terms were better than Barry Goldwater's and that restraint on North Vietnam's side would be the best guarantee that American forces did not become more deeply involved. But they did nothing about two other fundamental problems Johnson faced—the unstable internal situation in South Vietnam and the lack of Allied, especially French, support for American policy.

The effort to convince America's allies that the world's fate was at stake in Vietnam raised the costs of failure to a new level. This was not well understood, if at all, at the time, because no one imagined the possibility of defeat, unless it proved impossible to get a stable government in Saigon. Soon after the Gulf of Tonkin resolution was passed by Congress, National Security Adviser Bundy gave an upbeat assessment of what even a limited military escalation could accomplish. The inability of the post-Diem regime to right itself was by far the most worrisome aspect of the situation, he suggested. The object of putting troops in, therefore, would not be to win any specific military objective but to improve morale. "It seems to me at least possible," concluded Bundy, "that a couple of brigade-size units put in to do specific jobs about six weeks from now might be good medicine everywhere."[54]

By mid-January 1965, Washington was feeling intense pressure. It was coming, however, not from Hanoi so much as Saigon. The Vietnamese saw that the guerrillas were gaining steadily in the countryside, said Bundy, who now teamed with Secretary McNamara to make a direct recommendation, not one merely responsive to LBJ's instructions. Meanwhile, "they see the enormous power of the United States withheld, and they get little sense of firm and active U.S. policy." Whatever reasons and claims were later made for the use of American airpower in Vietnam, it was concern about morale—on both sides of the struggle—that triggered the sustained bombing of the North. Bundy and McNamara insisted that "the worst course of action . . . [was] to continue in this essentially passive role which can only lead to eventual defeat and an invitation to get out in humiliating circumstances." The best course was "to use our military power in the Far East and to force a change of Communist policy."[55]

Johnson decided to send Bundy to Vietnam to see for himself. While he was there, the NLF launched an attack on the American military installations at Pleiku that killed seven and wounded over one hundred. Bundy visited the hospital and was deeply moved. According to David Halberstam, Johnson himself believed that it changed Vietnam for Bundy. He had been used to poets and intellectuals at Harvard, now he faced men in pain. Later, still according to

Halberstam, Johnson told his national security adviser, "Well, they made a believer out of you, didn't they. A little fire will do that."[56]

This bit of Johnson lore via Halberstam needs to be regarded with more than a pinch of salt. Bundy has also been quoted as saying, "Pleikus are like streetcars—such an opportunity for retaliation arose regularly."[57] Perhaps it would be best to say that Vietnam had an emotional impact on Bundy and that Pleiku heightened his concern. The grave weakness in the American posture in Vietnam, he insisted in his report to the president, was the widespread belief that the United States did not have the "will and force and patience and determination to take the necessary action and stay the course."

This is the overriding reason for our present recommendation of a policy of sustained reprisal. Once such a policy is put in force, we shall be able to speak in Vietnam on many topics and in many ways, with growing force and effectiveness.[58]

An interesting dissent to this course was lodged by the CIA's William Colby, who would remark to Bundy that a fatal error was being made by concentrating on fine-tuning the next increment of bombing North Vietnam. Instead major attention should be given to how to meet the challenge at the village level. "You may be right, Bill," answered the national security adviser, "but the structure of the American government probably won't permit it."[59]

It was a telling point. Colby interpreted the remark to mean that the Pentagon could only fight a war in the ways it knew how, and there was no organization in the structure that could fight in any other ways (essentially a failure of imagination). The concept could not be challenged. Bundy may have meant, however, that Congress could not have been moved to continue support of the effort in Vietnam without the drama of bombing raids. But the essential problem facing Johnson was that he and his advisers believed they did not have time to formulate and carry out a policy to combat the challenge in the villages. At a National Security Council meeting on February 18, 1965, for example, Johnson expressed the fear that any hint of a negotiated settlement would give the wrong impression to Saigon. "Under these circumstances Saigon might begin its own negotiations very quickly and without our knowledge or participation."[60]

Increasingly, the feeling in Washington was that Saigon was not the proper authority to negotiate peace. The bombing had been started not to win the war but out of desperation to prevent political collapse in the South. Given that situation, a dangerous assumption that South Vietnam could not be trusted with its own future, at least until a stable government had been achieved, began to be taken for granted: Vietnam was too important a decision for the Vietnamese. An unsigned National Security Council memorandum of February 1965 explained why. The author began his comments with a blunt statement that historians of the future might designate the 1960s as the decade when "our civilization fashioned so painfully since the Reformation could be said to have reached its end." If that happened, it would likely not be because of nuclear cataclysm but as a result of a new polarization of the world between the poor, the restless, and the nonwhite peoples, led or pushed by China, as opposed to Europe and North America. If that happened, "we will find ourselves in a virtual state of seige."

The West, of course, still can survive as a political grouping and even as a culture. We will still maintain overwhelming military power in the sense that we could at any time reduce the land mass of Asia and of Africa to ashes. But this would provide us with slim comfort. . . .

In the last analysis, the West must preserve (or at least not willingly and voluntarily default) its access to, communications with, and benign influence on the peoples of Asia and Africa. We have much that is worthwhile to offer and much to gain. Our society and theirs can be enriched and nourished by the two-way flow of ideas and goods and peoples. China has chosen to slam its doors, at least for the present. We and the other peoples of the world cannot afford to see any more doors close, for every door that closes quickens the pace of rich-poor, colored-white, North-South division of the world.[61]

The vision of China as the ultimate enemy in Southeast Asia forced Bundy to think about the possibility of war. What was the American object in Vietnam? he asked himself in late March 1965. The "cardinal" interest was "*not* to be a Paper Tiger," "not to have it thought that when we commit ourselves we really mean no high risks. [T]his means, essentially, a willingness to fight China *if* necessary."[62]

Johnson's advisers had all realized that the bombing campaign, Rolling Thunder, would not win the war—only buy time and impress both Vietnams with American determination. Large-scale troop deployments came under consideration soon after Rolling Thunder got under way, first as perimeter forces designed to prevent any repetition of the surprise attack at Pleiku and then, without public notice, as at least semioffensive units.[63]

Bundy had tried his hand at several draft messages for Johnson to deliver to Congress, or on some public occasion, to prepare the nation for the escalation or "Americanization" of the war. With the Teach-In Movement gaining momentum (largely in response to Rolling Thunder), Bundy looked for some "dramatic packaging" that could win back straying liberals. On March 30, 1965, he sent Johnson a memo that proposed the establishment of a Southeast Asia Development Corporation, to be formed by the nations of the region and to which North Vietnam could belong once there was a settlement of the war. The industrialized nations of the world could be invited to contribute resources. The tasks of this new organization should include various projects, for example, "the Mekong Valley—bigger and more imaginative than TVA; and a lot tougher to do." [64] It might even be possible to involve the United Nations in this other war in Vietnam.

Johnson used some of the ideas in the memo when he went to Baltimore on April 7, 1965, to deliver a major speech on Vietnam at Johns Hopkins University. In the speech, the president talked about wanting negotiations and brought forth the plan for a Mekong Valley Authority. The speech did win back, at least temporarily, many liberal critics, but while the other war—which cynics called exporting the Great Society to Vietnam—was launched with great fanfare, it was essentially a sideshow to the debates over military steps to win the war.

Stung by criticism from his former Harvard colleagues, Bundy wrote a letter to the *Harvard Crimson*. "Both individual advisers and individual actions are fair targets for critical judgment," he wrote, "but no useful purpose is served by assuming that Dr. Strangelove is in charge down here." His own role, he protested, had been exaggerated, "especially by Harvard men, who often see the world through glasses that magnify the work of those who have frequented Harvard square." This typically Bundy-style putdown left the reader with two impressions, one, that the Harvard elite was not as important in the nation as it thought it was, and two, that Bundy was indeed more in the know than a college professor residing in Cambridge, Massachusetts. The heart of the long letter, which managed to touch on nearly every challenge to administration policy, was Bundy's placement of blame for any future enlargement of the war on the other side. Once again, all the emphasis was on credibility and how that famous Harvard graduate, John Kennedy, had "redeemed" American failures at a crucial point in the cold war:

The initiative in attack has come from others, not from us. The risks of a real enlargement are least when our will is clear and our temper cool. [Crisis management again!] We are not paper tigers, and it would be a very great danger to the peace of all the world if we should carelessly let it be thought that we are. This is the lesson that we learned in failure and redeemed in triumph by John F. Kennedy over Cuba. . . . The truth is that we are not tigers at all. We are strong and loyal friends whose purpose is peace and progress, in Asia as elsewhere. The work of development—for all countries—awaits us. The door to discussion—with all countries—is open. But in the present case, as so often before, the way to peace lies over the hard road of determination. *It has been so since 1940 for us all.*[65]

Secretary of State Dean Rusk was famous, of course, for invoking the "Munich Analogy" to explain why the United States could not let Ho Chi Minh take over all Vietnam. Bundy's analogy here is a bit more subtle. The threat is that U.S. failure in Vietnam will encourage not a big attack like Hitler's blitzkreig but a gradual deterioration. There was nothing subtle about Bundy's handling of a television debate with "teach-in" critic Professor Hans Morgenthau, however.

The national security adviser had been scheduled to appear at the National Teach-In, held in Washington on May 15, 1965. He was absent that day because he was in the Dominican Republic, attending to the presumed Communist threat in that revolution, an intervention that brought down new criticism on the administration and saw the split between Johnson and Senator Fulbright, chairman of the Senate Foreign Relations Committee, become permanent.[66] In the national teach-in, a team of critics had debated a team of administration supporters. Bundy agreed to join another team for a debate on CBS television on June 21, 1965. It soon turned into a one-on-one match between the national security adviser and Morgenthau. Bundy's tactic was to confront the professor with his past mistakes and erroneous prophecies. Turning over card after card containing Morgenthau's statements, Bundy clearly relished reading back the professor's words and confronting him not on Vietnam but with his doomsaying views from yesterday and before.[67]

Bundy dealt with critics inside the administration somewhat differently. The most prominent of these was Undersecretary of State George Ball. In spring and early summer 1965, Bundy wrote memos that reflected many of the questions and doubts Ball posed. But on July 1, 1965, the national security adviser recommended that the president "listen hard" to Ball and then decide in favor of his brother, William Bundy, assistant secretary of state for the Far East, who had offered a scaled down version of Defense Secretary McNamara's plan for putting combat troops into Vietnam.[68]

The important point, as political scientist Larry Berman notes, was that Bill Bundy's proposal was not a compromise at all but a way "for getting into the war as quietly as possible."[69] Ball had proposed, on July 1, 1965, that the United States extricate itself by a negotiated withdrawal. Rusk and McNamara both felt that Ball's paper should not be argued before a large group, "that it is exceedingly dangerous to have this possibility reported in a wider circle." Bundy took a curious position on this, suggesting to the president that the inclusion of other voices, prointervention voices, might be helpful, where, it seems, Rusk and McNamara did not want to talk about the possibility of withdrawal at all. But he agreed with the two secretaries.[70]

Ball did have his day in court during the discussions at the end of July, but the decision was to go ahead with a plan to send 100,000 combat troops to Vietnam. The Johnson administration had passed the point of no return. At the end of 1965, Bundy and McNamara pressed Johnson to accept a bombing pause, in part because critics continued to charge that Washington had not gone the "full distance" in seeking negotiations but also because it had become clear that the war required more troop deployments in 1966 and steep budget increases. "We should expect that it will not lead to negotiations, but it will strengthen your hand both at home and abroad as a determined man of peace facing a very tough course in 1966. It is quite true, as I have argued before, that the bombing is not what started the trouble, but it is also true that we have a great interest in proving our own good faith as peace lovers."[71]

Bundy was quite right in believing the pause would not lead to negotiations. Leaders in Hanoi had also made up their minds. And he was also correct in assuming that the exercise was really about will and determination. What was missing from an analysis of the war, however, was Bundy's own statement that the "bombing is not what started the trouble," in the sense that the war in Vietnam that counted was the war in the South. If that could not be won, and there were still no indications beyond the consistently overly optimistic "body counts" that it was being won, bombing pauses were part of a "losing" strategy at home that would not satisfy liberal critics and only further alienate conservatives.

The bombing pause strategy, as defined by Bundy, therefore, only confused the basic issues in the war and confirmed the problematic assumption that those who held out against the bombing were really "causing" American defeat. As the bombing pause strategy absorbed both defenders and critics of the war, moreover, the debate shifted away from questions about whether the U.S. military in Vietnam was capable of defeating the enemy—whatever the numbers of American troops deployed—and whether the Pentagon concept offered anything but stalemate at constantly higher levels to outflanking the critics. "If we give up the bombing," said Bundy in a memo about resumption in late January 1966, "when we get nothing but a brutal

'No' from Hanoi, we will give them a wholly wrong signal and strengthen the hard-liners among them. They will reach the conclusion that we are weak and ready to quit, and the chance of moving to a peace settlement will go down, not up. All our evidence shows that the people who talk about an indefinite suspension are working against peace and not in favor of it."[72]

On the slippery slope of that proposition, Johnson slid toward a military imbroglio in Southeast Asia and political disaster at home. A few weeks after writing this memo on ending the bombing pause, Bundy resigned to head the Ford Foundation. Before leaving Washington, Bundy appeared on NBC's news program, "Meet the Press." The stated American objective in Vietnam was to allow the people of the South the right of self-determination. This was the reason given by Washington, therefore, that Hanoi's insistence that the Saigon government had to be dissolved as a precondition of negotiations could not be countenanced. Afterward, supposedly, the decision of whether or not the NLF could be elected to power was up to the Vietnamese. But it was always left fuzzy.

Caught unaware by a question concerning a possible coalition government, Bundy danced around the issue as best he could. People who wanted to live in peace and had different political opinions should create no problem. "It is when you talk about the usefulness of putting Communists in a position of power and responsibility that I think you are in trouble."[73]

About a year later, Bundy wrote in *Foreign Affairs* a reaffirmation of his faith in the administration's strategy, while trying to take into account certain of the views of the critics. On the bombing, he now insisted, contrary to liberal criticism, that it had been carried out with the greatest care and was "the most restrained in modern warfare." It was wholly wrong to charge the president and secretary of defense with recklessness. "What they deserve instead is the understanding support of those who want restraint, as they continue to resist pressures from the few who do believe in greatly widening the war as a means to ending it."[74]

Whereas he had once sought to put the onus of risking a prolonged war by sending the wrong signal to Hanoi on those who wanted to end the bombing, Bundy was now attempting to shift the responsibility for holding the "hawks" in check to the "doves." He also suggested that while it was good "on balance" that Vietnam was the first televised war, "it remains a striking fact that this time we get our dose of *The Naked and the Dead* not afterward, but instantly."[75] The implied comparison with World War II, and secondarily with Norman Mailer's semimuckraking novel, was clever juxtaposition but not likely to deter further criticism, or even distract the public as his earlier chastising of Morgenthau had done.

But the central argument of the piece was a retreat to the old postwar fear of the repercussions of a new "isolationism" at home and abroad. At home the consequences of defeat would be, he insisted, "heavy reaction." Abroad, while the United States could not assure peace and progress, "there is no safety yet for free men anywhere without us, and it is the relation between this astonishing proposition and the complexities of each part of the world that makes the conduct of our foreign affairs such an overwhelming task."[76]

There was, he concluded as well, a decisive difference between raising the cost of aggression and trying to "win" by "defeating" Hanoi. Once again the concept emerged as the guiding principle of American military and political strategy: this was a war between two nations. And now he did not talk about the problem of the postwar government in South Vietnam but suggested that the war might end as the struggle in Greece had ended after World War II, with the Communists folding their tents and disappearing back into the countryside. "If the Communists do decide that their present purposes exceed their capacity, may they not prefer a private decision to a public admission?"[77]

In fall 1967, McNamara's doubts about the efficacy of the concept, especially the bombing strategy, was a key factor in Johnson's decision to summon a council of cold war "wise men" to reconsider the war in Vietnam. There were many other issues to consider besides Vietnam itself, such as the deepening seriousness of the balance of payments problem.

Johnson needed to impress the nation with the thought that he was seeking the best advice possible; but he also needed to see if there really was any advice they had to offer. Bundy chaired the sessions in November 1967 and reported back to Johnson that there was no sentiment for getting out—except for Ball's by now well-known dissent. The group took into account McNamara's concern that the bombing was not really accomplishing anything in the way of interdiction and dismissed it as too narrow a conclusion. The bombing was essential, it still appeared to them, as a political weapon in Vietnam and to keep the hawks on board at home.

There were doubts expressed about the way the war was going on the ground. The group's advice was for Johnson to become more involved on the tactical level. Bundy's rationale for this was a fascinating combination of historical analysis and immediate necessity. The commander-in-chief should visibly take command of a contest, said Bundy, that was more political in its character than any since the Civil War, during which Lincoln at last took charge of the military strategy. "I think the visible exercise of his [the commander-in-chief's] authority is not only best for the war but also best for public opinion—and also best for the internal confidence of the Government. Briefings which cite the latest statistics have lost their power to persuade. So have spectacular summits."[78]

Perhaps without fully realizing it, Bundy and the wise men had raised the possibility that the government was in danger of coming apart—not from outside criticism, although that focused attention on the issue, but from an internal breakdown. The rationale for the war now also included, however subtly suggested, the necessity to see it through to prevent that breakdown from happening. Bundy expected, for reasons of hope more than anything else, that if Johnson led a review of military strategy on the ground, something could emerge that would gradually increase chances of success and gradually decrease the cost in American lives and money:

There just has to be an end of the cost of build-up at some point, and we ought not to let anyone believe that the dollar in Vietnam doesn't matter. It matters like Hell to our ability to stay the course.[79]

The next time the wise men met was in the aftermath of the 1968 Tet Offensive. There had been a complete turnaround in attitudes toward the war in that group. Before them was General Westmoreland's request for another huge troop deployment. The enemy had been turned back this time, but Westmoreland wanted another 200,000 troops to pursue his "victory" to a conclusion. Bundy pondered the alternatives without much optimism: "Great fall-off in support. Hell of a statement now is 'here they come again, with $30 billion now forever instead of $25 billion.'" "In World War II, 'prevail we will' would work," said Clark Clifford, "because conditions were right. Now they aren't." Arthur Goldberg asked the final question, "Can we continue this effort without erosion of public confidence."[80]

The upshot of the sessions the wise men held and their meeting with Johnson was the decision for a partial bombing halt in the hope that peace negotiations could begin. Johnson also took himself out of the 1968 presidential race so as to seek peace. In mid-August, Bundy wrote the president that he now felt, after years of taking the opposite side, that a full bombing halt was necessary and in American interests. He insisted that his reasons were quite different from those of doves and leftists. His reasons, however, did correspond in many respects to those of the doves and the leftists.

A bombing halt was, he said, a "grave" question. "What I hope for is a decision of imaginative courage, not *because* of soft-headed pressure from doves, but really *in spite of* them. I think stopping the bombing is now the right course for those who want to defend the gains we have made in Southeast Asia since 1964." [81] The response from Johnson was a negative, drafted by Rostow, Bundy's successor as national security adviser. It was good, said the response, "to enjoy again the sharpness and clarity of your mind." Then it continued with this reading back to Bundy of his own previous assumptions and studied way of dealing with dissent, with the barest touch of "Tory reasonableness": "I know it's hard to believe on the outside, but the simple fact is the other side is not yet ready for a settlement. I do not despair that they might be ready sometime in the weeks and months ahead—although I am not counting on this." [82]

At the end of October, Johnson went ahead with a full suspension of the bombing. It was really the beginning of "Vietnamization," although it was undertaken in an effort to save Hubert Humphrey's candidacy. Johnson went back to the LBJ ranch to brood about the war, with, among others, Doris Kearns. [83] Bundy left the Ford Foundation and became a professor at New York University, where he became a student of the foreign policy of both nuclear superpowers in the atomic age and a powerful commentator on ways of avoiding the ultimate catastrophe. [84]

McGeorge Bundy's central concern as the formal holder of the office of national security adviser in the Kennedy and early Johnson years had been the effective functioning of the presidency. While he also performed specific diplomatic missions for LBJ, what really paved the way for the freewheeling style of his illustrious successor, Henry Kissinger, was his reorganization of the National Security Council as the president's quick response vehicle as opposed to the ponderous State Department.

With Kissinger's arrival in the basement of the White House, the national security adviser's role became too visible for the good of either the president or his counselor. The special circumstances of the Nixon years explain part of the reason that happened, but Bundy's activism redefined the scope and power of the office and prepared the way for someone with Kissinger's special talents and ego. At times, the ability to control the flow of information does become the ability to shape the outcome, however subtle or indirect the understanding of the situation between the principals might be.

Harry Hopkins with hand grenades? Mac Bundy was much more than that.

NOTES

1. Sidney Hyman, "When Bundy Says, 'The President Wants—,'" *New York Times Magazine*, December 2, 1962, 30–31, 132–133.

2. Max Frankel, "The Importance of Being Bundy," *New York Times Magazine*, March 28, 1965, 32–35, 96–97.

3. Thomas Paterson, ed., *Kennedy's Quest for Victory: American Foreign Policy, 1961–1963* (New York: Oxford University Press, 1989): 11.

4. David Halberstam, *The Best and the Brightest* (New York: Random House, 1972): 60.

5. "A Message to Teachers" [June 28, 1918], in Arthur S. Link et al., eds., *The Papers of Woodrow Wilson*, vol. 48 (Princeton: Princeton University Press, 1985): 455–456.

6. Quoted in Lloyd C. Gardner, ed., *Wilson and Revolutions: 1913–1921* (Philadelphia, 1976): 66–69.

7. Quoted in William Appleman Williams et al., eds., *America in Vietnam* (New York: Anchor Press/Doubleday, 1985): 247–248.

8. Ibid.

9. "JFK's McGeorge Bundy—Cool Head for Any Crisis," *Newsweek*, March 1, 1963, 20–24.

10. Milton MacKaye, "Bundy of the White House," *Saturday Evening Post*, March 10, 1962, 82–84.

11. Hyman, "When Bundy Says," 30–31, 132–133.

12. Ibid. A less exalted treatment of the "Bundy tradition" was uttered by British journalist Henry Fairlie, who wrote about their instinctive commitment to the establishment: "When has any Bundy ever rebelled, apart from his mother, who resigned from the Daughters of the American Revolution when it had the insolence to ask from her a fee of twenty-five dollars to authenticate her genealogy?" *The Kennedy Promise: The Politics of Expectation* (New York: Doubleday, 1973): 176.

13. Ronald Steel, *Walter Lippmann and the American Century* (Boston: Little, Brown, 1980): 523.

14. Arthur M. Schlesinger, Jr., *A Thousand Days: John F. Kennedy in the White House* (Boston: Houghton Mifflin, 1965): 207.

15. Fairlie, *The Kennedy Promise*, 174.

16. MacKaye, "Bundy of the White House," 82–84.

17. John P. Burke, Fred I. Greenstein, with collaboration of Larry Berman

and Richard Immerman, *How Presidents Test Reality: Decisions on Viet Nam, 1954 and 1965* (New York: Russell Sage Foundation, 1989). The way Kennedy organized the National Security Council and indeed his presidency, commented Henry Fairlie, meant that only minds of the "same bent" had access to the Oval Office. "The advice which John Kennedy invited was, for this reason, dismayingly thin." *The Kennedy Promise*, 176.

18. Roger Hilsman, *To Move a Nation: The Politics of Foreign Policy in the Administration of John F. Kennedy* (New York: Doubleday, 1967): 6.

19. Fairlie, *The Kennedy Promise*, 135.

20. George Ball, *The Past Has Another Pattern: Memoirs* (New York: W. W. Norton, 1982): 187–188.

21. Fairlie, *The Kennedy Promise*, 135.

22. Halberstam, *The Best and the Brightest*, 160–161.

23. Such symbols took on special importance in Kennedy's mind. On learning that two "Communist-oriented" nations had requested Peace Corps volunteers, Kennedy told Secretary of State Dean Rusk, "If we can successfully crack Ghana and Guinea, Mali may turn to the West." Paterson, *Kennedy's Quest for Victory*, 15.

24. Wayne S. Smith, *The Closest of Enemies: A Personal and Diplomatic History of the Castro Years* (New York: W. W. Norton, 1987): 68–70.

25. Fairlie, *The Kennedy Promise*, 180–181.

26. Walter LaFeber, *Inevitable Revolutions: The United States in Central America* (New York: W. W. Norton, 1983): 149–150.

27. Paterson, *Kennedy's Quest for Victory*, 135–138.

28. James G. Hershberg, "Before 'The Missiles of October': Did Kennedy Plan a Military Strike against Cuba?" *Diplomatic History* 14 (Spring 1990): 163–198.

29. McGeorge Bundy, *Danger and Survival: Choices about the Bomb in the First Fifty Years* (New York: Random House, 1988): 395.

30. Ibid., 415–416.

31. Hershberg, "Before 'The Missiles of October,'" 166.

32. Ibid., 170–171.

33. See James G. Blight and David A. Welch, *On the Brink: Americans and Soviets Reexamine the Cuban Missile Crisis* (New York: Hill and Wang, 1989).

34. Paterson, *Kennedy's Quest for Victory*, 142.

35. See "White House Tapes and Minutes of the Cuban Missile Crisis: ExCom Meetings, October 1962," with an introduction by Marc Trachtenberg, *International Security* 10 (Summer 1985): 164–203. See also Bundy, *Danger and Survival*, 391–462.

36. "White House Tapes," 188.

37. Bundy, *Danger and Survival*, 452.

38. W. W. Rostow, "Beware of Historians Bearing False Analogies," *Foreign Affairs* 66 (Spring 1988): 863–868.

39. Bundy, *Danger and Survival*, 462.

40. Halberstam, *The Best and the Brightest*, 347.

41. *Foreign Affairs* 42 (April 1964): 353–365.

42. Fairlie, *The Kennedy Promise*, 135.

43. Paterson, *Kennedy's Quest for Victory*, 235.

44. Ibid., 234.

45. Andrew Krepinevich, *The Army and Vietnam* (Baltimore: Johns Hopkins University Press, 1986): 5.

46. James C. Thomson, Jr., "How Could Vietnam Happen? An Autopsy," *The Atlantic Monthly* 22 (April 1968): 47–53.

47. The Senator Gravel Edition, *The Pentagon Papers*, 4 vols. (Boston: Beacon Press, 1971), II: 738–739.

48. Ibid., 782–783.

49. Ibid., 789–792.

50. Ibid., 792–793.

51. Quoted in Krepinevich, *The Army and Vietnam*, 95.

52. Bundy to Johnson, May 22, 1965, and Bundy to Johnson, May 25, 1964, The Papers of Lyndon Baines Johnson, The Lyndon Baines Johnson Library, Austin, Texas, National Security Files, Bundy Memos to the President, Boxes 1 and 2.

53. Lunch Notes, August 4, 1964, McGeorge Bundy Papers, Johnson Library, Box 1. See also, William Colby, *Lost Victory: A Firsthand Account of America's Sixteen-Year Involvement in Vietnam* (Chicago: Contemporary Books, 1989): 181. The North Vietnamese attack "was clearly a retaliation for a covert raid the previous night by maritime forces the CIA had initiated and turned over to the Department of Defense." For McCone quote, see "The 'Phantom Battle' that Led to War," *U. S. News and World Report*, July 23, 1984, 56–67.

54. Bundy to Johnson, August 31, 1964, Johnson Papers, National Security Files, Bundy Memos for the President, Box 2.

55. Bundy to Johnson, January 27, 1965, Johnson Papers, National Security Files, Bundy Memos for the President, Box 2.

56. Halberstam, *The Best and the Brightest*, 521.

57. George C. Herring, *America's Longest War: The U.S. and Vietnam, 1950–1975* (New York: John Wiley, 1979): 130.

58. Bundy to Johnson, February 7, 1965, Johnson Papers, National Security Council Meetings, Box 1.

59. Colby, *Lost Victory*, 179.

60. Minutes of National Security Council Meeting, February 18, 1965, Johnson Papers, National Security Council Meetings, Box 1.

61. Unsigned Memorandum, February [?], 1965, Johnson Papers, National Security Files, International Travel, Boxes 28–29. The memo has notes in McGeorge Bundy's handwriting, but the basic themes were common enough in Bundy's day and in that of his successors, Walt Rostow and Henry Kissinger.

62. "Vietnam—what is our interest there and our object," draft memo, March 22, 1965, Johnson Papers, National Security Files, Files of McGeorge Bundy, Box 17.

63. For the background to and details of all these decisions, see Larry

Berman, *Planning a Tragedy: The Americanization of the War in Vietnam* (New York: W. W. Norton, 1982): chap. 3.

64. Bundy to Johnson, March 30, 1965, Johnson Papers, Files of McGeorge Bundy, Box 17.

65. Draft, April 20, 1965, Johnson Papers, Files of McGeorge Bundy, Boxes 18–19. Emphasis added.

66. Bundy's role in the Dominican crisis needs more analysis than is possible in the space available here. That he believed the Communist danger was real and that the American intervention was justified seems clear. See, e.g., Bundy to Rusk, May 26, 1965, Johnson Papers, National Security Files, Dominican Republic, Boxes 49–54. For the general framework of the intervention, see Walter LaFeber, "Latin American Policy," in Robert Divine, ed., *The Johnson Years, Volume One* (Manhattan: University Press of Kansas, 1987): 63–92, and Abraham F. Lowenthal, *The Dominican Intervention* (Cambridge: Harvard University Press, 1972).

67. *New York Times*, June 22, 1965, 1–2.

68. Berman, *Planning a Tragedy*, 70–94.

69. Ibid., 94.

70. Bundy to Johnson, July 1, 1965, Johnson Papers, National Security Files, Bundy Memos to the President, Box 4.

71. Bundy to Johnson, November 27, 1965, Johnson Papers, National Security Files, Vietnam, Boxes 91–95.

72. Bundy to Johnson, January 24, 1966, Johnson Papers, National Security Files, Vietnam, Boxes 91–95.

73. Transcript of February 20, 1966, Johnson Papers, Files of McGeorge Bundy, Boxes 15–16.

74. "The End of Either/Or," *Foreign Affairs* 45 (January 1967): 189–201.

75. Ibid.

76. Ibid.

77. Ibid.

78. Bundy to Johnson, November 10, 1967, Johnson Papers, Reference Files, Miscellaneous Vietnam Documents.

79. Ibid.

80. Notes of March 19, 1968, Johnson Papers, Meeting Notes Files, Box 2.

81. Bundy to Johnson, August 15, 1964, Johnson Papers, National Security Files, Vietnam, Boxes 92–95.

82. Draft, August 22, 1965, Johnson Papers, National Security Files, Vietnam, Boxes 92–95.

83. Doris Kearns, *Lyndon Johnson and the American Dream* (New York: Harper and Row, 1976), is really all about his brooding over Vietnam. But see esp. chap. 9.

84. Bundy, *Danger and Survival*.

CHAPTER 8

And Then There Were None!
How Arthur H. Vandenberg and Gerald P. Nye Separately Departed Isolationist Leadership Roles

WAYNE S. COLE

In the depression decade of the 1930s, before World War II, Republican Senators Arthur H. Vandenberg of Michigan and Gerald P. Nye of North Dakota were among the more vocal, powerful, and uncompromising of America's "isolationist" leaders. At the close of World War II, in the middle of the 1940s, both Vandenberg and Nye were removed from the ranks of isolationist leadership—Vandenberg through conversion to bipartisan internationalism and Nye through rejection by voters at the polls.

Uncompromising and unyielding in his commitment to traditional patterns in American foreign affairs, Nye was defeated in 1944 and never again won election to any public office or appointment to any position calling for judgment on foreign policy matters. More flexible and adaptable, Vandenberg adjusted to political realities at home and abroad and moved on to provide leadership for bipartisan forces undergirding America's internationalism, collective security, and containment policies in the nuclear age. History sees Nye as a symbol and remnant of an obsolete, parochial, misguided, and almost irresponsible approach to foreign affairs that had long since outlived its usefulness. History finds in Vandenberg the wisdom to recognize the errors of his earlier ways and the statesmanship to help guide America, Congress, and his own Republican party toward enlight-

232

ened policies and institutions for the protection of peace, security, and freedom—the United Nations, the Marshall Plan, containment, and the North Atlantic Treaty Organization. In that sense, Vandenberg helped shape responsible contributions to the "Long Peace" that continues to serve Americans and billions of others nearly a half-century later.

By examining those two persons in depth, one may uncover and reveal some of the elements that led the United States to turn away from the traditional noninterventionist and unilateral policies it had pursued through much of its early independent history and to embrace multilateral leadership roles through the decades since World War II. There were similarities in the backgrounds and performances of the two men, but there were also fundamental differences. Those differences were extraordinarily significant both for the careers of those men and for the future of the United States in world affairs.

Both Vandenberg and Nye were born late in the nineteenth century in the Upper Mississippi Valley Middle West—Vandenberg in Grand Rapids, Michigan, in 1884, Nye in Hortonville, Wisconsin, in 1892. Both could trace their ancestry back to the colonial period in American history. Both were reared in politically concerned Republican families, and both remained loyal Republicans throughout their lives. Neither graduated from college. Neither was a lawyer. Both had been newspapermen: Vandenberg was editor of the *Grand Rapids Herald* from 1906 until he went to the Senate twenty-two years later; Nye was editor of small town newspapers in Wisconsin, Iowa, and North Dakota from the time he graduated from high school in 1911 until he went to the Senate nearly fifteen years later. Though both were patriotic, neither ever served in the U.S. armed forces. Both were too young for service in the Spanish-American War; both were married and had dependents during World War I; and both were senators and past middle age during World War II.[1]

Both men gained their Senate seats initially by appointment—Nye as a young man of thirty-three in 1925, Vandenberg at the age of forty-five in 1928. Both served more than three terms in the senate—Nye for nearly twenty years until 1945, Vandenberg for nearly twenty-three years until his death in 1951. Both were fervent isolationists until after the Japanese attack on Pearl Harbor on December 7, 1941, and neither explicitly repudiated or apologized for his noninterventionist views and activities.

At 5'10" and less than 160 pounds, the lean young Nye was three inches shorter than Vandenberg and more than forty pounds lighter.

His smoothly combed brown hair provided a youthful, almost boyish, appearance. Vandenberg's dark, graying, and thinning hair, along with his formidable build and posture, provided a more distinguished (some thought pompous and posturing) appearance and style.

Both married twice and fathered children. Vandenberg's first wife, a talented pianist, bore them three children before her death; his second marriage was to a Chicago journalist and socialite. Nye was first married in 1916 to a Missouri nurse and, after a quiet divorce in 1940, then married an attractive Iowa schoolteacher; he had three children by each of his wives.

Both men were serious, earnest, and hardworking. Neither was good at small talk, and neither really felt comfortable in Washington's party circuit. Neither was ever involved in any financial or political scandal. Neither was a part of or really accepted by the "eastern urban establishment." Both became talented and moving orators, Nye more than Vandenberg. Both were more effective in committee and in winning press attention than in engineering enactment of specific legislation (though Vandenberg eventually became far more effective than Nye in legislative matters). Both were mentioned as possible presidential nominees—Vandenberg much more often and more seriously than Nye. Neither ever won nomination or election to any executive office, and neither ever held any judicial position. Until Vandenberg represented the United States at the San Francisco conference that drafted the United Nations Charter in 1945, neither had had any formal diplomatic experience.

Both men served on the Senate Foreign Relations Committee. Vandenberg chaired that powerful committee during the Republican-led 80th Congress, helping to shape America's containment policies in the early years of the cold war from 1947 to 1949. Nye did not become a member of the Foreign Relations Committee until nearly three-fourths of the way through his Senate career, when he replaced the legendary William E. Borah of Idaho who had died early in 1940. But Nye never became the power on the committee that Borah had been—or that Vandenberg was to become. Instead, Nye's greatest prominence on foreign policy matters came as chair of the Munitions Investigating Committee, in his battles on neutrality legislation, and in his speaking engagements across the country (including those he gave under the sponsorship of the America First Committee in 1941).

Senator Nye and Senator Vandenberg were co-authors of the resolution calling for creation of a select committee to investigate the munitions industry. Both were prominent in that Senate investigation from 1934 to 1936—Nye as chair and Vandenberg as one of the committee's more active members. Their views on the findings and recommendations did not differ greatly, except that Nye was part of the committee majority favoring government ownership of munitions industries, while Vandenberg was part of the minority that favored reliance on strict government control of private munitions companies.[2] Both played active roles in the background and enactment of the neutrality laws of 1935, 1936, and 1937. Both favored mandatory legislation and opposed the discretionary provisions sought by internationalists and the administration. Both vigorously opposed President Franklin D. Roosevelt's efforts to revise those neutrality laws away. Both failed in those efforts.[3]

Neither Vandenberg nor Nye ever voted for Roosevelt in any of his four campaigns for the presidency.[4] Though both conferred with FDR on specific matters—domestic and foreign—and though both had official social contact with him, neither was close to the president personally or politically. Roosevelt actively courted some prominent prewar isolationists such as Hiram Johnson of California, George Norris of Nebraska, Burton K. Wheeler of Montana, and Robert M. La Follette, Jr., of Wisconsin to win their support for his domestic New Deal program. Neither Vandenberg nor Nye, however, won much stroking of that sort either early or late in FDR's White House career.[5] In 1940, Senator Nye supported and campaigned for the nomination of Vandenberg for president in Republican primary elections. Both Vandenberg and Nye considered Abraham Lincoln their favorite president and the one who came closest to their political ideals.[6]

The two men had much in common. It should not have been surprising to find Vandenberg and Nye battling shoulder to shoulder on behalf of noninvolvement by the United States in European wars and in opposing President Roosevelt's increasingly bold aid-short-of-war internationalism before Pearl Harbor. Both Vandenberg and Nye voted for the declarations of war against Japan, Germany, and Italy after the attack on Pearl Harbor, and both supported America's war efforts against the Axis during World War II.

Nonetheless, there were certain clear differences and contrasts between Arthur H. Vandenberg and Gerald P. Nye. And those differences ultimately sent them off in different directions on American foreign affairs during and after World War II. Those differences would remove both men from the leadership of American isolationism but would do so in strikingly different ways.

An obvious difference with fundamental roots involved their views on domestic economic, social, and political issues. Both Vandenberg and Nye over time became increasingly concerned about excessive presidential power in general (what a later generation called "the Imperial Presidency") and about President Roosevelt's power in particular.[7] Nonetheless, before World War II, Nye of the northern Great Plains cattle and wheat state of North Dakota was an agrarian radical or progressive on domestic issues. Vandenberg, who was from Michigan, with its mixed agricultural and industrial economy and its combination of rural, small town, and urban populations, had sympathy for agriculture, could find accord with progressives on some issues, and never had any love for Wall Street.[8] Vandenberg, however, was never the agrarian radical or progressive that Nye was. He was an undoctrinaire conservative on domestic issues.[9] During most of his years in public life, Nye was to the left of Roosevelt and the New Deal; Vandenberg was to the right of Roosevelt and voted against much of the New Deal.

It has become conventional wisdom to equate isolationism with conservatism and internationalism with liberalism. It is commonly assumed that if an individual was an isolationist, he or she probably was a conservative on domestic issues. Similarly, it is commonly assumed that if an individual was an internationalist, he or she must be comparatively liberal on domestic issues. One can, in fact, identify specific individuals for whom those assumptions were accurate. Nonetheless, as often as not, that bit of conventional wisdom is mistaken. More often than not in the 1930s, leading isolationists were progressives or liberals on domestic issues, while many dedicated internationalists were conservatives. Such was the case with Nye and Vandenberg.

Given his mixed constituency in Michigan and given the unpopularity of business conservatism during the depression decade of the 1930s, it would have been politically unwise for Senator Vandenberg unequivocally to oppose all of FDR's New Deal relief, recovery, and reform measures. And Vandenberg never was one to fall on his sword battling for or against an issue. Instead, the Michigan senator operated from a "yes but" or an "on the other hand" posture in analyzing New Deal proposals.

In 1934, as he faced the voters in his quest for another term in the Senate, Vandenberg wrote that in his campaign he credited the New Deal with advantages that he could "conscientiously applaud" and recognized that America could not "go back to the 'old deal.'" He proposed "to develop . . . the progressive attitude of a new Republicanism which shall operate on a basis of 'social responsibility without socialism.'"[10]

When he converted those campaign words into actual votes on specific New Deal measures, however, they were negative more often than affirmative. Vandenberg voted against the AAA, the NRA, the TVA, Reciprocity, work relief, the Wagner Act, the Holding Company Bill, the "soak-the-rich" tax bill, court packing, and many other administration measures.[11]

In striking contrast, Nye had sharpened his political teeth in the spirited progressivism of Fighting Bob La Follette's Wisconsin, Woodrow Wilson's New Freedom in the second decade of the twentieth century, the agrarian radicalism of the Nonpartisan League after World War I, as one of the pridefully raucous "Sons of the Wild Jackass" in the 1920s, and as one of those progressive Republicans on whom President Roosevelt depended to help win enactment of much of his New Deal program in the 1930s. Nye temporarily broke with Roosevelt on the NRA, but that was because he saw it as benefiting big business against small business, the farmer, labor, and the "little guy." Like other western agrarian progressives, Nye really was not confident of Roosevelt's commitment to progressivism as they defined it. He thought the Democratic party would return to its old conservative ways after FDR's New Deal had run its course. One of Senator Nye's many criticisms of Roosevelt was that in refocusing his attention to foreign affairs in the latter part of the 1930s, the president was turning away from his earlier progressivism and was reestablishing big business, big military, and big government to their powerful, oppressive, and exploitive ways in America. Late in his career, Nye became disenchanted with big labor, but his compassion and empathy were always with the little guy, the weak, the downtrodden. He always feared and distrusted concentrated wealth and power, the high and the mighty, including big business, big finance, big government, big military, and (eventually) big labor.[12]

Appropriately, Vandenberg's political ideal before he entered the Senate (the person about whom he had written two or three worshipful books) was Alexander Hamilton of New York, the ideological father of the conservative Federalist party and of business conservatism in America under the Constitution. In 1938, Vandenberg called for a political coalition that "would again put Alexander Hamilton and Thomas Jefferson in partnership for the common good."[13] In contrast, Nye's conception of the good life (like Thomas Jefferson's long before) was fundamentally rural, agrarian, small business, and small town. Vandenberg's Alexander Hamilton was never Nye's ideal.[14] Vandenberg was no liberal on domestic matters.

There were also significant contrasts between Vandenberg and Nye in their respective political styles and tactics. Both Vandenberg and

Nye had substantial political talents in their separate ways; they could not have risen to such prominent positions in public life without those talents. But their styles and tactics differed.

Nye tended to put his head down and flail away in direct frontal assaults on his adversaries. His were uncomplicated direct battles on behalf of the hardworking debtor farmer, small businessman, and little guy against the privileged, creditor, wealthy, powerful, and exploitive elites in the urban Northeast. There was nothing terribly complicated, subtle, or devious about Nye's political tactics; he fought for the downtrodden good guys in rural and small town America against the powerful and exploitive bad guys in the urban Northeast and abroad.

In contrast, Vandenberg preferred coalition politics, with emphasis on building political coalitions cutting across party, economic, and sectional lines to accomplish shared objectives. In the 1930s, he particularly envisaged bipartisan coalitions on the conservative side of domestic concerns; during and after World War II, he conceived of bipartisan coalitions on the side of internationalism, collective security, and (during the cold war) containment. Always his coalition politics cut across party lines, abjured playing politics with national concerns, included an active role for Congress, and envisaged the accomplishment of broad-based unity to serve higher goals at home and abroad.

Nye's political tactics worked best in a homogeneous socioeconomic environment. The Upper Mississippi Valley that produced him and the North Dakota that he served had their diversity. There was ethnic diversity—Russian-Americans, Norwegian-Americans, German-Americans, Scotch-Irish, and Anglo-Saxons. There was religious diversity—Roman Catholics, Orthodox Catholics, Lutherans, Methodists, Presbyterians, and others. There were farmers, and there were small businessmen. There were property owners and people without productive property. There were differences between the rich and the poor (though those class differences were much less sharp than in most other parts of the country and in most other parts of the world).

Much more striking, however, were the widely shared interests and values of a rural, agricultural, small town, small business, producing, debtor, egalitarian society that felt conflicts of interest in its dealings with railroads, bankers, financiers, cities, big business, big government, big military, the East, and urban elites. Nye operated from an agrarian progressive base in a state that had little industrial or urban development. On state levels, he and his fellow agrarian progressives had no great need to construct complicated political coalitions cutting across broad socioeconomic lines. In battling for the little guy against privilege, they found it easy to rally the people on the farms and in the small towns of the West behind them.

Nye's temperament and style fit those patterns. He thrived on aggressive no-holds-barred battles for the little guy against the powerful privileged classes of the great cities in the East (and abroad). Those crusades and political tactics could and did work impressively well on the local, state, and regional levels on the Great Plains. But on the national level in the increasingly urbanized, industrialized, capital-surplus, pluralistic, bureaucratic America of the twentieth century, those crusades and tactics were almost certain to fail. And they did—on both domestic and foreign policy issues.

For Vandenberg of Michigan the circumstances, political tactics, and temperament were different. Aggressive crusades cutting across social and class lines would not work in the pluralistic political environment of Michigan as they did in the comparatively homogeneous rural society of North Dakota. And, in any event, that was not Vandenberg's style. Throughout his public career, he found fascination in trying to build broadly based bipartisan coalitions on both domestic and foreign policy issues.[15]

At the very beginning of the Roosevelt administration, Vandenberg applauded pleas "for nonpartisan action" in the economic crisis.[16] In the 1936 presidential campaign, Vandenberg endorsed the "Landon-Knox coalitionists" in opposition to "the Roosevelt party."[17] In 1937, he heartily cooperated with the "bipartisan" strategy in battling against FDR's "court packing" proposal, putting Democratic Senator Burton K. Wheeler and other Democrats and progressives (including Nye) up front in the contest against the president's proposal, while conservative Republicans (including Vandenberg) stayed back in the shadows.[18] He expected that some of the 1938 congressional and senatorial elections would "be laboratory demonstrations of the means by which a new coalition (built around the Republican nucleus)" could "produce a triumphant realignment of political parties."[19] In 1938, he boasted that he had "been talking about coalition—the need for a truly national government to meet this crisis—ever since 1934." In his view, coalition was "a state of mind long before" it was "a mechanism." He alluded to Lincoln's tactic in 1864 using "the regular Republican machinery under the temporary pseudonym of a 'Union convention' which nominated a Union ticket, ran a Union campaign, and won a Union victory with a Democratic nominee for Vice-President." Vandenberg was not recommending Lincoln's formula or a new party, but he thought the important thing at the time was "to encourage the coalition state of mind." Thus, "mechanism" would "take care of itself." It was in that context that he called for "a coalition which would again put Alexander Hamilton and Thomas Jefferson in partnership for the common good, precisely as they once cooperated to save America from Aaron Burr." Though he did not say so explicitly, it was reasonable to conclude that Vandenberg saw Roosevelt in the role of Burr in that scenario.[20] In 1938–39, Vandenberg urged approval of a "profit-sharing resolution" that conceivably might have served as a basis for accord or coalition between labor and management.[21]

In December 1941, after the Japanese attack on Pearl Harbor, Senator Vandenberg wrote to President Roosevelt urging creation of a Joint Congressional Committee on War Cooperation to be elected by the two houses of Congress.[22] The Michigan senator wholeheartedly cooperated as a member of Secretary of State Cordell Hull's Committee of Eight senators to deliberate on the proper structure for the forthcoming United Nations Organization. That secret and influential committee included four Democrats, three Republicans (including Vandenberg), and one Progressive.[23] Vandenberg responded cautiously but affirmatively in 1945 when first President Roosevelt and later President Truman named him (along with Democrats) to represent the United States in the deliberations at the San Francisco conference to draft the United Nations Charter.[24] And Republican Vandenberg was the central architect in the Senate building bipartisan bases for containment foreign policies during the Truman administration after World War II.[25]

More fundamental were differences between Nye and Vandenberg in the socioeconomic constituencies they served in public life. The America that Senator Nye identified with and spoke for (and that most other western progressive isolationists spoke for) was overwhelmingly rural and small town. It was an America consisting largely of farmers on the soil and of small businessmen buying from and selling to those farmers in countless small towns scattered across the prairies and Great Plains. The former were largely wheat and cattle farmers on the Great Plains and corn and hog farmers on the rolling prairies.[26] It was the America that William Jennings Bryan and his Populists identified with and spoke for.[27] It was the America of Arthur C. Townley's Nonpartisan League,[28] of countless agrarian progressives over the years such as the La Follettes of Wisconsin, Borah of Idaho, Hiram Johnson of California, Wheeler of Montana,

George W. Norris of Nebraska, Arthur C. Capper of Kansas, Henrick Shipstead of Minnesota, and many others before and since.[29] A century and a half earlier, it was the America of Thomas Jefferson of Virginia.[30] With variations rooted in time and region, it was the America of most people who lived and worked and died in what is now the United States during the first three centuries after Europeans began to colonize that huge part of North America.

Nye's United States was productive, debtor, egalitarian, democratic socially, Republican politically, patriotic, Christian, largely white, hardworking, and family oriented and had its ethnic roots in northern and western Europe (particularly in Germany, Scandinavia, and the British Isles). It was the America that rapidly conquered the "Last American Frontier" in the latter part of the nineteenth century and in the early years of the twentieth century. It was the America that blanketed Nye's North Dakota.[31]

But it was also the America that was rapidly waning relative to the burgeoning cities with their booming industries, expanding financial resources, ethnic and cultural diversity, sharp class divisions, more cosmopolitan and larger world perspectives and interests, and growing power in shaping and controlling American values, political parties, and government policies—domestic and foreign.[32] A person born and reared on the land or in the small towns of North Dakota could feel like a stranger in a foreign country when visiting great urban metropolitan centers in the eastern part of the United States, then and now.

The population of North Dakota never reached 700,000 during Nye's years in the Senate and generally declined later. Fryburg in western North Dakota had a population of only about 300 when he first located there in 1916, and it has declined substantially since then. Cooperstown farther east, where he lived when he went to the Senate in 1925, had a population at that time of less than 1,500. The largest city in the state, Fargo, had 20,000 people when Nye arrived in 1916 and had not yet reached 40,000 when his Senate career ended in 1945. The state capital, Bismarck, had approximately 6,000 people in 1916 and not much more than 20,000 when his Senate career ended. Those small cities and villages were largely marketing centers for the rural population. North Dakota was (and remains) one of the most sparsely populated states in the union. What little manufacturing it had largely involved the processing of agricultural products such as flour milling and meat packing.[33]

In Nye's years there, North Dakota had almost nothing in the way of defense industries and ranked at or near the bottom among states in the defense contracts it received from the federal government.[34] The per capita income in those years (and most of the time since) was below the national average (and lower on the farms than in the towns and cities). Despite the earnest efforts of the Nonpartisan League and of the state's progressive legislators, the people of North Dakota had little or no control over the prices they received for the products they produced and sold, over the prices or quality of manufactured products they purchased or of the services they required. Such matters were either controlled on the world markets (as with wheat) or by urban businessmen, bankers, and railroad entrepreneurs residing outside the state and even outside the region—in Minneapolis–St. Paul, Chicago, New York, or London. Quite literally, North Dakota (and the greater part of the Great Plains) was a "colonial" area economically—producing raw materials for markets they did not control and buying and borrowing from urban sources wholly outside their control.[35]

At the same time, North Dakota was at the geographic center of the North American continent, approximately 1,500 miles from the Atlantic and Pacific oceans. Under those circumstances, it was little wonder that Nye's constituents had difficulty working up any enthusiasm or felt immediacy for involvement in European affairs. One need not be apathetic or ill-informed in North Dakota to doubt whether the Kaiser's huns or Hitler's panzer divisions were likely to come smashing across the horizons. At the same time, it was not unjustified to see themselves as exploited and to find their exploiters in the cities of America, in railroad boardrooms, in Wall Street banking houses, and even in the government in Washington, D.C.

Farmers, townspeople, and politicians from the Great Plains put those pieces together in various ways, and the intensity of feelings varied over time and place, but nearly all could subscribe to the general perspectives sketched here. It was a socioeconomic-political scenario that did not give developments in Europe high priority; the very real difficulties that those farmers and townspeople confronted in their daily lives were much closer to home. They had little difficulty explaining massive naval building programs and involvement in foreign wars as foreign policy projections of the "selfish interests" of the great cities of the East.

All that made it easy for Senator Nye to rally political support in North Dakota. But the farmers and townspeople so numerous in North Dakota (and historically within the United States) were, in the twentieth century, rapidly slipping to a minority status within the United States generally. Farmers were already in a minority in the United States (though not in North Dakota) when Nye first went to the Senate in 1925, and they have steadily declined in numbers, percentages, and power in the decades since. Today fewer than 2 percent of the American people actually make their livings as farmers, and many of those get parts of their incomes from nonfarm sources. Less than 30 percent of the American people are classified as rural (farming and small town).[36] Despite some advantageous political institutions and talented political spokesmen, rural America, for which Nye spoke on domestic and foreign affairs, has dwindled to an almost insignificant political minority by the final decade of the twentieth century. And those farmers who remain have been so integrated into urban institutions and values that they are not even a shell of what they were when Nye was a senator from 1925 to 1945 (or what they had been early in American history when Jefferson was secretary of state, vice president, and president). American isolationism has had a multitude of roots, but insofar as it was rooted in Great Plains agriculture and in rural and small town America, it was doomed to defeat by the changing American society and economy in the twentieth century.

When turning from the Great Plains and Nye's North Dakota to Senator Vandenberg's Great Lakes state of Michigan,[37] one encounters a strikingly different socioeconomic-political environment.[38] Almost everything in Michigan was different, at least in degree. Michigan was different from North Dakota in the 1920s when Vandenberg and Nye first entered the Senate, it became more different during the two decades those men served in public office, and it became even more different during the course of the twentieth century. To a striking degree, Nye's North Dakota was a latter-day manifestation of the older America—of Jefferson's land of farmers. And the foreign policy projections of that older America (as personified in Senator Nye) were those of isolationism. In sharp contrast, Vandenberg's Michigan was a vivid manifestation of the new America—of Hamilton's urban business, commercial, industrial, and financial America. And the foreign policy projections of that newer America (as personified in the later Senator Vandenberg) were those of internationalism, collective security, and containment.

North Dakota's homogeneous society; Michigan's diversity and cultural pluralism. North Dakota's egalitarianism; Michigan's sharp class divisions. North Dakota's rural and small town society; Michigan's increasing urbanization. North Dakota's agriculture; Michigan's heavy industry. Landlocked North Dakota in the middle of a huge landmass; Middle Western Michigan with its Great Lakes shipping and developing access via the later St. Lawrence Seaway to worldwide export markets. North Dakota with almost no defense industries; Michigan labeled the "Arsenal of Democracy" during World War II. Born in the nineteenth century, Vandenberg identified with and served that earlier Middle Western farming-mining-forestry economy and its traditional foreign policy projections through more than half of his Senate career. But along with his state and nation, he changed course during World War II and the early cold war. Michigan (and the United States generally) became something new in the twentieth century; Vandenberg (and his foreign policy perspectives) caught up with his state and the nation and became something new along with them.

There was farming in Michigan—but with a difference. The soil was richer, the rainfall more plentiful, natural hazards less destructive, products more varied and adaptable, urban markets larger and closer at hand, and the percentage of farmers and hence the degree of dependence on agriculture much less than in North Dakota. Important parts of Michigan's industries involved the processing of agricultural products, for example, breakfast cereals and dairy products. Though such industries were much larger than in North Dakota, they constituted a smaller proportion of the state's manufacturing than they did in North Dakota. And forestry, mining, and shipping supplemented agriculture in the state's economy even in the nineteenth century in ways that were impossible for North Dakota.

Important though agriculture, forestry, and mining were in Michigan, in Vandenberg's lifetime heavy industry—particularly the automotive industry—became far more important. With Ford, General Motors, Chrysler, and a host of lesser manufacturers centered in Michigan, the state became the focal point for one of the most gigantic and influential heavy industries ever, both within the United States and worldwide. In the depression decade of the 1930s, management and labor within the automotive industry clashed violently. Nonetheless, both management and labor (and much of the rest of the state and even the nation) were bound together with the future of that industry broadly defined.

And when defense production, rearmament programs, Lend-Lease aid to the victims of Axis aggression, and World War II itself required unprecedented quantities of guns, airplanes, tanks, and ships, Michigan's industrial moguls profitably converted from automotive production for civilians to the production of every sort of military equipment to satisfy the insatiable requirements of the United States and its UN allies. America's "Arsenal of Democracy" turned out war goods in huge quantities. The Ford Motor Company spent $100 million to build the gigantic Willow Run Bomber Plant that produced thousands of huge four-engine B-24 heavy bombers. The state built $778 million worth of new manufacturing facilities to supplement those that converted to war production. In the course of World War II, Michigan produced some $27 billion worth of war goods, more than produced in any other state. Though attention focused on Greater Detroit and its huge manufacturing facilities, many other smaller cities in the state similarly contributed to the production of war goods. And the massive war production attracted many thousands of workers ranging from black migrants from the South to local housewives.[39]

The end of the war in 1945 brought reconversion to satisfy pent-up civilian consumer demand for automobiles and countless other consumer products in the postwar era. And then came the Marshall Plan and the European Recovery Program, the cold war, the North Atlantic Treaty Organization, the Military Assistance Program, Korea, and Vietnam.

Some of the western agrarian progressive isolationists serving Great Plains states earnestly tried to win defense contracts and war production orders for their constituents. Senators Capper of Kansas, Norris of Nebraska, and even Nye of North Dakota (among others) sought such plums and boasted of the advantages their states offered for war production.[40] They met with some successes, but none of the Great Plains states outside the South had the natural and industrial advantages that Michigan, on the Great Lakes, commanded.

Vandenberg did not have to get involved in the messy (and politically divisive and damaging) contests between labor and management or between blacks and whites. He did not even have to come hat in hand to plead for defense contracts for his constituents. Defense, war, cold war, and containment required the industrial products that Michigan's heavy industry could and did profitably produce in quantity. Vandenberg doubtless was moved by honest, earnest, patriotic concerns and mature wisdom in departing his earlier isolationist ways and in helping to guide his state, his party, and his nation to internationalism, collective security, and containment. But the wisdom of his ways was more conspicuously apparent in the urbanized industrialized state of Michigan than it was in Nye's landlocked farming state farther west on the northern Great Plains.

Included in Michigan's population were many German-Americans,

Irish-Americans, Italian-Americans, and Scotch-Irish whose ethnic inclinations tended to reinforce Vandenberg's isolationism. But it also had a large Polish-American population, along with many Finnish-Americans and persons of English, French, and Canadian descent, who added weight on the "interventionist" side even before Pearl Harbor. The unfortunate plight of European Poles at the hands of Communist Russia during and after World War II reinforced the political currents in Michigan on behalf of American multilateral involvement in Europe. In the cold war setting, one could even envisage Michigan's German-Americans calling for a larger American containment role in the face of Soviet challenges, in contrast to their isolationist inclinations when Germany was the adversary. Samuel Lubell had found in German-Americans a major base for American isolationism before Pearl Harbor, but in 1951 when the Soviet Union was the adversary, he asked rhetorically, "If Germany is overrun, will German-Americans vote 'isolationist'?" In the decade of the 1940s, the ethnic influences in Michigan generally were on the side of Vandenberg's developing internationalism and containment. And Vandenberg was alert to those patterns. Earnest foreign policy concerns of significant ethnic groups supplemented and reinforced the state's urbanization and heavy industry on the side of multilateral involvement in European affairs.[41]

Now it may have been that by nature, Vandenberg was simply more intelligent, wiser, better informed, more practical, more cosmopolitan, more responsible, more adaptable, and more realistic than Nye. But one would be hard-pressed to provide objective proof of that—unless one started from the assumption that by definition, those qualities identified with internationalism, collective security, and containment per se. Through the press, radio, and then television, both Vandenberg and Nye were exposed to information about Hitler's Nazi Germany, Mussolini's Fascist Italy, Japan's militarists, and Stalin's Communist Soviet Union. In their roles on the Foreign Relations Committee and in contacts in public life, both men had better access to relevant information on world affairs than most people. Until near the end of World War II, one would not have expected Vandenberg to have been significantly better informed than Nye on such matters. But the states each served (i.e., the domestic constraints and pressures operating on each of them from within the United States) were radically different. And those differing domestic circumstances for the two men projected into radically different roles for the United States in world affairs.

On December 19, 1944, on his fifty-second birthday and a little more than a month after defeat at the polls in his unsuccessful bid for election to another term, Nye took the floor and delivered his farewell address to the Senate. He spoke pridefully and without apology for his efforts to keep the United States out of World War II. He warned that the victories in that war would not be followed by any "golden age for America." He predicted that America would be burdened by ever-mounting debts to pay for the military forces essential for the role the United States had elected to accept for itself in world affairs. He forecast that the United States would "be involved in every quarrel between our partners in this new world order" and that when World War III erupted, the United States would "be in it from the first day." Nye contended that the only way the United States could stay out of World War III was "by minding our own business. By keeping out of these entangling alliances. By developing our own markets here in this hemisphere and devoting our strength honestly and solely to the defense of our own territory." He cited historian Charles A. Beard's book, *The Open Door at Home,* to bolster his argument that it was possible for the United States "to find, in our own domestic market and in trade which we can easily develop on friendly terms with our neighbors in this hemisphere, all the prosperity we need for our American people."[42]

But the America of that time (and of today) was not listening. Senator Nye's speech got little attention. It was, in effect, a funeral dirge for his political career and for American isolationism. Nye tried to regain a seat in the Senate in the elections of 1946—but was again defeated. He died in Washington, D.C., in 1971 at the age of seventy-eight. By that time, one of Nye's sons had been seriously wounded in combat in Vietnam. His youngest son was serving as an air force pilot in Southeast Asia. And at the moment the former senator died, the United States was pressing on with its unpopular war in Vietnam that ended with defeat after his death.[43]

On January 10, 1945, three weeks after Nye delivered his farewell address, Vandenberg took the Senate floor to deliver the most important address in his public career. He did not mention, repudiate, or apologize for his isolationist or noninterventionist views and efforts before Pearl Harbor. And he did not abandon the critical views he had always held of Franklin D. Roosevelt. Vandenberg did say, however, that the oceans had "ceased to be moats which automatically protect our ramparts." He did urge guarding American self-interest and building American military power. And as he had many times earlier, Vandenberg advanced critical and distrustful views of the So-

viet Union's role in world affairs. He called for continued Allied unity
for defeating the Axis and for planning the peace.[44] (Both Nye's
speech and Vandenberg's oration preceded Roosevelt's meeting with
Churchill and Stalin at Yalta and America's use of atomic bombs on
the Japanese cities of Hiroshima and Nagasaki.) Vandenberg's speech
won widespread and highly favorable attention. It proved to be, in
effect, a triumphal processional for his emergence as the leading Republican spokesman in the Senate for the bipartisan consensus behind America's internationalism, collective security, and containment
policies after World War II. Like Roosevelt, Vandenberg was moving
with the currents in Michigan, in the United States, and in the Western world; he was on his way to the pinnacle of his career. In contrast,
Nye was beaten, rejected, and (with his foreign policy views) cast on
the political junk heap.

To understand the directions the United States has pursued in
world affairs, one must take a careful look abroad at world conditions,
power distribution, and national interests. One must probe in depth
the minds, temperaments, and character of the persons who guided
American policies abroad. But one must also look in depth at both the
enduring and the changing characteristics of the domestic socioeconomic-political conditions that helped mold American views, policies, and actions on foreign affairs. One must look at them in Nye's
North Dakota, in Vandenberg's Michigan, and in the whole of the
United States. It is there that one most clearly discerns why some
Americans and their leaders found the transition from traditional isolationism to internationalism natural and long overdue and why others (fully as earnest, honest, patriotic, and even intelligent) could find
that transition ever so difficult and (in their view) unnecessary and
unwise. Since it was Nye and his America that were fading way, he
and his traditional foreign policy views (deeply rooted in the soil
tilled by Americans over the course of three centuries) inevitably
must suffer the disdain and abuse that comes with being on the losing side. And it was Vandenberg's (and Hamilton's and Roosevelt's)
America that triumphed in the twentieth century, in both domestic
and foreign affairs.

In radically different ways, both Arthur H. Vandenberg and
Gerald P. Nye departed the leadership roles they had played so
prominently before Pearl Harbor on behalf of noninvolvement in European wars. Nye and his rural and small town America were cast
aside—along with foreign policy projections of that older America.
Vandenberg and his increasingly urbanized and industrialized mod-

ern America changed course and triumphed—along with internationalist and containment foreign policy projections of that newer
America.

NOTES

1.   On Nye, see Wayne S. Cole, *Senator Gerald P. Nye and American Foreign
Relations* (Minneapolis: University of Minnesota Press, 1962), and Wayne S.
Cole, "Gerald P. Nye and Agrarian Bases for the Rise and Fall of American
Isolationism," in John N. Schacht, ed., *Three Faces of Midwestern Isolationism:
Gerald P. Nye, Robert E. Wood, and John L. Lewis* (Iowa City: Center for the
Study of the Recent History of the United States, 1981): 1–10. Both publica-
tions are based on research in the Gerald P. Nye Papers and on extended
interviews and conversations with Nye from 1956 to 1971. The Nye papers
are deposited at Herbert Hoover Library, West Branch, Iowa.

On Vandenberg, see Arthur H. Vandenberg, Jr., ed., with the collaboration
of Joe Alex Morris, *The Private Papers of Senator Vandenberg* (Boston: Houghton
Mifflin Co., 1952), and C. David Tompkins, *Senator Arthur H. Vandenberg: The
Evolution of a Modern Republican, 1884–1945* (East Lansing: Michigan State
University Press, 1970). Both are based on research in the Arthur H. Vanden-
berg Papers that are deposited in Bentley Historical Library, University of
Michigan, Ann Arbor, Michigan.

2.   For a detailed scholarly study of the munitions investigation, see
John Edward Wiltz, *In Search of Peace: The Senate Munitions Inquiry, 1934–36*
(Baton Rouge: Louisiana State University Press, 1963). See also Cole, *Senator
Gerald P. Nye*, 65–96, esp. 71, 92.

3.   The best scholarly history of enactment and revision of the neutrality
legislation is Robert A. Divine, *The Illusion of Neutrality* (Chicago: University
of Chicago Press, 1962).

4.   Interview with Gerald P. Nye, Chevy Chase, Maryland, July 27, 1959.

5.   For a scholarly study of President Franklin D. Roosevelt's relations
with leading isolationists, including both Vandenberg and Nye, see Wayne S.
Cole, *Roosevelt and the Isolationists, 1932–45* (Lincoln: University of Nebraska
Press, 1983).

6.   *Knoxville News-Sentinel*, May 5, 1935, C-7, Nye Papers.

7.   On Vandenberg, see Arthur H. Vandenberg, "Is the Republic Slipping?" *Review of Reviews* 93 (June 1936): 68; Vandenberg to Howard C. Lawrence, January 5, 1938, Vandenberg Papers; and Vandenberg, "'United We
Stand—,'" *Saturday Evening Post* 210 (April 30, 1938): 25, 79–81. Of central
relevance on Nye, see Brent Dow Allinson, "Senator Nye Sums Up," *Christian Century* 52 (January 16, 1935): 80–81; *Congressional Record*, 74th Cong., 1st
sess., 1935, 79:460.

8.   James Couzens to John Carson, October 30, 1934, James Couzens Pa-

pers, Library of Congress, Washington, D.C.; Ray Tucker, "Marked Man," *Collier's* 95 (March 9, 1935): 38; *Literary Digest* 120 (July 13, 1935): 38.

9.   For examples, see Vandenberg to Couzens, August 3, 1934, Couzens Papers; Arthur H. Vandenberg, "An Answer to the President," *Review of Reviews* 92 (August 1935): 23–24; Arthur H. Vandenberg, "Vampires on the Blood Stream of the Public Credit," *Vital Speeches of the Day* 2 (July 15, 1936): 643; A. H. Vandenberg, "Hash by the Billion! Wanted a Tax-Saving Diet," *Saturday Evening Post* 209 (August 29, 1936): 10–11, 61–64; Arthur H. Vandenberg, "The Republican Indictment," *Fortune* 14 (October 1936): 110–13, 178, 183–84; Vandenberg to Thomas W. Lamont, December 2, 1937, Vandenberg Papers; *Newsweek* 10 (December 6, 1937): 16; Vandenberg, "Pump-Priming Adventures," *Vital Speeches of the Day* 4 (May 1, 1938): 424–425; and Milton S. Mayer, *Men Who Would Be President: Try to Find Vandenberg*," *Nation* 150 (May 11, 1940): 587–588.

10.   Vandenberg to James Couzens, August 3, 1934, Couzens Papers.

11.   "Voting Record of Arthur H. Vandenberg," [1933–1936], n.d., Lowell Mellett Papers, Franklin D. Roosevelt Library, Hyde Park, New York.

12.   Cole, *Senator Gerald P. Nye*, 8, 18, 21–22, 30–41, 46–56.

13.   Vandenberg, "'United We Stand—,'" *Saturday Evening Post* 210 (April 30, 1938): 81.

14.   Cole, *Senator Gerald P. Nye*, 3–13.

15.   Tompkins, *Senator Arthur H. Vandenberg*, 144–145.

16.   Vandenberg to Ernest Kanzler, March 7, 1933, Vandenberg Papers.

17.   Vandenberg, "The Republican Indictment," *Fortune* 14 (October 1936): 113.

18.   Vandenberg diary entries, February 18, March 2, May 13, [1937], Scrapbook #9, Vandenberg to William E. Evans, May 24, 1937, Vandenberg Papers; Vandenberg, "The Biography of an Undelivered Speech," *Saturday Evening Post* 210 (October 9, 1937): 25, 32, 35, 37; and Cole, *Roosevelt and the Isolationists*, 213–216.

19.   Vandenberg to William E. Evans, May 24, 1937, Vandenberg "Diary," February 6 and 18, March 2, May 18, [1937], Vandenberg Papers; Cole, *Roosevelt and the Isolationists*, 213–216.

20.   Vandenberg, "'United We Stand—,'" *Saturday Evening Post* 210 (April 30, 1938): 25, 79, 80–81.

21.   Vandenberg to Mrs. Robert L. Bacon, August 15, 1938, Vandenberg to Donald Despain, February 24, 1939, Vandenberg Papers.

22.   Vandenberg to Roosevelt, December 15, 1941, Official File 419, Roosevelt to Vandenberg, President's Personal File 3529, Franklin D. Roosevelt Papers, Franklin D. Roosevelt Library, Hyde Park, New York.

23.   Vandenberg, *Private Papers*, 90–125; Cordell Hull, *The Memoirs of Cordell Hull*, 2 vols. (New York: Macmillan Co., 1948): 2, 1656–1685.

24.   Vandenberg, *Private Papers*, 139–140, 146–159, 165–169.

25.   Harry S. Truman, *Memoirs of Harry S. Truman: Years of Trial and Hope* (Garden City, N.Y.: Doubleday & Co., 1956): 172; David R. Kepley, *The Col-*

lapse of the Middle Way: Senate Republicans and the Bipartisan Foreign Policy, *1948–1952* (New York: Greenwood Press, 1988): 2–3, 7–8, 56–59.

26. For analyses of the agrarian bases for Nye's roles in public affairs, including the positions he took on foreign affairs, see Cole, *Senator Gerald P. Nye,* esp. 3–13, 24–41, 227–235. See also Cole, "Gerald P. Nye and Agrarian Bases for the Rise and Fall of American Isolationism," in *Three Faces of Midwestern Isolationism,* 1–10.

27. The most detailed scholarly biography of Bryan is Paolo E. Coletta, *William Jennings Bryan,* 3 vols. (Lincoln: University of Nebraska Press, 1964–1969) For a recent perceptive scholarly account, see LeRoy Ashby, *William Jennings Bryan: Champion of Democracy* (Boston: Twayne Publishers, 1987).

28. On the Nonpartisan League, see Robert L. Morlan, *Political Prairie Fire: The Nonpartisan League, 1915–1922* (Minneapolis: University of Minnesota Press, 1955).

29. For a scholarly study of many of those western agrarian progressives in the Roosevelt era, see Ronald L. Feinman, *Twilight of Progressivism: The Western Republicans and the New Deal* (Baltimore: Johns Hopkins University Press, 1981). See also Russell B. Nye, *Midwestern Progressive Politics: A Historical Study of Its Origins and Development, 1870–1958* (East Lansing: Michigan State University Press, 1959).

30. The most detailed scholarly biography of Jefferson is Dumas Malone, *Jefferson and His Times,* 5 vols. (Boston: Little, Brown, 1948–1974). See also Charles A. Beard, *Economic Origins of Jeffersonian Democracy* (New York: Macmillan Co., 1915), esp. 415–464; Beard, *The Idea of National Interest: An Analytical Study in American Foreign Policy* (New York: Macmillan Co., 1934): 50–56, 84–88, 166–168, 549–551; Gilbert Chinard, *Thomas Jefferson: The Apostle of Americanism,* 2d ed. rev. (Ann Arbor: University of Michigan Press, 1957): 132–136, 211–214, 326–330, 351–352, 396–399, 468–488, 491–497; and Merrill D. Peterson, ed., *Thomas Jefferson: A Reference Biography* (New York: Charles Scribner's Sons, 1986), esp. 1–24, 385–398.

31. For scholarly histories of North Dakota, see Elwyn B. Robinson, *History of North Dakota* (Lincoln: University of Nebraska Press, 1966), and Robert P. Wilkins and Wynona H. Wilkins, *North Dakota: A Bicentennial History* (New York: W. W. Norton & Co., 1977). For descriptions and analyses of North Dakota's society, economy, and politics, see Melvin E. Kazeck, *North Dakota: A Human and Economic Geography* (Fargo: North Dakota Institute for Regional Studies, 1956), J. M. Gillette, *Social Economics of North Dakota* (Minneapolis: Burgess Publishing Co., 1942), Robert L. Vexler, *Chronology and Documentary Handbook of the State of North Dakota* (Dobbs Ferry, N.Y.: Oceana Publications, 1978), and Federal Writers' Project of the Works Progress Administration for the State of North Dakota, *North Dakota: A Guide to the Northern Prairie State,* 2d ed. (New York: Oxford University Press, 1950). My thinking on the socioeconomic-political patterns in North Dakota was greatly enriched by Elwyn B. Robinson, "The Themes of North Dakota History" (mimeographed article originally presented as an address at Seventy-

Fifth Anniversary Conference, University of North Dakota, November 6, 1958).

32. For a scholarly study by an able historian focusing on the declining and minority role of farmers in the United States, see Gilbert C. Fite, *American Farmers: The New Minority* (Bloomington: Indiana University Press, 1981).

33. Kazeck, *North Dakota*, 35–37, 135–195, 230; Gillette, *Social Economics*, 68–74, 86–142, 196–199; Federal Writers Project, *North Dakota*, 64–95, 121–48; and Vexler, *North Dakota*, 20–30, 141.

34. *Congressional Record*, 77th Cong., 1st sess. (1941), A1603–1605; *Des Moines Sunday Register*, March 26, 1961; *Des Moines Tribune*, November 10, 1960.

35. That emphasis on North Dakota and the Great Plains as "colonial" areas exploited by eastern urban business interests is a central theme in Glenn H. Smith, *Langer of North Dakota: A Study in Isolationism, 1940–1959* (New York and London: Garland Publishing, 1979).

36. *Washington Post*, November 24, 1982, A3, February 10, 1988, A17, September 4, 1984, A17, May 24, 1987, A3, January 7, 1990, A14, September 30, 1990, H2, February 21, 1991, A1, A12; *Time*, May 15, 1978, 14–15, March 27, 1989, 66–68, October 9, 1989, 30–36, September 24, 1990, 53–56.

37. Among scholarly histories of Michigan, see M. M. Quaife and Sidney Glazer, *Michigan: From Primitive Wilderness to Industrial Commonwealth* (New York: Prentice-Hall, 1948), and F. Clever Bald, *Michigan in Four Centuries*, rev. ed. (New York: Harper & Brothers, 1961).

38. For convenient studies describing and analyzing Michigan's social structure, economy, and politics, see Lawrence M. Sommers, with Joe T. Darden, Jay R. Harman, and Laurie K. Sommers, *Michigan: A Geography* (Boulder and London: Westview Press, 1984), Lewis Beeson, ed., *This is Michigan: A Sketch of These Times and Times Gone By* (Lansing: Michigan Historical Commission, 1949), and Stephen B. Sarasohn and Vera H. Sarasohn, *Political Party Patterns in Michigan* (Detroit: Wayne State University Press, 1957).

39. Quaife and Glazer, *Michigan*, 360–362; Bald, *Michigan*, 432–436; Sommers, *Michigan*, 119; and Alan Clive, *State of War: Michigan in World War II* (Ann Arbor: University of Michigan Press, 1979), esp. 1–213, 234–244.

40. For examples, see Capper to Henry L. Stimson, August 6, 1940, Capper to Henry A. Wallace, July 9, 1940, Capper to William S. Knudsen, August 7, 1940, Capper to F. W. Brinkerhoff, May 5, 1941, Capper to Samuel Wilson, May 31, 1941, Arthur Capper Papers, Kansas State Historical Society, Topeka, Kansas; George W. Norris to Chester C. Davis, July 19, 1940, November 27, 1940, January 29, 1941, Norris to Clifford Townsend, April 23, 1941, Norris to Morris L. Cooke, June 26, 1941, Norris to General Harry K. Rutherford, July 23, 1941, Norris to Guy V. Doran, November 28, 1941, George W. Norris Papers, Library of Congress, Washington, D.C.; *Congressional Record*, 77th Cong., 1st sess., 1941, 87, pt. 2: 2201.

41. Tompkins, *Senator Arthur H. Vandenberg*, 173–174, 228–229; Vandenberg, *Private Papers*, 147–156, 185–186, 243–244, 313–314; Samuel Lubell,

"Who Votes Isolationist and Why," *Harper's Magazine* 202 (April 1951): 29–36.

42. *Congressional Record*, 78th Cong., 2d sess., 1944, 90: 9683–9689.

43. *Washington Evening Star*, July 19, 1971; interview with Gerald P. Nye, College Park, Md., March 29, 1971; and Marguerite Nye to author, December 10, 1971.

44. *Congressional Record*, 79th Cong., 1st sess., 1945, 91: 164–167; Vandenberg, *Private Papers*, 126–145.

SELECTED PUBLICATIONS OF
FRED HARVEY HARRINGTON

INDEX

Selected Publications of Fred Harvey Harrington

BOOKS

God, Mammon, and the Japanese: Dr. Horace N. Allen and Korean-American Relations, 1884–1905. Madison: The University of Wisconsin Press, 1944.

Fighting Politician: Major General N. P. Banks. Philadelphia: University of Pennsylvania Press, 1948.

Hanging Judge. Caldwell, Idaho: Caxton Printers, 1951.

The Future of Adult Education: New Responsibilities of Colleges and Universities. Foreword by John W. Gardner. San Francisco: Josey-Bass, 1977.

ADDRESSES

The University and the State: Inaugural Address by Fred Harvey Harrington, President of the University of Wisconsin, October 20, 1962. Madison: University of Wisconsin Press, 1962.

ARTICLES

"The Anti-Imperialist Movement in the United States, 1898–1900." *Mississippi Valley Historical Review* 22 (1935): 211–230.

"Literary Aspects of Anti-Imperialism." *New England Quarterly* 10 (1937): 650–667.

"Beard's Idea of National Interest and New Interpretations." *American Perspectives* 4 (1950): 335–345.

"Politics and Foreign Policy." In Alexander DeConde, ed., *The Encyclopedia of American Foreign Policy.* New York: Scribner's, 1978.

"'Europe First' and Its Consequences for the Far Eastern Policy of the United States." In Lloyd C. Gardner, ed., *Redefining the Past: Essays in Diplomatic History in Honor of William Appleman Williams* (Corvallis: Quadrangle Press, 1986.

BOOK REVIEWS

Expansionists of 1898, by Julius W. Pratt. *Mississippi Valley Historical Review* 24 (1937): 94–95.

The Far Eastern Policy of the United States, by A. Whitney Griswold. *Mississippi Valley Historical Review* 26 (1939): 126–127.

The Road to Teheran, by Foster Rhea Dulles. *Mississippi Valley Historical Review* 31 (1944): 154–155.

The Time for Decision, by Sumner Welles. *Mississippi Valley Historical Review* 31 (1944): 448–449.

Ten Years in Japan, by Joseph C. Grew. *Pacific Historical Review* 13 (1944): 473.

Arkansas, by John Gould Fletcher. *Journal of Southern History* 13 (1947): 573–574.

The Memoirs of Cordell Hull. Mississippi Valley Historical Review 35 (1948): 335–337.

Rock of Chickamauga: The Life of General George H. Thomas, by Freeman Cleaves. *American Historical Review* 54 (1949): 892–893.

The Confederate States of America, 1861–65, by E. Merton Coulter. *Mississippi Valley Historical Review* 37 (1950): 334–336.

The American Mind, by Henry Steele Commager. *Journal of Southern History* 17 (1951): 104–106.

Herbert Hoover's Latin-American Policy, by Alexander DeConde. *American Historical Review* 56 (1951): 991–992.

The United States as a World Power, by Samuel Flagg Bemis. *Mississippi Valley Historical Review* 38 (1951): 343–344.

Seven Decisions that Shaped History, by Sumner Welles. *Pacific Historical Review* 20 (1951): 417–418.

The American Record in the Far East, 1945–51, by Kenneth Scott Latourette. *Mississippi Valley Historical Review* 39 (1953): 792–793.

Open Door Diplomat: The Life of W. W. Rockhill, by Paul A. Varg. *Pacific Historical Review* 22 (1953): 416–417.

The China Tangle, by Herbert Feis. *Mississippi Valley Historical Review* 40 (1953): 568–569.

The American Tradition in Foreign Policy, by Frank Tannenbaum. *Pacific Historical Review* 24 (1955): 426–427.

Russia Leaves the War, by George F. Kennan. *Mississippi Valley Historical Review* 44 (1957): 165–166.

The Decision to Intervene, by George F. Kennan. *Mississippi Valley Historical Review* 45 (1959): 685–687.

The Purpose of American Politics, by Hans J. Morgenthau. *American Historical Review* 67 (1962): 1050.

Index

mas Mann, Undersecretary of State for Latin American affairs in the Kennedy and Johnson administrations, was instrumental in turning the United States away from the Alliance for Progress and back to a hard-line policy. A former Harvard dean, McGeorge Bundy influenced the Kennedy–Johnson experiments in global social engineering and the escalation of the Vietnam War.

The rise of the United States to the status of the world's lone (and often highly perplexed and frustrated) superpower cannot be understood without understanding these nine influential men and their roles in recent American history. The volume also stands as a tribute to Fred Harvey Harrington, professor of history and former president of the University of Wisconsin–Madison. All of the contributors began their distinguished careers as students of Harrington.

Thomas J. McCormick is professor of history at the University of Wisconsin–Madison and author of *China Market* and *America's Half-Century: U.S. Foreign Policy in the Cold War.*

Walter LaFeber is professor of history at Cornell University and author of *America, Russia, and the Cold War* and *The New Empire: An Interpretation of American Expansion, 1860–1898.*